What Some Peo

"Brilliant! This book will make you laugh, cry and reflect on the great work that teachers do. A Grade 9 read!"
Marcia Dixon, Award-winning Journalist,
***The Voice* newspaper**

"This book will strike a chord with teachers. By reading this, people will have an understanding of how some kids fail themselves! It was so engrossing."
D. Carryl, Primary School Teacher

"Julz has crafted a genius publication out of her 20 years in education. A warts-and-all insightful, funny, touching, and honest diary of the highs and lows of the new social worker/ psychologist/substitute parent – known as the teacher. Can't wait for the movie!"
Kevin Jones, Father of five

"One minute I laughed 'til I cried, and the next minute my jaw just dropped in shock. Julz lays herself bare and I think people will appreciate her candour. I can see this becoming an unofficial teacher training manual - especially for BAME teachers. I'll certainly be recommending this book to the teachers I know."
Jackie Raymond, Sub Editor, *Keep The Faith* magazine

"*39 Weeks*, Wow! Funny, inspirational, motivational. Everything you've ever wanted to know about real teachers is contained in this gem of a novel. Reading this is a must."
Dorothy Hall, Charity CEO

"*39 Weeks* is entertaining and well written. It's a real treat for every teacher, parent and person who loves young people. I couldn't put it down. An entertaining and thought-provoking read."
Lyz Bailey, Humanistic Counsellor

Just Julz

Julz is a senior leader in an inner city comprehensive and has been working in education for 20 years.

Her career experience has included, Marketing, Promotions, Public Relations and Print Journalism for a national newspaper, Screenplay Writing and Script Editing for an Independent production company, Broadcast Production and Journalism for ITN and Television Production, and Presenting for Channel 4 and ITV1.

In her first year of teaching she was chosen by the government's teacher training agency to be the face of a teaching resource for newly qualified teachers across the UK and was nominated for a prestigious Lloyds Bank Teaching Award for Best New Teacher in a secondary school.

Her teaching was graded by Her Majesty's Inspectors OFSTED as Outstanding and, as a Head of Year, led her Year group to historic GCSE success.

Her work within the local community has earned her many awards including two for her Community work and a 'Respect Making A Stand' Award from former Prime Minister Tony Blair.

Julz is a trustee for a national charity, a treasurer for a local community project and a primary school governor.

She is married with three children.

39 Weeks

Life Behind The School Gates

Julz Bremmer

Published by BlackJac Media

Paperback: ISBN 978-0-9933 168-4-5
eBook: ISBN 978-0-9933 168-5-2

Copyright © BlackJac Media 2018

Publisher: Bailey McKenzie
Sub Editor: Jackie Raymond
Cover Design: Andy Pryor Vik Osipova
Layout: Charlotte Mouncey
Editorial Consultant: Yazmin McKenzie

For orders and enquiries, call: +44(0)20 7429481305

www.blackjacmedia.com

To my wonderful mother
fantastic children
beautiful family - both past and present
and great friends.
Not forgetting all my inspiring pupils
and colleagues

'cos no man is an island.

Luv Julz x

Train up a child in the way he should go
and when he is old,
he will not depart from it.

Proverbs 22:6

Foreword

As far as I'm concerned, teachers carry out one of the most important and challenging tasks in the world: they help shape the minds; influence the world view, and help to draw out the great potential that lies within the young people that sit in their classrooms. This task can be made even more difficult when carried out within an inner-city environment.

In this book, *39 Weeks: Life Behind The School Gates*, teacher Julz Bremmer brings to the fore the fun to be had, the challenges that are faced, and the goals that can be attained. It provides interesting and insightful episodes about the teaching profession, which take the reader on a fascinating journey through the ups and downs of teaching pupils in an inner-city school.

We meet Julz, a cast of teachers, support staff and, more importantly, the students themselves, and discover what happens when teachers believe in the latent talents that lie within all the pupils they encounter: they set about the task of drawing them out and making a phenomenal difference.

I spent half a day shadowing Julz, and felt like I was on the set of BBC's *EastEnders*. The whirlwind of emotions I experienced in the four hours watching her deal with students, parents and the curriculum was indescribable.

This book will make you laugh, cry and reflect on the great work that teachers do. It will also make you aware of some of the seemingly insurmountable challenges teachers and pupils have to overcome in order to achieve, and all of this action takes place within the 39 weeks of an academic year.

Brilliant! Definitely a Grade 9 read!
Marcia Dixon, *The Voice* newspaper

Introduction

I'd always wanted to teach, but I also wanted to be rich, so my ambition was put on the back burner while I sought fame and fortune.

Most of you know that, until you have achieved your burning desire, the fire is never extinguished. I was finally at peace when I was appointed to my first teaching post, and officially became a real 'Miss'.

What became evident in my first year was how things had changed so dramatically from when I was at school or, as one child succinctly put it, 'in the olden days'!

By watching the students and sharing their lives, I began to realise how fortunate I had been as a kid. What I thought I hated about growing up and resented in my childhood had actually saved me from a life of destruction: religion, strict parenting and a strong Caribbean family unit.

So, unlike today, I was a child who did not succumb to peer pressure; I learned to hand wash and iron at an early age; mastered the art of making rice and peas in my teens, and my virginity was something to be proud of.

I was brought up to believe that education carried value; it was important and, even though I thought university was for middle class White children, my parents expected me to achieve the highest standards and grades.

The Caribbean provides some valuable lessons we can pattern; no, not to beat your children, but to be their parents, not their mates, and to be clear and consistent with expectations: *"Hard ears pickney walk two time,"* meaning, a child, who does not listen, will learn the hard way.

In my household, the language of my youth was peppered with Caribbean proverbs - wise words of wisdom designed to reprimand and educate but, more often than not, they amused. To this end, I have added, for your pleasure, some of my favourite phrases at the end of each episode.

I have written *39 Weeks: Life Behind The School Gates* for you to have an insight into my reality of what goes on behind the school gates. It is set in a mixed comprehensive, located in a deprived London borough, and is written from my personal experience as a teacher of 20 years, who is part of the school's Senior Leadership Team.

The educational backdrop when I started writing was that of concern regarding the achievement of African Caribbean pupils, in particular boys. Many educationists and professionals have strongly vocalised their opinions as to the reasons for this failure, but perhaps, after reading my book, you may take their comments with a slice of cake and custard, and see that there are many factors affecting achievement.

I hope my book, at best, makes you realise that not only in Africa should 'the village' raise the child, but also in Hackney, Haringey, Handsworth, or Harlem and your own back yard.

I also hope my accounts will shock, shame, inform, amuse but, more importantly, make you take an active role in your child's schooling or in the education system.

We need you as school governors, school helpers or for you to dedicate a few hours' support in classes, for example with pupils' reading and with school trips.

Respect is due to organisations like: *The Kiyan Prince Foundation, One Teen, Soapbox TV, Manhood Academy, 100 Black Men of London, The Original Investigator, One Hand Can't Clap, Eastside Young Leaders Academy, Westside Young Leaders Academy, Mentor Kings, The King's Peace Treaty, The Solution Room, Father 2 Father, I Can Project, The Black Child Agenda, Leaps & Bounds Educational Services, Aleto Foundation, Ultra Education, National Association of Black Supplementary Schools (NABSS), Diamond Enterprise School, The 4Front Project, Aspire Prep, Code 7, Supakids, The Basement Dance Studio, Pray for London, Pray for our Youth, The Man Den, Steppaz, Hood 2 Good, G.A.N.G., SOKBKOOS, The Crib,*

Generating Genius, The Safety Box and Blak Sox who are already making a difference.

There are so many groups – too many to mention here – which are doing fantastic work with our children, but you can check out the ones above on your social media platforms.

Respect is also due to the professional organisations who are and have been committed to the professional development of BME teachers: Rosemary Campbell-Stephens, with her inspiring Investing in Diversity and pre-NPQH courses, and the Network for Black Professionals. Along with Diane Abbott MP, who in 2002 brought the discourse to the fore with the 'London Schools and the Black Child' initiative. All this has definitely been a way forward.

We cannot afford to lose our offspring to overflowing prisons; the gun and knife crime epidemic; the teenage pregnancy trend, and drug culture. We should turn off our TVs; unplug the Wii, PlayStation and Xbox 360 Kinect; switch off the Wi-Fi on our iPhones, smartphones and tablets, and spend quality time with our children.

My prized investment is my dining table, where we sit daily as a family to share experiences, talk to each other and eat.

Being a teacher was the best decision I have ever made.

Having seen Obama occupy the White House, I truly believe that, in 10 years' time, I will be sitting in my rocking chair, surrounded by grandchildren, and I'll switch on the television and listen to the British Prime Minister addressing the nation, and I'll be saying to my family: "I taught her!" ☺

JB x

Contents

SPRING TERM

HALF TERM BREAK

SUMMER TERM

HALF TERM BREAK

EPILOGUE

GLOSSARY

AUTUMN TERM

Week Beginning 4ᵗʰ September

New Beginnings

One of the things I love about teaching is the Autumn term. Not just the weather changing from humid to cool, or the colour of nature gradually moving from yellow to brown but, for a teacher, September was an excellent excuse for any poor experiences from the previous terms to be eradicated, and for any negative attitudes from students or staff to be thrown out like old text books, with everyone starting on a clean page.

Like January, the beginning of an academic year is an opportunity for me to revisit professional resolutions, and start afresh on the ones that failed miserably. For students, it's a new start and a chance to create targets and set goals; for staff, a chance to show off their newly recharged energy, recaptured over the six-week holiday period.

My summer break was bittersweet.

My grandmother, a Pentecostal minister, had been diagnosed with terminal cancer, and we were told she had six weeks to live and, with each week, her health deteriorated.

The whole family moved into her semi in east London to be with her. There were over ten of us, and it was like living on Walton's Mountain. Everyone naturally adopted a role: my mum and aunt would rotate the cooking and bath routines; and others would shop, organise Gran's medication, or do the radiotherapy run.

The young ones would fight over Henry the hoover and furniture polish, ensuring the house was spick-and-span. Even on her deathbed, Gran still believed that cleanliness was next to godliness.

Number 23 was a revolving door, with numerous church brethren popping in and out, and bringing hope and positivity through their singing and prayers.

By week three, the muscle in her right eyelid had stopped functioning and closed permanently, but she adorned an eye patch and would bravely play the role of 'Jack Sparrow' with the grandchildren.

Every morning, I would snuggle up next to her under the duvet, and read in my best voice a page from her *Daily Bread* and *The Word For Today* booklets. She would lie back, close the left eye, smile, nod, and then whisper "Amen" at the end of each session.

I would later retreat to the garden to continue to write outstanding (that's overdue, not brilliant) schemes of work, organise seating plans, and double-check student set lists.

By week four, I was still bogged down with this. If my friends could see me now, I thought, they really wouldn't bother to 'hate' on teachers for having 13 weeks' holiday a year.

At the beginning of week five, I had finished reading to Gran, and I was stopped in my tracks by her humming. It was an old gospel favourite: *'If I Can Help Somebody As I Walk Along, Then My Living Shall Not Be In Vain'*. I returned back to her bedside, held her hand and joined in. Halfway through, she paused and whispered, "My work is done."

The statement shocked me, and reality hit in those four words that were simple and clear. I left the room, locked myself in the downstairs loo and, for the first time in five weeks, wept uncontrollably.

On Day 41 of my summer holiday, Grandma Bailey died.

As the Good Book confirmed, she had 'fought a good fight, finished the course and had kept the faith.' So it wasn't a time to cry, mourn or have regrets. Characteristically, being the beginning of September, it was that time again to reflect, evaluate and review.

Top of the list was being a teacher.

Was this something that I really wanted to continue doing?

Hard work. Naughty kids. Marking. Assessments. Ofsted. More marking. Stress. Rude parents. And even more marking!

It was crystal clear: life was too short. Was *now* the time to do something different? Have some fun? Live life, maybe?

The bedroom without Grandma was empty and lifeless. I sat on her bed hoping for just a spark of inspiration, and I struggled to come up with an answer, instead thinking back to when she was alive...

I had just achieved promotion as Head of Year, and visualised the excitement and joy on her face when I told her the good news. She wasn't a touchy feely woman, but I've never forgotten that hug of pride she gave me, which was *just that little bit longer* than the one she gave my brother when his single hit the national charts.

I smiled at the memory.

Often we equate success with wealth or celebrity, but I had learnt, by working with children over the years, that teaching meant more. It was a vocation, and being given the responsibility of moulding young intellects and influencing enquiring minds was a precious gift. I was a talented teacher; had a special relationship with parents, and was loved and respected by my students, their families and colleagues. What more could I ask for?

I leaned over and picked up her photo from the bedside table. She was smiling back at me in her Sunday best. And it was at that moment, that it all began to slot into place.

My mind drifted back to the good old days. My grandmother was standing on the church rostrum, leading the devotional service. She was singing with the congregation at the top of her voice: "*If I can help somebody as I walk along, then my living shall not be in vain...*"

Thanks, Grandma.

The students filed into the classroom, looking immaculate in their new September uniform, and I logged into SIMS as they began sitting at their desks.

I smiled, as I gazed at the twenty-eight pairs of eager eyes looking at me expectantly. Hmmm. Watch out children, I thought, as I moved towards the interactive whiteboard.

Miss Bremmer's in the house, ready to shake things up and raise achievement.

Bring. It. On!

"If yuh nuh see mammy, yuh seek granny."

Grandparents are important in the family support network.

EPISODE 2

Week Beginning 11th September

The Early Days

My early days as a new teacher were a massive learning curve. I lie; at times, it felt like a baptism of fire! The 14-year-old boys sported low-batty trousers, outgrown jumpers, were twice my size, and would stand by my classroom door as I entered, grinning widely, begging to carry my books with their awkward, broken voices, or would enthusiastically yell, "Yu alright, Miss?" I would try to disguise my nerves and gaze up at the 5' 10" teens, scuttle to my desk, and reply in my best teacher voice, "Good morning."

The hip language of my schooldays may well have been Latin, because the new school street talk had significantly changed. For me, a student of the 80s, the vibe was: 'safe', 'bad', 'wicked' and 'hard'! For them, it was 'nang', 'piff' and 'clapped'. Even now, it's all systems change, with 'lit', 'spice' and 'muggy'.

Now, you tell me, with their wide vocabulary and unique writing skills, I'm surprised 'Street' is not a Modern Foreign Language. How is it these kids can't get a good GCSE grade in French or Spanish, but they can learn street code from scratch - and in double-quick time? It's beyond me. It is a skill to text-talk or DM, so much so, my son can blatantly leave his Snapchat open, knowing full well that I can't read or understand a word, apart from the basics: CBA (can't be arsed); WUU2 (what you up to); PAW (parents are watching), or LMFAO (laughing my...) - oh never mind!

Being a class tutor for the first time was an amazing experience. All new teachers dream of being given their own group of twenty-eight 11-year-olds, whom they can support, shape and bond with. I was thrown in at the deep end, and given a group of 14-year-olds in my rookie year. My role was primarily caretaker for the group whose teacher had been on long-term sick leave. It was awkward. I wasn't their real tutor, so they could play up, knowing I wouldn't be there for long.

They were a nice bunch, and I was shocked to discover that their tutor was not likely to return. She had been out of school for six months, and had been diagnosed with a terminal illness. It didn't sit well with me, knowing she had been with them close to four years, and had spent time daily with these students. At some point soon, she would die and they wouldn't be prepared. I pleaded with senior management to somehow inform them gently, but my request fell on deaf ears.

I decided to take matters into my own hands and work with the group during registration to create a book for her. I got each student to contribute to a page of writing and design. They each wrote her a letter, letting her know how they were doing individually, and I took photographs to go with their texts. We received a beautiful note of thanks from her partner, days after we sent the book, saying Ms Mac had cried buckets and loved the gesture. A fortnight later, I was breaking the news to the group that she had died. I was so glad they had been given the chance to talk to her via their letters. For most, it eased the grieving process. And from then on, they became *my* group, *my* babies, and the bonding process began.

In the beginning, the girls were cautious of me: "Who's this young Black teacher?" I would get in early with treats, and create a space for them to chat and laugh as I supported with homework. The boys were surprisingly easier to crack, and would each greet me with a massive hug each morning, and tell me how they loved me being their tutor. I felt well and truly blessed.

After a PSHE session, Sean Allen asked if we could have a chat. He sat at my desk and blurted out, "I think I've got gonorrhoea, Miss."

I chuckled. His face became serious.

"It's not funny, Miss. I really do." I continued to smile and explained: "The reason I'm laughing is because you've misunderstood what was taught this morning. You can't have gonorrhoea; it's a sexually transmitted disease. You can only contract it if you're having sex," I reassured him.

"I know, Miss," he snapped back. "I'm not *that* silly." He then began to accurately describe his symptoms.

"But you're only 14!" I responded in shock.

"Come off it, Miss," he laughed. "What's *that* got to do with anything?"

I was gobsmacked. I went to see the Head of Year, Mr Guide.

"But they're only 14, sir!" I repeated. "They're babies. They hang out in my room in the mornings, and give me big hugs..." I paused. I looked down at my double D chest and froze.

"Oh. My. God. They hug me every morning. *All* of them! Oh my God, oh my God..."

Sean Allen did me a massive favour. From that day on, the darling 14-year-old boys in my tutor group remained confused as to why our morning greeting was now a handshake! Oh my Gawwwwwd!

Being a young Black, female teacher had its advantages in my inner-city comp, but also its setbacks. One student, Ashton Barnes, was insistent that I was 'his girlfriend', and would daily call me 'his woman'. No matter how much I reprimanded him or put him in detention, he would continue. Ironically, spending 20 minutes after school with me seemed to be a reward rather than a punishment. In the corridor he would wink at me, in the playground he would blow kisses and, when I called the register in the morning and afternoon, he would reply, "Present, Babes." It was getting ridiculous!

I sought advice and help from Mr Guide. He just laughed and, in his baritone voice, said I would find a way to sort it. I now know he was giving me the opportunity to solve this myself, but it was frustrating and getting very embarrassing.

Early one morning, I had my light bulb moment.

I called the register. "Ashton Barnes?"

"Yeah, Babes," he replied. The tutor group chuckled.

"Ashton Barnes?" I repeated firmly.

"Yeah, Babes," he yelled louder. The tutor group laughed. With that, I picked up the mobile on my desk. It was connected and, on the other end, was Ashton's mum, who had been listening to the conversation.

"Hi, Mrs Barnes. Yes, that was your son. Sure…" I responded. "Ashton, it's for you."

The tutor group gasped in unison, as Ashton froze, open-mouthed.

"Come, come, Ashton," I continued. "I haven't got all day." He got up and took the phone.

"Yes, Mum. Yes, Mum," he responded, as he walked out of the room. The group were still in shock.

"Now, shall we continue? Sarah Brown?"

"Present," she replied and, as Ashton returned and handed back my phone in silence, I could hear one of the students whisper: "Dark. Miss B's dark, man, dark!"

Even after that experience, it still took time for me to grow into the role. Whenever a student vexed my spirit, I would go home seething and return the next day, and the very same kid, who had caused me a sleepless night, would be waving at me, genuinely happy to see me and excitedly yelling: "Good morning, Miss Bremmer," like nothing had happened. Huh? I didn't get it.

What also surprised me was how, as a teacher, the students somehow didn't see you as being human, and so you were not allowed to be upset, hurt or angry if they decided to get rude. This, however, was not always possible.

"Get out!" I stopped the lesson for the third time, and was not prepared to do it again. Eddie Maynard just sat there.

"You need to move. And you need to move fast because you're wasting my time and the class's time."

Eddie kissed his teeth and started to rise from his seat. I stood still, seething as I watched him ever so slowly take his time. Patience, Julz, patience, I was telling myself, because what I *wanted* to do was drag him by the jumper and shove him outside.

He finally exited the classroom and I continued to teach. Every so often, I could hear a kicking sound, and the classroom door would open and close. I knew it was Eddie, and I was starting to get irritated. By the fourth time, I had had enough. I walked over to the door and caught him on his fifth attempt to disrupt.

"Move from my door, Eddie."

"Make me," he replied.

"Don't make me make you, Eddie, cos you won't like it." My voice was serious. My tone was deadly. His foot was still jammed between the door and the hinge.

"I'm gonna count to three," I continued. Damn, I thought, why did I say that? The whole class was now watching this soap opera unfold and, if Eddie didn't move his foot, what was I going to do next?

"One!" I said loudly and measured. Oh God, help me, I thought. Mek him move him foot. Please, God.

"Two!" We were now staring each other out, but his foot was showing no signs of shifting. Oh nooo! Come on, Lord, do this for me, please, I silently begged. Mek him move him foot.

"Three!" I shouted, and simultaneously his foot moved. Hallelujah. Thank You, Jesus! I silently screamed.

I joined Eddie outside in the corridor. He began walking towards the Isolation Room.

"Don't play with me, boy. Do that again and you're in trouble, big time!" I shouted down the corridor.

He turned.

"Oh shut your mouth, you fat bitch," he yelled.

I was frozen. Bitch? Maybe. But FAT?!!! Whaaaaaaa?! I saw *red*, and instantly began to chase him.

"Noooo!" he shouted, as I got closer and was ready to jump him.

"Not you, Miss," and pointed behind me. "Her!"

I swiftly looked round, and there behind us, past the classroom, stood Josephine, a large... well, OK, fat, Year 10 student, sticking her fingers up at Eddie.

I ground to a halt. Oh my God! Me and my temper, I whispered to myself. I nearly lost it!

I swiftly headed back to my class, who by now had flooded into the corridor. Trying to regain my composure, I shooed them back into the room.

As they exited at the end of the lesson, I could hear their comments. Summarised, it was how the action outside the room was more exciting than *Macbeth*, the text we had been reading.

Note to self:

1. Don't make threats you can't keep
2. Think before you do
3. Lose at least two stone!

"Puss and dog nuh have di same luck."

What works for one, might not work for another.

EPISODE 3

King Solomon's Legacy

Growing up, I was an avid reader, who loved books. My vivid imagination allowed the novels to transport me to places that only existed in my dreams. I would read my CS Lewis favourite over and over, and would often mind-travel from Pembury Estate to Narnia. I was the sixth member of the Famous Five, the eighth member of the Secret Seven and, when I was grown, I was Bridget Jones: single, overweight and a budding journalist, waiting for Mr Darcy to sweep me off my feet!

Being raised in a Pentecostal family, my daily reading diet consisted of many magnificent Bible stories: Joseph and his Technicolour Dreamcoat; David and Goliath; Daniel in the Lions' Den... These tales were enchanting, entrancing and inspiring.

The narrative structure follows a theme and plot, and embedded within this is the set-up, the conflict and the resolution. This traditional format was a pattern I was familiar with. However, I quickly learnt that, in school, student stories and incidents did not always follow this template. I had to always be prepared for the unexpected.

Janine was a first class joker. Her humour was sometimes refreshing on a stressful day and, at other times, it unwittingly caused more harm than good. Following a fight with Sharon Anderson, they had both been sent to me to issue a punishment. Sharon was a sensible, focused student, so I was intrigued to find out what had happened - especially in light of the fact that Janine was the one sporting a bruised eye, and half the weave from the front of her head was missing.

"She tried to disrespect me, Miss," Sharon said calmly.

"It was a joke!" Janine responded.

"Well, I didn't find it funny." Sharon's tone was still calm.

"That's because you're nasty," Janine goaded.

Sharon switched. She dived at Janine, trying to grab another piece of her weave.

"Stop!" I interrupted firmly. "Sharon, if you do that again, I'm going to exclude you."

"Yes, Miss," she said, her head now bowed.

"Janine, let's start with you. From the beginning."

"Well, Miss..." Janine began. "Shaun Reid bet me £1 that he could get any girl to show him their knickers."

She paused.

"Carry on," I demanded. "This sounds interesting."

"Well, we went up to Tarika Johnson, and he said to her, 'Eee-yuk, you're wearing the same knickers you had on yesterday.' Tarika got vex, and started shouting that he's a liar because she had spotty ones on yesterday, and then said, 'Look,' and she lifted up her skirt to show him that she was wearing yellow ones today. I had to give him the pound. I thought that if I had a go, I could make some money, so I did the same thing to Sharon."

"And she hit you for accusing her of wearing the same knickers?" I pre-empted.

"Sort of," she replied. "When I told Sharon that she had the same knickers on that she was wearing yesterday, she said, 'So what, they weren't that dirty so what's the big deal wearing them again for another day?' Some of the girls in her tutor group were there, and starting calling her 'dutty baggie' and she just went mad."

Eee-yuk! I thought. I knew I had to punish Janine for her behaviour, but thought perhaps I should also penalise Sharon for being so nasty!

I quickly learnt that it wasn't always easy to spot the liar. No matter how hard I stared at a student, the nose of the one telling fibs was not going to grow, so I had to work out very quickly how to deal with and resolve any conflict that presented itself.

My first rule was to always listen to both sides, then get the students to write their versions down. (Sometimes the truth gets lost in translation from the verbal to written account.) In the event of a fight, if the instigator cannot be uncovered, both the students would be punished.

Most of what I had to deal with was straightforward but, every so often, I would be challenged with a dilemma, which called for astute handling.

Two students were rolling along the corridor floor, punching and kicking each other. Surprisingly, no one had said to the other 'Your mum', which was a popular reason for a fistfight. Instead, the affray was over a football.

"My dad got it for me from Spain," Steven Taylor screamed.

"Liar!" Felipe Carter yelled. "I got the football off my nan."

"Prove it!" Steven shouted.

"She lives in Barcelona and spent the summer with us. She bought me this football," Felipe said.

"Liar!" Steven yelled.

"You mean *you* are!" Felipe shouted.

"Now cut it out, boys," I interjected.

This was going nowhere. I was stuck, and looked to the hills for some divine intervention.

Ping! Another light bulb moment. This situation called for a King Solomon Judgment.

For those of you not familiar with the 'Good Book', let me get you up to speed.

Two women came to King Solomon with a problem. They lived in the same house and both had baby sons, three days apart. One night, one of the women rolled onto her baby and he died, so she swapped her dead baby with the one that was alive. In the morning, when the other woman went to feed her son, she saw that he was dead. But when she looked at him in the light, she knew he wasn't her son.

Both women argued in front of the King that the living baby belonged to them. They argued back and forth until finally he said:

"Both of you say this baby is yours. Someone bring me a sword." A sword was brought and Solomon ordered: "Cut the baby in half! That way each of you can have part of him."

"Please don't kill my son," the baby's real mother screamed. "Your Majesty, I love him very much, but give him to her. Just don't kill him."

The other woman shouted: "Go ahead and cut him in half. Then neither of us will have the baby."

Solomon said, "Don't kill the baby." Then he pointed to the first woman: "She is his real mother. Give the baby to her."

Everyone in Israel was amazed when they heard how King Solomon had made his decision. Solomon knew the real mother would never allow her child to be killed. The Israelites realised that God had given him wisdom to judge fairly.

I took both the boys into the canteen, and asked a kitchen assistant for a knife.

"OK, boys, seeing as you can't decide who this ball belongs to, I'm just gonna cut it in half, and you each can have a piece." I hovered the knife over the top of the ball.

"Go ahead, Miss," Steven said calmly. Then began to raise his voice: "Cut it up. Go ahead and cut it up!"

"Noooooo!" Felipe yelled. "I can't let you do that. Please, Miss, I beg you. I'd rather Steven have my ball than you damage it."

I smiled as I put the knife down, and picked the ball up. I handed it to Felipe, who was in shock.

"Here you go, Felipe, I think this belongs to you."

Felipe was ecstatic and grabbed the ball and skipped away, happy. Steven was fuming.

"Be thankful I'm not taking this further," I warned Steven. "Now clear off!"

Later that day, I was called to Reception. Someone was waiting for me in the foyer. It was Mr Taylor, Steven's father. He was an accountant, and looked like he had just come from work, as he was suited and booted.

"Good afternoon, Miss Bremmer."

"Hello Dad," I replied.

"I won't keep you, because I know you are very busy, but I thought I'd pop in and drop off a receipt. It's for a football that I purchased for my Steven. I bought it from the Nou Camp Stadium in Barcelona. I assumed you might need it to purchase another one just in case you can't get the original ball back."

He smiled, then winked before he added: "Have a lovely evening." Then left.

I was stunned.

I opened the receipt. 'FC Barcelona leather football. 35 euros.' How embarrassing!

This never happened to King Solomon! How could I have got it so wrong? Bloody Felipe!

I guess I need to do a lot more work on the wisdom bit. Oh shame...

"Mark twice, cut once."

Take time to make the right decision.

Week Beginning 25th September

No One Forgets A Mad Teacher

L ittle Shelly was the Year group sweetheart. Vietnamese, softly spoken, impeccable manners and a delight to teach. So, when her loud-mouthed classmate, Janice, dragged her into my office, literally, complaining about her treatment in a lesson, I had to sit up and listen.

Mrs Hannah was a bully. Janice had not understood a question, and Mrs Hannah had caught Shelly trying to explain it. Her punishment? To stand on the desk in the Science lab for the rest of the lesson—45 minutes!

Shelly was in tears as Janice outlined the incident in detail, and she reluctantly nodded after each of Jan's 'innit, innit'.

Now, if I'm honest, I had heard about Mrs H's sanctions, but put it down to overzealousness. Students were kept in at break, because headings in exercise books had not been underlined. Lunchtimes were taken away for crossing out words without using a rubber, and an hour after school was given for talking in her class but, this time, she had taken the biscuit.

What a wicked woman, I thought, as I prepared to go over to S Block. This is it!

"Please, Miss," Shelly whispered, "please don't let me go back there, please, Miss, please."

I took her hand, gave it a comforting squeeze, and assured her I would deal with the situation.

Catherine Hannah was waiting for me, as I entered her lab without knocking. She had that sickly sweet smile on her face, and began overloading me with small talk.

"About Shelly…" I abruptly interjected.

"Oh, she's doing so well. Just today I had to praise her for an excellent piece of work, and got her to stand on the table so that all the students could see her and clap…"

"Bull!" I interrupted.

"Now, you listen to me," Catherine Hannah hissed viciously. "I've been teaching way longer than you, and maybe you don't agree with some of my classroom strategies, but they have got me results, the best in the department, in fact!"

I was horrified. First, at her Mr Hyde transformation, and second, at the barefaced cheek of her justifying her poor behaviour.

"Let me tell yuh someting, 'oman." (It's amazing how we all become Caribbean when we are vexed.) "I may have been teaching for a significantly shorter period of time than yourself." (And then take on the Queen's English again.) "But you are bang out of order. You owe Shelly an apology, and I want her moved to a different teaching set from tomorrow."

"Will you be mentioning this to your Line Manager?" Catherine's tone was more contrite and slightly humble.

"No," I confirmed. Catherine looked relieved. "But I *will* be talking to her parents, so I suggest you think of a better excuse to tell them if they decide to take this further."

As I left the lab, it gave me great pleasure to see Mrs Hannah nervous.

It just didn't seem the right moment to tell her that Shelly's parents could not speak a word of English. So, when I had called to explain the incident to them, they hadn't a clue what I was going on about.

Across the block, Otis was being a prat. He was a champion pain in the butt, but a harmless, cheeky chappy. It was only five minutes into the lesson, and he had been kicked out. I'd received a message to say he was wandering around, and left instructions for him to be sent to my office when he was eventually picked up.

He turned up outside my door half an hour later, red-faced, snotty-nosed, and crying his eyes out.

"Mr Gordon tried to kill me!" I stood by the door, looking at the little scamp in shock. "Help me, Miss, help me. Mr Gordon tried to kill me!"

I told Otis not to be so silly, and together we headed to Peter Gordon's teaching room. Surprised, I saw Peter outside, shaken, while the students were running riot, clearly relishing the opportunity not to do any work.

I replaced Peter with a cover teacher, headed back to my office, and the three of us sat down.

Mr Gordon began. He had been teaching, and Otis had been standing at his classroom door, waving and making faces at the students inside. He signalled for Otis to go away, and continued with his starter activity. Otis ignored his instructions, and continued with his tomfoolery, which was creating a disruption in the class. When Mr Gordon yelled at the door, Otis decided to gob a large amount of phlegm onto the glass window.

Mr Gordon was silent, and I urged him to continue. He said the students in the class began to go wild; he saw red and chased after Otis, cornering him by the staircase, and it was at this point he tried to strangle him.

"See, I told you, Miss," Otis confirmed. "Mr Gordon tried to kill me!"

Shit, I thought. Shit. I asked Otis to wait outside so I could have a word with Peter in private.

"Are you *crazy*?!" I yelled when we were alone. I explained that I would have to report the incident, and set up a meeting with Otis Davis' mum. She was down the school in an instant.

"You dirty mare!" Otis' mum yelled, when I retold the incident. She then began whacking the 13-year-old around the head. Mr Gordon and I were frozen. "I am so embarrassed," she continued. Mr Gordon and I were still stuck to our seats. "I would have more than strangled the filthy sod!" she shouted. "Just wait till I get you home, Otis." She then apologised to Mr Gordon, and began pushing Otis out of my office.

Because Ms Davis had been so supportive, and Otis repentant, I did not exclude him for his nasty actions, but he was given a

Saturday detention. The compromise allowed me to issue Peter Gordon with just a warning. Mediation was also arranged, and he had to apologise to Otis, but worse, clean the dripping gob from his classroom door.

We all make mistakes - both students and teachers - and hopefully can learn from them. I don't see my role as one of crucifying students when they do wrong nor, likewise, members of staff.

Catherine Hannah stopped speaking to me after the desk incident with Shelly, but my relationship with Mr Gordon went from strength to strength, with him often seeking advice and support on how to deal with difficult students.

The next day, outside my door was a small box, beautifully wrapped. Inside was a brown, seated statue. It was bald and naked with a large round tummy. I thanked Shelly for her thoughtfulness, and she was surprised I knew the Laughing Buddha was a gift from her.

That was easy, I thought, as I secretly smiled to myself. It was the spitting image of Catherine Hannah!

"If yuh nyam egg, yuh muss bruk de shell."

Actions have consequences.

EPISODE 5

Watch Your Back

In all walks of life there are haters: people who mean you no good, and are just waiting for you to stumble. My mother always taught me to kill any negative vibes with kindness. She would say: "God is not sleeping when it comes to wickedness," and would refer back to the Bible. She would quote the book of Numbers: 'Whom God blesses, no man can curse' and also Isaiah chapter 54: 'No weapon that is formed against thee shall prosper.'

I remember reading about UK pop star, James Blunt, who was a singing superstar in 2005. In his career, he successfully clocked up five Number 1 chart hits; won two Brit Awards; two MTV Video Music Awards and two Ivor Novello Awards, as well as receiving five Grammy Award nominations. He sold 20 million albums and 17 million singles worldwide. And, even with all this, the Marmite singer was being hated on by Twitter trolls and labelled 'Mr Boring', until his killer putdowns turned him into an online sensation.

Some of his classic responses to those who decided to have a go at him included the following:

Twitter Troll: *James Blunt has an annoying face and a highly irritating voice*

James Blunt: *And no mortgage*

Twitter Troll: *James Blunt, why have you only got 200k followers?*

James Blunt: *Jesus only needed twelve*

Twitter Troll: *I try to hate James Blunt but I can't*

James Blunt: You obviously went to one of those schools where everyone got a prize

Gwaarn, James, with your bad self. You tell 'em! I so love the rise of an underdog.

One of my leadership talents lay in training, nurturing and supporting colleagues to reach their full potential, along with building teams and executing new projects. So I get a great thrill when I see staff grow, achieve promotion, or embrace challenges they never thought possible. Someone being better than me at a task has never bothered me; the outcome, as long as it benefited the students, was what really mattered, and I know many teachers have that attitude. So it still surprises me when I hear about a hater, and that I have to watch my back.

Jest is a sneaky guise, but it is important to be aware of, as Maya Angelou once said: "When people show you who they are... Believe them!"

I vividly remember returning to school after a sabbatical, and was excited about my return. I stood looking out of the window at the children running around the playground without a care in the world, and was soaking up the back-to-school buzz in the General Office, glad to be back, only to be greeted by 'glass half empty' Len, a character who mirrored Grantly in the BBC's *Waterloo Road*.

"Good morning," I chirped, with a beaming smile.

"Like a dog returning to his vomit," he scowled back at me.

In one simple sentence he had dampened my rising spirit, and I was furious that I had allowed him to. More so, because I hadn't or couldn't think of a cutting comeback fast enough. No weapon... No weapon... I repeated and, head high, walked out of the office.

Someone, who had bags of cutting comebacks, was tiny Vanessa. She was 4' 11", and what she lacked in size, she certainly made up for in passion and a quest for justice. As a senior postholder in a department, she took her role very seriously and, when she was on the warpath, monitoring books and assessments, everyone locked themselves away in their classrooms, ensuring they were up to date.

No one went unnoticed and, as a senior staff member and close friend of Vanessa's, even I didn't get a squeeze.

"I know you're in there!" she would shout, rapping on my locked office door.

"Go away, V!" I yelled from inside.

"Your literature trial exam marks are not on the system. You have 'til the end of the day, or I'm going to name and shame you!" she shouted back. I could hear her heels clacking down the corridor, and her banging on the locked classroom door of another poor teacher, who was also late with their marks.

I put the folder with the unmarked papers - that had been sitting in my bag for over a week - onto my desk with the mark scheme, and began to tackle the papers before she returned.

"I've got a problem."

It was late Friday evening, and still in school were those I affectionately termed as the 'no-lifers'. V, who was one of us, sat in the chair in front of my desk.

"Fire away," I replied.

"I've just been flicking through some books, and noticed that Robert hasn't marked his Year 10s since the beginning of term."

I glanced at my computer screen. It was 5th October.

"Oh dear," I frowned. "Not good." Robert Black was one of the school's deputies. He was a character - a teacher who was one of a kind. He had an incredible sense of humour and, like the girl with the little curl in the nursery rhyme: 'When he was good, he was very, very good, but when he was bad, he was horrid!' To be fair, he was excellent at his job and juggled many hats, each very successfully. His whole-school roles, one of which was Teaching and Learning, kept him extremely busy but, then again, he only taught two classes a week!

"Talk to him on Monday," I said. "*Gently*!" I emphasised. "He of all people knows the importance of marking and feedback. Set up a flexible monitoring schedule to make sure he's on top of things, and maybe even sit in with him and standardise the marks..."

"Nope," V butted in. "I'm going to report him."

"What?" I looked at her face to ascertain whether or not she was having a laugh.

"I'm serious," she confirmed. "Robert is not above the rules and, if he breaks them, then he needs to face the consequences."

This woman must have tripped in her mega heels and bumped her head, was my first thought.

"So tell me something," I began. "If Robert is one of the Deputy Heads of the school, and higher in rank than our Head of Department, tell me who in the world are you going to report him to?" I queried.

"The Head Teacher, of course," she replied confidently.

"Have you lost your mind, V?" I said incredulously. "Talk to the man. What you wanna grass him up for? Maybe he needs support. He's probably under the cosh. Do not report him to the Head!"

"You see. That's your problem, Julz. You're always trying to find the happy medium. Sometimes you need to do what's right and to hell with the consequences."

"It's not about a 'happy medium," I replied. I felt offended. "It's about trying other ways before you use your final option. It's also about exercising wisdom. If Robert finds out you've reported him, believe me, your days in this Department will be numbered."

"Sometimes you have to be Rosa Parks," V stated, again with confidence.

"You what?" I exclaimed. She's never going there. "You're going to compare your and Robert's situation to a Civil Rights activist?"

"It's about standing up for what is right. I'm doing this for the children!" And with that, she left.

"Don't do it, V!" I shouted down the corridor. But she had gone. I was gobsmacked. Oh boy. This was not going to be pretty. Robert would not just crush Vanessa, but annihilate her, and there was nothing I could do about it.

On Monday afternoon, as I was skimming though my emails, Vanessa's name was in the recipient section of my Inbox. I clicked 'Open'.

Her message was brief: 'The Deed Was Done'.

Oh boy. I slumped back in my seat, dreading the repercussions.

Surprisingly, a week passed, nothing. Two weeks, nothing. By week three, it was still quiet and I breathed a sigh of relief. Maybe I had got it wrong. The grapevine had confirmed that the Head had spoken to Robert about his books, and V had confirmed they had since been meticulously marked and were up to date. She was swanning through the corridor, like a puss in high-heeled boots with the cream.

By week four, the Appraisal schedule was released, and I had four lesson observations to conduct. I glanced down the list and noticed who was earmarked as Vanessa's observer. Robert Black. Uh oh. *This* should be interesting. I kept quiet and waited.

V's feedback grade from her Lesson Observation was 'Unsatisfactory'. According to Robert, the teaching and pupil progress were poor. A repeat observation was booked in for the following week. The outcome grade: 'Unsatisfactory'. V was fuming.

V loved being in the classroom; she came alive when she was teaching. Her classroom was decorated imaginatively, and everything was colour coordinated. She had a tendency to over plan her lessons, and was ambitious with activities, but an unsatisfactory teacher? No way.

Discussions were under way about what would be put into place to support V as a 'failing teacher'. She was fit to explode.

This was not good. And telling her 'I told you so' was not appropriate. To cap it off, the Head of Faculty resigned as she was relocating to Scotland, so there was a vacant Head of Faculty post. This should have been V's, as she was second-in-charge. The job was advertised nationally and an external candidate, who 'just happened' to be a mate of Robert Black's, ended up being appointed. To support department relations, V was sidelined to a post where she was in charge of a much smaller cohort, managing one member of staff.

To add further insult to injury, her classroom, which was her pride and joy, was given to another teacher. The rationale? She was teaching smaller groups, so a large teaching space was not necessary. Seeing V wheeling her suitcase, which housed all her books and resources, around the building from lesson to lesson was a sorry sight, but I knew it was a result of her punching above her weight. Robert Black was definitely in the heavyweight category compared to V's flyweight status.

Sheila Bennett was a teacher with the stamina but not always the skills to make the right call. However, it was always the kids first with her. Not a problem, you may say, but it was when she put the children before her colleagues. As a result, some members of her team would be irritated, but Sheila's heart was pure gold. Her loyalty was a beautiful quality and, if you could have bottled her enthusiasm, you would have made a fortune. I loved working with her. She never said No; was always keen to learn; a great sport; genuine and open, and ready for a challenge. To me, Sheila was the ideal workmate.

When I was called into the office of a senior leader, I was surprised that Sheila was the main topic of conversation.

"What's Sheila like to work with?" they probed.

"Great," I replied.

"Honestly?" they continued, seriously.

"Sorry?" I responded, confused.

"Be honest," they snapped.

"She's great. She's great," I repeated. I felt awkward, but needed to continue, because I could sense doubt. "I never have to ask her to do anything twice; she always does things with a smile; the kids love her; she's enthusiastic..."

"Rubbish!" I was stopped in mid flow. "From my understanding, she's uncooperative, divisive and a troublemaker!"

I sat shocked, with my mouth open. Am I missing something here? I wondered. Am I being stupid or something? This conversation could not be real.

"We are talking about Sheila?" I felt the need to clarify.

"Yes. Sheila."

I paused. Am I going mad? Where was all this misinformation coming from? Part of my role was to work with people, make judgements and act accordingly. If it looked like I couldn't even get the character of the person who was working closest to me right, what did that say about me professionally?

I then felt guilty about thinking about myself when it was Sheila's reputation being slandered. No! This was out of order. I knew what I was talking about. I had to stand up for her.

"I'm not sure where you are getting your information from, but I stand by what I've said. Sheila is a great worker, fantastic with the students, and an asset to this school."

"Then we will have to agree to disagree, then." The statement was sharp and firm. The abruptness in tone confirmed who was in control of this discussion. And it wasn't me.

"I understand Sheila's applying for promotion externally."

"Yes," I replied.

"And you are helping her?"

"Yes," I replied again.

"Good."

Good? *Good*? What did *that* mean?

"It would be great if she left of her own free will rather than being pushed," was the senior leader's next statement.

I began to visualise Sheila being held over a cliff by the school's senior management, and there was no way of me saving her without falling off with her.

The awkward silence in the office spoke volumes. Clearly I had been dismissed. I left the office vexed. Someone was telling porkie pies about Sheila. Should I tell her? Should I confront the person I thought it was? After some thought, I realised Sheila was better off out of here, away from the haters, and I was going to work hard to help her secure the promotion she deserved.

Both V and Sheila moved on to new schools. Vanessa's integrity served her well, as she used this and her energy to set up her own supplementary school. As her own boss, she was at liberty to do and say what she liked.

Sheila leaving was certainly the best move she ever made. At her new school she flew up the career ladder to Head of Year, and then quickly progressed to Assistant Head, and ended up as the Head of an International school in the Middle East, working from 7am to 1pm with a salary that was income tax free.

Back in cold Blighty, I was studying poetry with my Year 10s. We were about to analyse *Not My Business* by Nigerian poet, Niyi Osundare. It was written in accusation of the murderous dictatorship of General Sani Abacha from 1993 to 1998.

"Simone, Mensah and Jasmine, can you read the first six stanzas, please?"

Simone began.

"They picked Akanni up one morning
Beat him soft like clay
And stuffed him down the belly
Of a waiting jeep.
What business of mine is it
So long they don't take the yam
From my savouring mouth?"

Mensah continued.

"They came one night
Booted the whole house awake
And dragged Danladi out
Then off to a lengthy absence.
What business of mine is it
So long they don't take the yam
From my savouring mouth?"

The poem brought me back to the lengthy discussions I used to have with Vanessa, about standing up and being counted. Was she right? Was I really a coward for not sticking up for my friend?

Did I sell Sheila down the river by not defending her more vigorously, and not telling her about the backbiters who were actively trying to mastermind her downfall?

I realised the poetry reading had stopped.

"Can Ade read the final stanzas, please?" I requested.

And the reality of the final verses hit home, as I listened intently with my head bowed.

Ade stood up.

"And then one evening
As I sat down to eat my yam
A knock on the door froze my hungry hand.
The jeep was waiting on my bewildered lawn
Waiting, waiting in its usual silence."

I believed that to effect significant change, I needed to be on the inside and, by being on the School's Leadership Team, I would be a part of the decision-making processes, be the voice for the voiceless, and I would also be in a position to support and help pull other colleagues up, who showed talent and who could make a positive difference to the school.

But, if I stood by and did not defend others, who would be there for me?

"Pit inna de sky, it fall inna yuh y'eye."

Be careful how you treat others.

EPISODE 6

Assemble Together

What I love about my school is the great sense of community, and the opportunity to 'fellowship' weekly in a whole-school Assembly. I say 'whole school', but what I actually mean is a Key Stage, because it was impossible to fit all our 1500 students in the Assembly hall at the same time.

Getting 900 kids from Years 7, 8 and 9 into the hall every Thursday is a military operation, but we have the logistics down to a T, with specific Year groups entering through particular entrances to ensure everything runs smoothly and like clockwork. Dismissal was just as important. At the end of an Assembly, students were keen to get up, put jackets on and make their way to their first lesson.

In the early days, to try and get the pupils under control, the Head would firmly state from the stage: "Please remain seated while we organise departure." A reminder signal for the students not to get up until a member of staff gave them the go ahead.

I had observed Assemblies at other schools, and the whole process of getting the students into the hall, waiting for the Assembly to start and dismissal were all done in silence. You could hear a pin drop. Our Head refused to take this approach. She didn't mind the chatter, as long as there was an orderly entry and exit with the silence from the students once the proceedings had begun.

My devotion and passion for Assemblies were not always apparent in the early days. Some staff, who had the responsibility of leading, did not prepare, so we were subjected to 35 painful minutes of random tripe that was guaranteed to get the student body snoozing.

Our kids loved to perform, so Assemblies became a great platform to showcase talent. Sadly, not all the acts selected to go on stage were ready to make their debut. In the early days, I would cringe each time I'd hear the phrase: "And now we have a dance." And as soon as the intro to a Vybz Kartel or Mavado track kicked in, uh oh, I felt a sense of foreboding. On stage would trot a group of oversized girls in crop tops and cycle shorts, and the shaking of the chests and whining of batties would begin.

I could see from the corner of my eye the staff in the Maths department, who were primarily from the Caribbean, watching uncomfortably as they prayed for a tropical storm to sweep the dancers away. I told the Head that if I ever had to stand through such slackness again, I would personally go on stage and twerk like Miley at the VMAs. Needless to say, dancing in Assemblies was banned, and an advert was put in the *TES* for a teacher of Dance.

With time, the quality of the themes and the content within Assemblies improved. And the pressure to produce a Thursday morning half hour epic production was on. The English department had aliens explaining to students the power of words and the Attendance team would get the crowd going, by rewarding the students who had a 100% attendance and punctuality record by spinning a wheel, and then randomly draw winners who would walk away that morning with a bike, an iPad, a Kindle or JD Sports vouchers.

YouTube was a great resource for inspiration. Two clips that the Head used for her Assembly presentations, which encouraged and motivated, have never left me. The first, the amazing story of Nick Vujicic, who was born with Tetra-amelia syndrome, a rare disorder characterised by the absence of all four limbs. Watching the video showed that overcoming obstacles was possible, no matter what, and that we shouldn't let our circumstances dictate our lives.

The other was the inspiring story of Great Britain's 400m runner, Derek Redmond, whose hamstring snapped during his semi final race at the Barcelona 1992 Olympic Games. His father ran onto the track to support and lead him off, but Derek was determined to finish the race, so his father said they would do it together. They did, showing great teamwork and that success isn't always the winning, but finishing - no matter what your position - is an acomplishment. When you don't give up, you cannot fail. Powerful viewing. Especially if you put the Westlife song, 'You Raise Me Up', under the Redmond footage. Guaranteed to get students weeping.

"Good morning, Key Stage 3," our Head announced. "This morning we have a special guest, who is from the RNIB, which stands for the Royal National Institute for the Blind."

On stage walked a middle-aged White man, wearing dark glasses and carrying a white stick.

"Good morning, children," the man beamed. "Lovely to *see* you all this morning."

There was an awkward silence. The students were unsure how to react. "I met my wife on a blind date," he continued.

Muffled sounds of laughter came from the crowd.

"My wife's a clever lady," he added. "When she's upset with me, she rearranges the furniture!" The laughter began to get louder.

"What I am trying to show you this morning," he added, "is that I am just like you. I can sing, dance, tell jokes – well, not very good ones – and, apart from my visual impairment, we are all the same. So I expect you to treat me as such."

He went on to talk about the great work the RNIB was doing to support the visually impaired to be independent, and demonstrated some of the tools that have helped them to lead normal lives. He walked over to a table on the stage, which had a few kitchen appliances displayed on it.

"This is an audible liquid indicator. You put it on the rim of a tea cup or mug, and when you pour boiling water into the cup, it will bleep before the water reaches the top." He held a boiling kettle in his right hand, and the students watched with baited breath, as the water filled the cup and then bleeped before any overflowed. They all clapped. He explained how a tool like that helped a blind person avoid being scalded by the water.

He then conducted demonstrations with a talking mobile phone and a navigation bracelet, which looked like a modern piece of plastic jewellery, but was actually a navigation system that uses GPS, voice commands and audio feedback to provide the blind with a level of independence that currently, for many, is impossible. The students were gripped.

His presentation ended with a story:

There was a blind girl who hated herself just because she was blind. She hated everyone, except her loving boyfriend. He was always there for her. She said that if she could only see the world, she would marry him.

One day, someone donated a pair of eyes to her and then she could see everything, including her boyfriend. Her boyfriend asked her: "Now that you can see the world, will you marry me?"

The girl was shocked when she saw that her boyfriend was blind, too; his eyelids were disfigured and unattractive. His physical scars made her feel nauseous, and his disability reminded her of what she once was, and so she refused to marry him. Her boyfriend walked away in tears. Before he went, he left her a letter. It read:

"My darling, I love you more than life itself. Be happy and take care of your eyes, dear, because before they were yours, they were mine."

The audience, both staff and students, were stunned into silence. One student slowly clapped, then another, then another. In less than 10 seconds, the hall erupted into massive applause and then screams of appreciation. Our blind visitor humbly bowed.

On stage, the Head was ready to close. She addressed the student body.

"Please remain seated..." she began.

And the whole hall belted back in unison:

"While we organise dismissal!"

I welcomed the positive vibe and smiled. Like a Sunday sermon, the students and I had been left with an uplifting message to take us through the week.

"I threw my corn but I didn't call any fowl."

You are who you show yourself to be, not who you say you are.

Week Beginning: 16th October

Have Car Will Travel

I learnt quickly from colleagues how to successfully manage classes. Consistency was very important, as well as making clear to students who was in charge. This didn't mean yelling and asserting your authority, but being clear about the rules and why the students were there: to achieve.

During my early months of training, I saw the ambitions of the newly qualified slowly die in front of the whiteboard, lots of tears, plenty of anger and, in the case of my starting mate Shola, after less than a term, she just picked up her bags and headed straight out the school gates, never to return.

It was like the kids were equipped with a 'fear-dar', some kind of aerial that would detect who they could mess with and who they could not. I was determined that any rays connected to me said RESPECT. In order for this to happen, I planned my lessons meticulously, ensured they were accessible and fun and, when students stepped out of line, I nipped it in the bud instantly. I soon discovered the word in the playground was: "Don't mess with Miss B", because when I was good, I was very, very good, and when I was bad, I was DARK. That suited me just fine.

I conducted an informal survey about sanctions very early on with the pupils, and they openly declared that detentions didn't bother them, but they would get irritated if I kept them behind at lunchtimes, or called them into school on a Saturday. The survey also revealed that the students didn't like their parents being telephoned by teachers, but what they feared the most were home visits. So no surprises, then, when I say it was upon that principle I built my sanction strategy.

I would schedule two hours into my routine for my weekly home drop-ins, on a Sunday after church. This would be primarily to catch up with parents, whom I'd had difficulty getting hold of, either because mobile and landline numbers were dead, or they had not attended scheduled meetings. If the mountain wouldn't come to Muhammad…

Some evenings after school, if I had Sky-plussed my favourite soaps, I would look at my planner and eeny meeny miney mo as to whose house I was going to pop into. I am ashamed to admit that, on occasions, I did feel a hint of delight when the troublesome student came home from 'playing out', and found me on their sofa, drinking squash and eating their biscuits.

I took my time picking up their eyeballs that had temporarily left their heads.

The whispers in Assembly quickly spread. "Miss was at my yard last night" and the sympathetic pained expressions of their peers was clear. They were not going to let this happen to *them*. But, like life, not everyone got the message. By not everyone, I mean Iqra Abdulrahman. She was a Somalian girl in Year 9, who wore a hijab.

She was feisty. She was aggressive. She was rude. And she was a pain in the backside. In fact, she was the one no one wanted to teach. I was lucky, or perhaps I should say *she* was. Her name was not on any of my teaching sets, so we had no reason to cross paths. Well, not until this particular day. It was a Thursday; school had ended an hour before, and I was knackered. Heading to my office to collect my bag for home, there was a small crowd of about eight students opposite, and a lot of noise.

Reversing and taking the long route to avoid this crowd did, for a microsecond, cross my mind; after all, one of the deputies was due on corridor patrol. But I decided to do the right thing and shoo everyone home. The mini crowd dispersed very quickly at the sound of my voice, but Iqra continued to curse a little boy whose back was against the wall. I stopped beside them and gently asked her to calm down, and she promptly replied that I should shut up.

Standing in shock, my instant response back was "Excuse me?" and she responded louder: "Shut up!"

By this time, she was facing me, one to one, and the little boy took the opportunity to run. Still in awe of her cheek, I began to chuckle. Then stopped. Then said very firmly: "You need to follow me so we can finish this conversation in private." Her speedy response to that was that I should f**k myself and, with that, she lifted her maxi skirt and ran.

I froze.

After what had seemed a lifetime, I melted, walked back to my office and action-replayed the scenario in my head. I was the bull, and all around me was crimson. Even the tiredness that had dominated my body decided to take a hike. I calmly logged onto SIMS, looked up her address details, jumped in my car and began to drive.

In less than five minutes, I was sitting outside her house. Ten minutes on, I was still in the car, staring at the dashboard and trying to wind down. I phoned a colleague to retell the story, and let him know where I was.

Twenty minutes on, I clicked off the call and calmly stepped out of the car. I pressed the doorbell.

A young African boy answered.

"Good evening," I said politely. "I'm a teacher from Iqra's school. May I speak to your mother, please?"

"She don't speak English," he replied.

Damn!

"Is there another adult in that does?" I probed. "An older brother, sister, aunty…?"

"I'll get my uncle," he interrupted and disappeared.

I could hear the sound of the Somalian language behind the front door, and a man in his thirties appeared, flanked by a crowd of eight or nine male and female relatives. I presumed the elderly lady on his right was Iqra's mother.

Oh my gawd.

"Good evening," I repeated in my best Standard English. I proceeded to confirm that he was Iqra's uncle, and that was her mother next to him. I asked if he would mind translating my conversation to the mother. He agreed.

"After school today," I said clearly. The uncle translated.

"Iqra was very rude to me." The uncle translated.

With each phrase, the group of relatives, who were still crowded by the door, would nod.

"I asked her to come to my office…" He translated.

"…to discuss an incident she was involved in." He translated.

"And she told me…" He translated.

"…to f**k myself."

He froze.

It was silent.

"Can you translate that, please?" My voice was firm.

"No!" said the uncle.

I gave him my Don't-mess-with-me teacher look, and in an even firmer teacher voice: "Can you translate that, please?"

He translated.

There was silence.

Then there was chaos.

The mother screamed and proceeded to faint. The other relatives began to scream. The sound of the Somalian language was everywhere and, in an instant, from nowhere Iqra flew through the air and landed on the floor in front of me. All of the relatives then began to batter her.

I was in a Jackie Chan film, and did not know how to turn off the DVD.

I yelled "Stop!" at the top of my voice and the situation, which mirrored a playground 'bundle', came to a halt. Iqra's uncle pulled her from the floor, and yelled an instruction in Somali.

Her head was bowed. "I'm sorry, Miss," she mumbled.

"Why?" I questioned. It was a habit for me to ask 'why' when someone was ordered to apologise.

"For saying bad words to you," she replied.

"Have I ever been rude to you? Disrespected you? Raised my voice at you?" I asked.

"No," she replied. Her head was still bowed.

"Look at me," I ordered. "Never in all my years in teaching has *any* student spoken to me like that. In fact, never in my *life* has anyone said anything to me so degrading. I feel upset, hurt and very offended. It's clear you come from a family that does not approve or tolerate that type of behaviour, and I suggest you take some time to carefully think about your actions and the effect it has on your family but, more importantly, the impression it leaves about you."

I realised the uncle was still translating and noticed that her mother had begun to cry.

I thanked him for his time and left. The sound of the whole family apologising filled the air as I got into my car. They were all still by the door, bowing and saying how sorry they were.

My mobile rang. It was my colleague, Endri, checking to see if I was still alive. How ironic.

I reported the incident to Senior Management when I got back to school. I would write the incident up tomorrow.

The following week a card arrived in the post. It was from Iqra. I sat at my desk and read its contents.

Dear Miss

I am really sorry for what I said. It was bad, and I know I should not hurt and upset you, nice teacher. I feel bad I say nasty things, and I am very sorry. I make my family shamed and you sad. My Mum say I am going school in Somalia next week, so I write to say goodbye and sorry.

Iqra Abdulrahman

Raaaaaaah. Back to Africa. I told my colleague. He said I should put the note in the staff newsletter and collect my brownie points, but somehow it didn't feel like a victory.

My impromptu visits didn't stop after this experience, but became fewer and less impulsive. However, when my naughty pupils wave and say, "See you tomorrow, Miss," for classroom management purposes I still think it is important to make a point of saying: "Really? Not if I see you sooner."

Their uncomfortable smiles confirm. They understand.

"Mischief come by di poun and go by di ounce."

It takes a little effort or few words to start a lot of trouble.

HALF TERM BREAK

EPISODE 8

Stressed Out

It's funny, we commonly associate stress with adults, who are experiencing financial or emotional problems, or are having a hard time at work or with their kids. But last week, I experienced a mountain of *teens* under pressure. What was more interesting, however, was the way their anxiety manifested itself.

There was an email in my inbox that had been sent to the Head Teacher, but I was copied in. The timestamp was 2.45am! It was Mrs Marshall. Her son David was stressed.

In school, David is a friendly, sociable kid, who should be achieving A* grades across the board, but he suffers from an affliction I have seen in Able, Gifted & Talented teens: lazybones-itis. He's a coaster who does the very minimum, but somehow manages to gets by.

The email highlighted that David was behind in English, Maths and Media coursework. The metaphor Mrs Marshall used to describe David was a 'gas pedal'. She believed that if pressed too hard, he was going to speed out of control and, as a school, we would be responsible for any collision, because we were piling the pressure on her son and, as a result, going down a 'dangerous road'.

I sent for David while I printed out his latest Progress Report. I knew that the new GCSE specification in English and Maths did not have a coursework component, so he couldn't be behind on those, and his report noted that he was up to date with all his Media projects. David looked repentant when I read him the contents of his mother's email, and justified himself by saying: "I'm sorry. I had to make up something to tell her, Miss. That woman is seriously stressing me out!"

Winding down in RE with a supply teacher was a group of young boys. I was told to pop into the class, after a member of staff had recognised a smell when they had gone in to deliver a message. When I entered the room, I couldn't understand how the supply teacher wasn't high. The room reeked of weed!

The spliff had long since been thrown out of the window, and the students all denied involvement or knowledge of anyone puffing marijuana, so I went into detective mode and decided to eliminate suspects.

"Everyone up, and stretch your arms out in front of you," I instructed the class.

Confused, the students slowly stood up and stretched their arms horizontally in front of them. I deliberately took my time as I walked past each one, cautiously smelling their fingers. I literally sniffed out two boys and they 'grassed' (no pun intended) on the final culprit. The pupils in the know explained to the confused member of staff and others the significance of my actions.

Parents were contacted; the boys were referred to the School Police Officer for compulsory Drugs Education sessions, and were suspended for four days.

Tyriek was a talented footballer and had been selected to be part of a Premiership Youth Academy, and his mother came in to speak to me because he couldn't be bothered to get out of bed at the weekends to attend the training because he said he was too stressed. He sat in my office in silence, refusing to speak. I decided to start by asking my stress icebreakers in front of his frustrated mum.

"Are you married?" I asked.

Tyriek looked confused. "No."

"Have you got a job?"

"No."

"Do you have kids?"

"No."

"A mortgage?"

"No." Tyriek began to laugh.

"Come on, Tyriek," I cajoled. "What is it that is making you feel stressed?"

His mum interjected. "I don't know what to do, Mrs Bremmer. His dad made an appointment with the GP to see if she can get him a mental health assessment."

"She what?!" Tyriek yelled. "I don't need to see anyone! I'm stressed cos you took away my phone and I can't snap my friends!"

Stress can also stop students from attending school. The technical term is 'school refuser'. You may scoff, but a school in south London was asked to apologise to the family of a girl it had prosecuted for poor attendance, after she was diagnosed as having school phobia.

I can remember when I was young, not wanting to go to school but, in my family, a cough, cold, even chickenpox wouldn't stop Mum from dragging us out of the house. Our arm needed to have fallen out the socket for us to get out of going to school. And it would have to have been the arm with the hand that we wrote with!

Vicky Skeete would get stressed at the mere mention of school. Frightened she would be fined, her mother, Miss Skeete, would take her to the school gate every morning, but Vicky would be distressed, get anxious and panic, which resulted in her returning home.

Miss Skeete would beg for support, because she was aware Vicky was falling behind with schoolwork, and recognised that the longer Vicky stayed at home, the harder it would be to integrate her back into school.

She said that Vicky spent each day either in bed or sitting alone in a chair, staring out of the window. Vicky even found it hard to engage with the tutor the school had provided, so Miss Skeete had got her GP to fast track a CAMHS referral to support Vicky.

At break, Sylvia Dunn came into my office to show me a YouTube movie clip. She was a social media junkie, who was constantly on Facebook, Twitter, Instagram, Snapchat and every other app going. She habitually kept me updated with funny films: a cat attacking a lady who had kicked snow at it; a three-year-old who wanted cupcakes; a professor filling a jar with sand, pebbles, golf balls and chocolate, and this one: a young Nigerian boy, who pranks his African dad by telling him he has got a girl pregnant. It was hilarious.

At the end of the movie, the phone screen went back to Sylvia's Facebook profile page. On the right was a montage of her friend's faces. Vicky was in the middle.

"Sylvia, can I have a quick look at something?" I asked.

"Sure, Miss," she said.

I clicked on Vicky's face. Up popped her profile page. I scanned her status updates.

'Jeremy Kyle is an idiot. #DNAsetup'

'Westfields with mum. Love Zara's new collection.'

I continued to scroll down.

'Nose pierced today.' This status had a photo! Well, well, well, I thought. "Sylvia," I asked, "how do you screenshot something from a phone?

This the Education Welfare officer needed to see. Stressed my backfoot! If Vicky wasn't stressed before, she and her mum very soon would be!

Stress also has a way of making students behave stupidly - both in and outside school. A member of the public reported that a group of around 30 boys were behaving poorly on the High Road. She phoned the school to say that boys, aged about 12 and wearing our uniform, were shouting and running wildly on the pavement and in the road.

The next morning I called the Year 8 supergrass to my office.

"What happened after school yesterday, Keon?"

"Oh you mean the fight, Miss? Well, I heard that Davis, Simeon and Abel were with about 30 Year 9s, and Simeon was arguing with three of these gypsy boys about some rubbish, and they were gonna fight, and one of the gypsy boys went away and came back about two minutes later with a crowbar and everyone just dust."

"Excuse me?"

"They ran, Miss, man. They ran. I heard that the crazy gypsy boy was chasing them with the crowbar."

I emailed the Heads of Year the names of the boys mentioned and to update me on their actions, then called Simeon to my office.

He sat down. His body language was defiant and confident.

"Do you know what a gypsy traveller is?" I asked.

"No." He looked confused.

I explained: "It's a group of people who normally don't have a fixed address because they are mobile, so travel where the work is."

"OK," Simeon responded.

I continued: "So if a gypsy traveller decides he's gonna buss your head with a crowbar, because you're waiting around with your idiot mates to fight him, where do you think the Police are going to look if they want to arrest him?"

"I'm not sure, Miss."

"You're not sure, Miss? You're not sure, Miss? Well, the Police are not sure either, Simeon, because the gypsy traveller ain't got no address! They're mobile. They probably won't find them because they don't have no fixed abode."

"This happened outside school, Miss. It's got nothing to do with the school."

"Oh yes it does when you are wearing school uniform, Simeon, and when concerned members of the public telephone the school about poor student behaviour on the street."

"Well, it weren't just me…"

"Well, I'm dealing with *you*. The other Year Heads are speaking with the other students, so don't watch that, think about yourself. I'm going to telephone your mum and tell her that you decided not to go straight home from school yesterday, but you and 30 boys waited on the High Road to fight three gypsies. Oops, sorry, I stand corrected, it was actually *two* gypsy boys, because one went away for two minutes to get a crowbar, right?!"

I put Simeon's mum on loudspeaker. She was stunned at the details.

"Simeon… Simeon… Simeon…" Her words were soft, slow, purposeful and… "Beg you tell me why, when I tell you every morning to come straight home from school, you decide to make mischief on the High Road?" Soft, slow, purposeful and… scary.

"I just needed to hang with my friends, Mum. I've been stressed," he replied.

"Well you better get your stressed backside straight home today, boy, because me and you have some unfinished business. I'm going to…"

I swiftly took the phone off loudspeaker and intervened. I did not want to be party to a conversation about beatings, because I would have a duty of care to report this.

"Mum, have a chat with Simeon when he gets home. I'm sure he realises how he would do things differently given the chance. Don't you, Simeon?"

His mum continued: "Don't you worry about Simeon. I'm gonna fix his backside this evening."

I glanced over at him. He is looking less defiant and less confident. Damn, what have I started? This boy is getting beats tonight. How am I going to sort this?

I continued speaking to Mum. "I've been looking into activities that I can introduce to support students and their stress levels, because it is becoming a recurrent issue among the children." I decide to use Mum's tack right back at her, and say my final sentence soft, slow and purposeful: "I will have a meeting with Simeon first thing tomorrow, and will be discussing with him your actions and the conversation you have at home this evening, because I will need to report back all the details to our Child Protection Officer. Hopefully then, we can put the incident behind us and move forward."

I put down the receiver and glanced at Simeon. He looked relieved.

Beads of sweat gathered on my forehead, which began to feel tight and painful.

I exhaled.

Boy, *I* feel stressed!

"Young bud nuh know storm."

The young and inexperienced don't
understand true troubles or hardships.

EPISODE 9

Friends In High Places

It's as though trouble knows when you've had a hard day, and you're feeling tired and starting to get agitated.

Earlier one morning, I had to represent the school at a Peace Breakfast, which brought together various industries within the community: education, the emergency services, the council and voluntary agencies. The aim was to share job roles, experiences and to network. A colleague had dropped out because of teaching commitments, which meant I was up at 5.30am; at the event for breakfast at eight; back in school by ten, and *still* had to teach my last four lessons.

By 4.30pm, I just wanted to get home, kick off my heels, run a seasoned bath, and soak the stress of the day out of my aching feet.

I was heading to the car park, imagining the lazy evening ahead, when I was mobbed by at least 10 students. "Miss, Miss! The man in the sweetshop is trying to kill Andrew. You need to come! You've got to come!" one child shouted.

"What?"

"The man in the sweetshop is sitting on his head, and he is having an asthma attack. You have to come *now*!" another yelled.

I phoned the school office for backup, and ran down the path with a group of 13-year-olds trailing behind me.

The door of the shop was locked, and I looked through the glass. I could see Andrew on the floor, with the shop owner standing over him. There was also a police officer inside.

I knocked on the door and caught the attention of the shopkeeper and the policeman. The policeman looked at me, then turned away. I knocked again, and shouted through the door that I was the teacher of the boy, and would like to come inside. The policeman then shouted that I should go away.

Thinking he had not heard me, I repeated myself, and he repeated his comment - this time louder: "Go AWAY!"

The group of students were still behind me, looking more confused than I was. I began to get angry. I called the school office again, this time instructing them to telephone Andrew's father, and then focused on the task in hand. Bloody cheek! This policeman *was* going to open this door to me, and he was going to do it *now*. I began to bang hysterically, demanding the door be opened, which must have irritated the shopkeeper, because he walked past the policeman, unlocked the door and let me in.

The policeman was furious.

Andrew got up off the floor, and ran towards me in floods of tears. As I comforted him, I introduced myself and directed my questions to the shopkeeper and another officer, who had emerged from the back of the shop.

The shopkeeper said he had caught Andrew putting a packet of chewing gum in his pocket, and attempting to walk out of the shop. He had told him to stop, but he continued walking, so he grabbed him and tried to retrieve the gum. Andrew had resisted and tried to get away, so he held him down.

Andrew flew into a rage. "Liar, liar! He's lying, Miss. I didn't take nothing!"

This sounded exactly like Andrew; sadly, he was a massive liar and a little thief.

I looked at Andrew. I looked at the shopkeeper. The shopkeeper looked frustrated, very upset and scared. It was clear he had been ripped apart by the policeman.

The rude copper, whom I had been ignoring, interjected. "We've heard all of this already, sir. I'm asking the questions, so please address your answers to me." He then turned towards me and, with disdain, began to raise his voice: "I don't know who you are, but *I'm* in charge. *I* ask the questions, not you!"

I turned to the shopkeeper and loudly asked for a pen and a piece of paper and then, even more loudly, repeated his police number (which was on his shoulder) and wrote it down. I then made a big deal of folding the paper elaborately, before placing it into my bag.

"Oh, so you're gonna report me, Missy," he said sarcastically. "Let me repeat my number just in case you've taken it down wrong." He began to slowly and sarcastically repeat his ID letters and numbers. His partner, the shopkeeper and Andrew looked shocked.

I began to smile. Damn facety man. I opened my mouth to respond, but it was at that moment someone began banging on the shop door. It was Andrew's dad. Andrew ran towards the locked door.

Both policemen began speaking to Dad at once.

I walked towards Ray, Andrew's friend, who was still waiting patiently outside the shop.

"Did he take the gum?" I asked. I was quiet, but very serious.

"Yes, Miss," he confirmed.

While the police agreed to take Andrew and his dad to the station, I was stood near the shocked shopkeeper, who kept saying that he had been in business for fifteen years, and nothing like this had ever happened to him.

I relayed events to my four colleagues who had arrived, and asked them to dismiss the last of the loitering students. I confirmed I would speak to Andrew's dad that evening, and explained I would collect witness statements the next day from Ray and the other students who were there, to confirm the shopkeeper's and Andrew's accounts. Instinct was telling me, though, that Andrew had been up to no good, and it wasn't fair that the shopkeeper be blamed. However, it was also clear that the shopkeeper had been heavy-handed. And two wrongs don't make a right.

I then patiently waited for the policemen to finish speaking with the shopkeeper, and then approached them, asking for a brief word. The rude one looked irritated, and began breathing loudly on purpose as I spoke.

"Firstly, I would like to thank you both for your time in dealing with this incident. But I'm letting you know, I will be taking this matter further with your superior. Areas specifically that solely relate to *you!*" I pointed at the cheeky copper, who seemed to find me amusing. "In particular, your attitude," I continued. "I want you to know that I take offence in you refusing to open the door when I arrived, choosing to ignore me." He looked smug, so I decided to step it up a gear. "I believe that if I were White and had said I was a teacher, that shop door would have been opened much quicker," I baited.

My colleagues, who were waiting for me, stared at me in shock.

"Oh, *that* old chestnut," he replied.

"Well, talking of old chestnuts," I responded, and opened my bag, and fished out a business card which I flashed in front of him. "Incidentally, I met one of yours this morning, your Borough Commander. We had breakfast together. Got on like a house on fire!"

The PC started catching flies.

"What was it he said now?" I smiled at his opened mouth. "Oh yes, 'You teachers do a sterling job within the community', and if there is anything he can do to support, I should just give him a call."

Both policemen stood frozen.

I turned to my colleagues, "You ready?" and with that, waltzed out of the shop.

"That was cold," one colleague mouthed, as we continued walking.

I smiled with fake innocence.

I reflected in the car on the drive home. It's outrageous to think that, in this day and age, in order to be heard you have to resort to your friends in high places.

"Nuh romp wid maaga cow, a cudda bull mumma!"

Don't underestimate people who may seem weak and insignificant, because you don't know what kind of powerful and influential people they have in their corner.

EPISODE 10

Week Beginning: 13th November

Ofsted

One of my Leadership areas of responsibility is Preparation for an Ofsted Inspection. Ofsted is the Office for Standards in Education, who inspect schools to promote improvement and to hold them to account for the public money they receive. Graded judgements of Outstanding, Good, Requires Improvement and Inadequate are made on the following areas:

- the quality of teaching, learning and assessment
- personal development, behaviour and welfare
- the effectiveness of leadership and management
- outcomes for pupils

Our school had two previous 'Outstanding in all areas' judgements, which we are very proud of, especially when our intake come to us with low baselines and inflated Year 6 results. We also have a high number of students with special educational needs and English as their second language. That said, teachers and support staff do an incredible job to ensure all students make significant progress; possess self-confidence and high self-esteem to ensure they achieve not only academic success, but also the ability to navigate life as a responsible citizen.

Most weekdays I would leave school at 6.30pm, and the site would still be buzzing with staff planning or teaching extracurricular clubs. You could also find students taking part in tuition sessions, completing homework, or simply doing extra revision. A lot of the children at the school do not have practical revision space in their homes, so many stay in school until they are up to date with their work. On a Saturday, the picture would be no different. At least 500 students would be in school, studying extra Maths, English, ICT catch-up, or taking part in Year 7 Booster classes, and this pattern was replicated during the school holiday period.

When you and your colleagues sweat like this - week in, week out - to ensure the students achieve their best, it is inevitable that when an Inspector calls to evaluate your provision, it is important that the feedback should reflect the amount of work put in. Therefore the expectation is that the feedback received is nothing less than glowing.

Our school has highly effective and robust systems in place to ensure student achievement across the board. We conduct termly self-reviews, where Departments and Intervention Heads would evaluate the provision and its impact. Data and benchmarks are used to set targets, and to track and monitor progress, along with Intervention strategies to provide support for students at risk of underachieving.

Teaching and Learning is at the core, and a key priority in all strategic plans. Monitoring, evaluation, marking and feedback are rigorous, and a comprehensive staff training programme is in place to address skill gaps and new educational priorities and initiatives. Sharing good practice in our organisation is key to improvement, and classroom doors are always open for shared observations, formal and informal walkabouts and school tours. Essential areas of classroom practice include seating plans, pen portraits and praise, and our ethos is to reinforce positive behaviour and a culture of success. Included on our school calendar, therefore, are Award and Reward Assemblies, and Learning and Behaviour Focus Weeks - all offering plenty of opportunities to reinforce high expectations and celebrate student success.

Students are given regular opportunities to sit trial exams, and the lead-up ensures their approach and attitude are right. To support them on the day of exams, we would provide water, a banana and a cereal bar, so they are in the right mindset to do their best. Final assessment grades would be distributed to students and posted home, similar to the August GCSE Results Day.

As stakeholders, the student voice is valued. Our School Council is an active force, and they meet weekly as a group and half termly with the Head and senior leaders. They even manage a small budget, which they use for mini projects and campaigns. Prospective teachers are interviewed by a student panel from across the Year groups, as part of the recruitment process – this often proves to be more daunting than sitting in front of the Head Teacher.

Staff are given the opportunity to shadow key posts in the school, which supports promotion ambitions, and there are plenty of opportunities - if you show promise and talent - to be promoted from within. Ex-students are also encouraged to apply for job vacancies that arise within the school, and I have often found myself working alongside professionals I taught Shakespeare to when they were twelve!

Most leaders make it their business to attend Year Group Assemblies and, in September, try to get to know all the Year 7 students' names by Christmas. That way, nothing gets past them.

So with all this in place, my role is to make sure our good practice is highlighted and everyone is prepared. We know we are doing great things with and for the students, and they are achieving and making excellent progress. Communicating that to the Inspection team is key, as is providing the evidence to support that we are still an Outstanding institution.

The norm is for Ofsted to give schools 48 hours' notice of their visit, but they are not obliged to. A school could therefore receive a call saying the Inspectors were in the car park, and the team would walk into the school and spend the next two days observing lessons, looking at student books, analysing progress data and interviewing students, subject leaders and governors. They would also scrutinise documents, survey parents, and then come up with a judgement based on their findings.

I was on sick leave when I got the text. I froze. It was from the Head, and had been sent to all staff: 'Ofsted Inspection this Wednesday and Thursday. Meeting in the Staff Room at 1.00pm'.

Lawd a mercy! Ofsted were coming *tomorrow*. I could not believe it!

My phone rang. It was Mum checking up on me.

"You resting?" she fussed.

"Of course, Mum," I replied. "I'm gonna have a nap now, so I'll call you later this evening."

I put the phone down. Paused. Jumped out of bed, and booked an Uber to take me to school.

The atmosphere in the building was calm. Too calm. There were no staff rushing around; the photocopy room was not overflowing and, when I popped into classes, it was business as usual. Staff, who were not teaching, were incredibly composed, printing off class data or updating pen portraits, seating and lesson plans, and members of Leadership were going over their 48-hour plan, which had been drafted as a To Do list reminder, while the site team were conducting routine health and safety checks.

That's the way we do it! I smiled.

Back in my office, I pulled out the Faculty Evidence Folder and checked all the relevant documents were inside.

Wow. Everything was in place. Maybe I should head back home and get back into bed before my mum realised I was not there.

I decided to do something nice for the team and create a special newsletter, to give them a boost before the Ofsted experience, so I typed 'school jokes' into the Google search engine:

A science graduate asks, "Why does it work?"

An engineering graduate asks, "How does it work?"

The business graduate asks, "How much will it cost?"

A drama graduate asks, "Do you want fries with that?"

I began to chuckle. Then stopped. Maybe I need to be more Ofsted-specific, I thought, trying to talk seriously to myself.

I typed 'Ofsted jokes' into the search engine:

How many Ofsted inspectors does it take to change a light bulb?

Six. One to change it; one to read the plan on how to change it; one to observe the changing; one to write it up; one to assess, and one to merely advise that the bulb's performance is not satisfactory or better.

Oh man, I don't think so. That would definitely stress them out. I scrolled down to see if I could find a better one.

Why should all Ofsted inspectors be buried 10 feet underground? Because deep down, they're nice people.

Now *that* was funny. Dry, but funny. I was still laughing to myself, when my office phone rang. I swiftly composed myself and answered it.

I instantly recognised the caller's voice. She was angry. In fact, angry was an understatement.

"Just going to 'have a nap', eh? You're supposed to be off sick and you're back in that school. Go on, kill yourself. Don't worry about your family. We'll just pick up the pieces when you drop down dead." And with that my mum abruptly ended the call.

I called an Uber, packed my Data and Evidence Folders in my bag, and headed home.

The Leadership team gathered in the Head's office to meet the Inspection team at 8.00am the following morning.

Once seated, I scanned the five faces and listened to their backgrounds, trying to come up with a first impression. The Lead Inspector, Richard, was a former Head Teacher. 'Fair but firm', I jotted on my notepad as he continued speaking. Dave was a bald Irish man, whose specialism was Humanities. 'Small eyes, hmmmm critical', I scribbled next to his name. Next was Oluwafemi, an African male and PE specialist. 'Smiley', I wrote. Then there was Hamid, the Asian male. He was the Maths specialist, and had refused to shake the hand of any female leaders, citing it went against his Islamic faith. 'Google Islam, women and handshaking' I scrawled. Finally we were introduced to Fred, a middle-aged, sour-faced male, the English specialist. Noooooo! was my first impression. Noooooo! He looked harsh.

I did seven joint observations with Fred. He wasn't as scary as I first thought; he was professional, and had good subject knowledge. Three of his Teaching judgements I felt were inaccurate, and challenged him, evidencing all my comments. He agreed with my points and improved the grades.

Maths was not so lucky. Hamid was very dismissive to the women he encountered within the department, which was a problem as both the Head of Faculty and Line Manager were both female. All his teaching judgements were challenged, but he refused to budge. He said he was confident to report that the majority of the teaching he observed in the department required improvement. The Head of Faculty demanded she be present when he justified his poor teaching judgements, in light of the fact that the majority of the students had made and were making not good but exceptional progress.

Horrible Hamid, as he was known by the Senior team, continued his reign of pain, and grilled the Head of Faculty in the Subject meeting, even on self-explanatory aspects of the data and was, ironically, very unhappy that students who received Pupil Premium funding were doing exceptionally better than those who weren't. Carolyn came out of her meeting frustrated and on the verge of tears. She was close to pulling off her wig and dashing it at him!

I led two subject meetings with Assistant Head Penny and, after hearing about the Maths experience, we decided to take control. We evidenced why the English department was outstanding; defended our RAISE data; highlighted the phenomenal progress made by our Pupil Premium students; described how we would sustain improvement; showed how our mapping supported SEN and AG&T students, along with SMSC development, and handed over book samples.

Fred dug deep, and tried hard to shake our defence; he requested more books to scrutinise, samples of students' trial examination answer papers and data over time for three of our looked-after children. He was very thorough, but Penny and I went into that room with the intention of showing Fred that our team were on top of their game. We also used the forum to sing the praises of other departments who had shared good practice, and we had since embedded some of the ideas because of the positive impact.

In a training session, a couple of years back, the Head had told staff about the Dutch Admiral principle:

There were two junior officers in the Dutch Navy who made a pact. They decided that when they were at navy social functions, they would go out of their way to tell people what a great guy the other guy was. They'd appear at cocktail parties or dances and say: "What an unbelievable person Charlie is. He's the best man in the Navy" or "Did you hear about the brilliant idea Dave had?" Their secret efforts influenced the perceptions that others held. Peers saw them as leaders and doers. Both men were eventually made admirals – the two youngest ever appointed in the Dutch Navy.

So we ensured we slipped into our conversation that we did DIRT (Dedicated Improvement & Reflection Time) with the students - an activity that was shared from Humanities. We mentioned we used marking and feedback stamps, which we had originally seen used in Science, and bigged up the Teaching and Learning team, who had standardised the use of the green pen, and the whole school was now using them in the same way.

The meeting finally ended after sixty-five minutes and, once outside the room, Penny and I breathed a sigh of relief.

"My head is pounding," Penny groaned.

"Ditto," I replied. "He was tough." I paused. "You were great," I grinned, and held out for a high five.

"You too, girl," Penny said in a fake American accent, as she slapped my palm.

We both began to laugh.

Taking five minutes, Penny and I chilled in my office. I removed my shoes and started on my leftover sandwich.

The phone rang. The Head's PA's name flashed on the display. I pressed the loudspeaker button.

"I need to schedule you and Penny in for another meeting with Fred. Apparently, he has more questions," she said.

"Noooooooooooooooooo!" Penny and I yelled in unison, while I put my face in my hands. Penny lay across the desk, giving up the will to live.

Surprisingly, the two days went by swiftly. My attitude remained constant. I had been on an Ofsted Inspector Shadowing course, and found that the schools with the best outcomes were the ones who operated normally, and who did not feel intimidated by the presence of the Inspectors. The Inspectors were visitors in our school. We knew we worked effectively and very hard on a day-to-day basis. They were just ordinary people doing a job and, in less than three days, they would be going back to their lives.

It was both inspiring and amusing to watch the Head in action. She meant business. It was like she was not just fighting for the right grade for the staff and students, but also for the community at large. Following meetings, she also ran around collecting evidence, along with rallying the senior troops at key points to see if we needed support. She made sure the Inspectors got a sense of our school, and knew that both the staff and students were incredible. She went through our strengths and weaknesses, as outlined in the SEF, and clearly explained our strategy to be even more effective.

The children were lionesses and, without prompting throughout the two days, would stop the Inspectors in their tracks. A group of students even waited outside the staff toilets for the Lead Inspector, so they could tell him how much they loved the school and how great it was.

On their final day, the Inspectors were invited to our weekly whole-school Assembly and, at the end, the Head addressed the capacity crowd.

"As you know, you are the best students in the whole world." The students, who were used to being told this, began to clap and scream.

"You are all *Outstanding*." They began to scream louder.

"And I dare anyone to say otherwise." The students began to scream.

Clearly, that last sentence was directed at the Lead Inspector, as the Head stared in his direction as she powerfully delivered the final statement. All of the Senior Leadership team began to roar.

At 3.00pm, the Judgement was in.

The Head, Richard (the Lead Inspector) and members of the Senior Leadership team headed to the staff room to break the news informally.

"Thank you for allowing us to visit your school," the Lead Inspector began. "We have enjoyed observing lessons and meeting you all and your wonderful students. Truly, they are a credit to you."

He paused.

"The judgement at this time is confidential, because it can change if challenged, so I ask that you do not tell anyone outside this room until it is officially posted on our website."

He paused again.

Staff members' eyes were transfixed on Richard's every word.

"However, our findings are as follows:

The quality of teaching, learning and assessment – Outstanding!

Personal development, behaviour and welfare – Outstanding!

The effectiveness of leadership and management – Outstanding!

Outcomes for pupils – Outstanding!

We find your school to be Outstanding in all areas."

The staff, who had looked tired, weary and worn when the Leadership team entered the room, had out of nowhere gained an extra boost of energy, and began to scream and cheer and kiss and hug the person nearest to them.

It was great to witness this honour given to such a well-deserving team of people. The damp eyes were evidence enough to show how much the judgement - but more importantly, the school - meant to them.

I decided to make a swift exit before I started to blub. I was drained. I was knackered. I needed to sleep.

"So what next?" Penny poked her head round my office door. "Fancy going for a drink with some of the team, or are you too mashed?"

"Drinking while I'm on medication? No way. You go. I've got to be somewhere," I replied.

Once the door was closed, I put my head in my hands and began to quiver. The prospect of my next move was strangely worse than OFSTED calling.

I had to face my mum!

"Wha gwaan bad a maanin,
cyaan kum gud a evelin".

It is unwise to spend valuable time worrying
about problems we cannot solve.

Mad Boyz

Sometimes I wish the penny would drop much sooner for some of my boys, and that they would take school and the opportunities it offered more seriously before it was too late. Knowing that the big, wide world would be twice as hard for most is enough to make me want to shake them into fixing up, but, for some of them, you have to accept: it just ain't going to happen. As my mother would say to my brothers and me when we were kids: "Those who can't hear, muss feel," meaning 'If you don't listen, you will suffer the consequences'.

Leo Black was typical of the Jamaican proverb. He was a bright lad, with supportive parents, but couldn't be arsed to get his finger out and focus. In Year 7, school was one giant fairground ride. In Year 8, he climbed out of a classroom window to try and get out of reading in a lesson. By Year 9, he still hadn't got it together and, in Year 10, did not take his Options seriously. By the time the examination period arrived in Year 11, he was lost. He sat the first Maths paper and struggled to answer any questions, because he had never been in a lesson long enough to learn. His Head of Year, Gideon, was broken, because he had spent a lot of energy and effort trying to 'save' Leo by giving him a mentor, and even picking him up from home and taking him to school. All efforts were without success. He watched Leo struggle to answer any questions on the paper, eventually giving up and spending most of the time with his head on the desk. This was the typical pattern for all his exams.

On the day of the exam for the second Maths paper, Leo didn't even show up. A reminder call went home, and his parents, who had always been supportive, embarrassingly said they could not get him out of his room. Leo arrived at school in August to collect his GCSE results, and was seriously shocked to see he had failed all his exams. Gideon went over to console him and was shocked to realised Leo couldn't fathom how he had failed all his exams. Which begs the question: at what point do students realise the consequences of their behaviour and how, as teachers, do we support them before it is too late?

Joe was a student straight out of a Marvel comic: *The Incredible Hulk*! What triggered him turning green were the words 'excluded' or 'sending you home'. He would do something incredibly stupid - like pour bubble liquid onto the floor, so someone would fall over and hurt themselves - and, when reprimanded, would weep like a baby.

"Joe, I've had to send Stephen to the hospital, because it looks like he's fractured his leg after slipping on the bubbles you poured onto the floor. Do you understand why your behaviour is unacceptable?" I questioned.

"Yes, Miss," Joe replied.

"Why?" I probed.

"Because someone got hurt, Miss," he replied.

"Yes, but also because deliberately pouring liquid on the floor like that is very dangerous. I'm sorry, Joe," I continued, "but I am going to have to call your mother and tell her I am recommending a five-day fixed-term exclusion for your behaviour."

As soon as I said the word 'exclusion', Joe slowly turned a shade of green and exploded. He began to kick the doors and the doorframe, ran into the corridor, and then began to try and smash the windows in the corridor doors. (Thank goodness they were shatterproof!) There was *no way* I was following him while he was in his monster rage. I had three kids at home who needed me! I radioed for a Learning Mentor, and alerted staff to not let any students out of their rooms until the situation was under control. The Head and three Learning Mentors and I found Joe under a staircase on the floor, curled up into a ball and sobbing uncontrollably.

"Don't let that sad picture fool you," I told them when I arrived. "He's mad! And a health and safety threat!"

It took another 'Hulk' incident for the school to move him on. I felt no remorse writing up the paperwork to put him out. Joe needed counselling and support with his social skills - much more than we could provide. When other innocent children are being put at risk, for me there is no discussion. Fortunately, that feeling was mutual across Senior Leadership.

I was convinced that some of the male students joining the school mid-term from Eastern Europe were slightly older - actually very much older - than they had declared. Gibaldi was one that raised my suspicions. The fact that, at 13 years old, he was close to six foot in height and had a very deep, baritone voice was definitely a clue. An even bigger one came on my birthday.

"Happy birthday, Miss," he said in his best English, and smiled shyly as he stood by my door.

"Why, thank you, Gibaldi," I smiled back.

He then placed an awkwardly wrapped package and a card on my desk.

"Oh, wow! You shouldn't have spent your money on me! That wasn't necessary."

"You nice teacher," he replied, and stood by my desk, still smiling.

I took that as my cue to open the card and gift.

I removed the card from the envelope.

'Happy Anniversary' was the bold headline across the top.

I laughed.

"It's Birthday, Gibaldi, not Anniversary," I tried to explain.

"Happy Birthday, Miss," he repeated.

He doesn't have a clue what I'm saying, I laughed to myself, and began to open the gift.

Inside was a see-through top. A very, *very* see-through top. I looked at Gibaldi. He was now grinning.

"Oh! Ermmm..." I said out loud.

"You like?" Gibaldi asked.

"Very nice, but not nice for Miss," I tried to be gentle.

"Very nice for Miss," Gibaldi confirmed, as his hands did an outline of large breasts.

Eghhh, I thought. I know about hormones, but no way was this boy 13!

"You know he nicked the card from George's shop, Miss," Nadia, a fellow student, confirmed. "It's the first one he grabbed, that's why it says Anniversary!" she laughed.

"And the top?" I enquired.

"Oh, that was his mum's. It has a little top thingy that goes under it, but Gibaldi said you would look nicer without it!" By now, Nadia was in hysterics.

"Eee-owwww!" I shuddered. "This is bad. So, so bad."

I summoned Gibaldi to my office and met him by the door. In my hands, I held up the see-through top.

"You like?" Gibaldi repeated with a wide grin, and that pervy tone.

"I'm afraid not," I said honestly. "But I know someone who does..."

He looked confused.

I opened my office door and yelled inside.

"Mrs Karvonio, you like? Yes?"

Gibaldi's mother approached the door and grabbed her top. She was furious. Gibaldi was in shock. She began speaking at speed in Kosovan. I couldn't translate, but someone was in big trouble. Big time! I thought. I like…? Yes, I like…. I like that *very* much!

Then there's the Mad Boyz, whom you just can't help feeling sorry for.

JJ was brought to me by a concerned member of staff. He had been seen in the playground, trying to set an aerosol can alight.

"Did you try and set fire to that can?"

"Yes, Miss," he said calmly.

"Why?" I asked.

"I just wanted to see if it would explode," he replied.

"And if I called your mum right now, what would she say?" I continued.

"I would get beats, Miss," he answered honestly.

I had time for kids who, when they were in trouble, were honest rather than told lies and wasted my time, but JJ's straightforwardness concerned me. I decided maybe shock tactics were needed on this occasion. I googled images of Katie Piper, Simon Weston and other people whose faces had burns, and explained that he could have ended up disfigured or, God forbid, another pupil could have been disfigured if they had been in the wrong place at the wrong time, and the can had exploded. JJ winced.

"Now you've seen these pictures, JJ, how would you do things differently?"

"Well," JJ replied, "I'd try my hardest, Miss, not to do it again, but I can't promise because I often do silly things and don't know why."

Oh my days! How do you punish someone for being so honest? I wondered.

"Well, if that's your hardest, JJ, I'm afraid it's not good enough. I respect your honesty, but don't appreciate it. You cannot go around lighting aerosol cans; it is dangerous."

"Yes, Miss," JJ replied.

"What's your target grade in Science?" I asked.

"4," JJ replied.

"And what's your current grade?"

"2."

Ahhh. That explains it. Clearly he didn't pass the Science module on gases.

"I'm not going to send you home, JJ, because you have been honest. Stupid, but honest," I began.

"Yes, Miss," he responded contritely.

"So, as punishment, I want a 250-word essay on 'Why it is Dangerous to Heat an Aerosol Can'. And you can start it this Saturday. You are expected in the school library in full school uniform at 9.00am."

"Yes, Miss. Thank you, Miss," JJ replied.

I looked at him and he smiled.

Mad, I thought, he's mad. Just like Sonny, but Sonny wasn't going to get away with his behaviour so easily.

Sonny was put in detention for disrupting the learning in an English lesson and, when spoken to, refused to leave the classroom.

"I ain't doing the detention. I don't care what anybody says. I won't, and you can't make me!"

One of the things I've learnt about disciplining a student, especially one of the seniors, is to avoid doing this in front of an audience.

"No big ting, Sonny," I said. "I'll be back for you later, and we can discuss this then."

The class began to snigger, and Sonny's temper began to boil.

"Oh, why don't you teachers just f**k off and leave me alone?" and with that, he got up, brushed past me and stormed out of the room.

I followed him and, once in the corridor, I called his name.

"Sonny, you need to stop and come here right now."

He turned around but continued walking. "Make me!" he yelled back. "If you're bad, make me, Miss, and see what will happen!"

Endri, a senior staff member, was ahead, stopped him in his tracks, held onto his arms and began to reason with him.

"Let him go, sir," I said firmly, as I approached them. "Let Sonny go, so I can see just how bad he is!"

By now, I was face to face with him, and maaaad!

Endri took one look at my face and swiftly dragged Sonny away.

"Let him go, Endri," I insisted firmly.

"I'm sorting this, Julz!" he replied calmly, as he pulled Sonny away from my presence. I was still fuming.

The next day, there was a note on my office floor. It had been slid under my door. It was from Sonny.

Dear Miss

I realise what I had done was wrong so me myself and I have chose to apologise without even having to be forced.

I was upset from this morning and was not in the right mind so I did what I had done. So I have decided to man up and apologise for what I have done and hopefully you will forgive me.

From Sonny

I kissed my teeth. Sonny was placed in the Isolation Room for his behaviour but had he learnt his lesson? Sometimes students have to think before they act, and realise teachers are human, too. I emailed his English teacher, and told her that Sonny would be out of her lessons for the rest of the week, so she should give him some work and someone would pick him up from her class tomorrow.

The following day I went to Sonny's English class. He was standing by the door with his work in his hand, waiting to be collected. He looked terrified as I approached. "Thanks, Miss," I said to the teacher. "Follow me," I said to Sonny and walked ahead. Sonny followed me as if he were heading for the gallows.

He entered my office and I told him to sit down. He looked nervous and continued to stand.

"D-Did you get my letter?" he stuttered.

"Yes," I replied.

"No one told me to write it. I did that myself, Miss," he quickly added.

"So you said in your letter." I was flippant.

"Am I out of English for the rest of the week?" he queried.

"Yep," I replied.

"Who will I be working with?" he asked quietly.

"Me," I said firmly, and looked him in the eyes and smiled.

He froze.

"You, Miss?" Sonny said. His voice began to shake.

"Yes, Sonny. Me. I am a qualified English teacher, you know," I grinned.

"Now sit down," I said in my best teacher voice, and pointed to the student desk I had in my office, "and turn to page 56 in your workbook. Today, we are going to look at how to summarise text."

For the next four days, Sonny was perfect: he arrived at my office on time, fully equipped and eager to learn. He earned several merits for great work and, if I had to admit it, I enjoyed teaching him. One to one, he was a model student. At the end of our final session, I gave him a Praise Postcard for the excellent effort he had made, and emailed his English teacher reminding her of Sonny's return on Monday, updating her on the work Sonny had completed, and how excellent his behaviour had been.

Monday was always a mad day for me: Leadership Briefing first thing; Year 7 Assembly during registration; teaching Period 1; a Line Management meeting Period 2, and Break Duty. I rushed to my office at the end of break to collect my documents for a Self Review meeting I had Period 3 and, to my surprise, Sonny was standing outside.

"What's up, Sonny?" I enquired.

"It's English now, Miss," he replied.

"I know, but you're back with your class," I reminded him.

"But I want to stay with you," he whined.

"What?" I was in shock. He could not be serious.

"Sonny, you were with me last week as a punishment," I confirmed.

"But I like staying with you, Miss. You make English fun," he smiled.

This child could not be serious.

"Sonny," I smiled. "I am going to count to ten, and if you are not inside your English class, sitting down, with your book in front of you, with today's date, the title and LO written down, then I will be sending you to spend some time with Mr Banjo."

"One..." Sonny stood in thought. "Two..." he began to run...

I followed him down the corridor and watched him enter his class, get seated, open his exercise book and start writing.

You know something, I thought to myself, some of these boys I teach are not just mad, they're absolutely crazzzzzzzy!

"Yuh shake man han, yuh nuh shake him heart."

Appearances can be deceiving.

Week Beginning: 27th November

One Size Doesn't Fit All

The effective triangular partnership of Parent, Teacher and Child is what I believe makes for a successful educational outcome. If any part of that triangle breaks down, then expect problems.

My school has always been a positive environment, where staff go over and above for the children, so it was hard for me in my early days of teaching to imagine another institution doing anything less. My school provides a free breakfast to all students who arrive in school before 8am. Where uniform is an issue, we have bought items for students: shoes, trousers, jumpers and, if finances have stopped a child participating in an educational experience, we have paid. We have even gone the extra mile and picked children up from home to ensure they are in school and receiving an education. These examples are just the tip of the iceberg.

However, I have come to realise that sadly, my school is an exception to the rule. I am called upon more and more frequently, because of my position and knowledge of education, to be an advocate for friends (or friends of friends) in meetings with Head Teachers or senior leaders, following incidents where their children have been suspended, threatened with a managed move, or with permanent exclusion from school.

Many of these incidents could be addressed more swiftly if parents were aware of school and educational policies, and how they can legally challenge any concerns they may have. I have been shocked with the illegal way some schools have operated and the threats they have levied on parents, and how these schools would have got away with blatant racism if they had not been held to account.

These experiences confirm that the English education system does not suit all children. One size most certainly does not fit all and, as a parent, you have to know your child and the factors and environments that allow them to grow effectively, and then make an informed judgement as to what is best for them to thrive academically.

I am a teacher but also a mother, and I know my children, who are my greatest investment. So when my eldest son, at 12 years old, began to play up at school, as a family we looked at his potential, the environment and the factors that were stopping him from achieving and eventually, after a series of discussions, which included my son, we made the tough decision to send him to the Caribbean to continue his secondary education.

Many parents I know have pre-empted a negative educational outcome and sent their child abroad to be educated. And for most, it's the best decision they have ever made. My friend Maureen was told by her son's teachers in the UK that he did not belong in a mainstream school. She decided to fight the decision, but her fear of him failing - and ending up on the school-to-prison trajectory - made her change her mind, choosing instead to pack up and move to Jamaica. Today, her boy Jay is excelling at his school in Kingston, and achieving top grades.

Others parents I know have made the brave decision to homeschool, because they have realised the traditional way of learning does not suit their child. Children can move on to study A levels without going down the traditional school route. Many homeschool students study at home, then sit GCSEs at an independent centre. Once successful, they then move on to a Level 3 qualification. This is often supported with Saturday Supplementary school sessions - an option that has proved successful within the Black community for over 40 years.

I read a post on social media from a mother, who had made the decision to homeschool her son. It spoke volumes, and I applaud her courage and admire her for not handing over her child to a system that she believed would fail him:

'On this day, January 31st, at 3pm, I am proud to say my son will officially be deregistered from mainstream school. I will not fight or exhaust my energy and efforts into an institutional system to accept my child or train him to get information. No longer will he be excluded from services and experiences that enhance his development while his unique abilities and spirit are classed as 'not normal'! My child is a product of me, so normality is something we do not subscribe to. So with great pleasure I embrace the next stage in our relationship as I homeschool my Prince.'

What many parents fail to realise is that they have a choice as to how they want their children educated, and what curriculum diet they want their child fed.

It is therefore essential, if your child is being educated in the mainstream system, that you engage with the school, keep up to date with their progress, and attend all meetings, so you are up to speed with their performance and any school policy changes.

I love Parents' Evening.

My colleagues and I sometimes play the game 'Spot the parent', and we try to guess who their child is. More often than not, you realise why a kid behaves a certain way when you see their parents' characteristics in action. At our school, we ask parents to come in and see us twice a year to get updated on their child's progress and, surprisingly for some, that's two occasions too many.

Our school keeps records of attendance, so the pressure is on not to be the Year group with the lowest turnout. My strategy to combat this is to collect the students, whose parents did not attend Parents' Meeting, the following day, and give them all an hour's detention. This ensures their parents get an earful from their kids when they get home!

Following my most recent detention, I had a call from an irate father, who wanted to know if it was true that I had told his son he was out of order for not coming into school for his report. I confirmed that it was true I had told all the children that, and stood by what I said. Another parent came in to complain to the Head Teacher about me giving their child a detention, because they could not attend as they were busy. "Too busy to phone the school and apologise for not being able to attend?" was my response. Parents get a year's notice and, if they can't turn up or contact the school to reschedule, I think it's bang out of order.

Eight parents came into school to cuss me off after my actions. I took the criticism gracefully and, at the same time, it gave me an opportunity to talk about their child's progress and discuss their child's report. I don't know about you, but that's what I call a result.

It's strange: parents won't come in for Parents' Evening, but can find the time to come down the school for the strangest of reasons. A mother sent the gran and two aunties to fight me for sending her son home for swearing at a teacher and slamming the door in his face; another refused to come in for their appointment when her son told a girl to suck his d*ck, but had no hesitation to rush down the school when their mobile phone had been confiscated. I even had a father, whom I had never met before (even though his daughter had been in my care for over three years), saying that if I didn't return his daughter's very expensive non-uniform hoodie, he was going to 'lick me down'. Ironically, two Learning Mentors intervened, and decided to remove him from the premises for his safety, because they knew what I could be like if I lost my temper!

You have to laugh, but honestly, sometimes I just don't get it. If these are the messages we are getting from parents, can we really expect better from the children?

I should add that there are the faithful ones, who consistently attend meetings, call the school, are up to date with their child's progress, and support the school in all matters to ensure their child excels.

Take Jacob's mum - a strong Nigerian, who will accept nothing less than her son leaving school with enough qualifications to ensure he becomes a top surgeon. Jacob is aware of his family expectations and works solidly. He can often be found in the library after school, completing homework, and is even in school on Saturdays. At this particular Parents' Evening she was furious. Jacob's report had all Level 8 grades and one Level 7. Level 8 is the equivalent to the old A* grade; Level 7 is an A grade. For Jacob's mum, the Level 7 stood out like a sore thumb.

She began to raise her voice: "Look, Miss, a 7, that is bad, a Level 7!" An embarrassed Jacob was close to tears.

"Look, Mum," I replied even louder. "Seven Level 8s, Mum, *seven*. That is fantastic! If Jacob were my son, I'd be buying him a car!" Ms Owusu looked even more shocked: "A car, eh? Home, Jacob!"

Relieved, Jacob slyly beamed, and I was left sighing. How do you find the happy medium?

Well first, I would encourage all parents to play an active role in their child's education. Don't just instinctively ask the question: 'How was school today?' without showing a genuine interest in the answer. If you ask a closed question, you will get a simple answer: 'Fine, good, OK.' Try asking an open question and probing further, so you can get a clearer picture of what is happening in your child's classroom.

I was stopped by a parent in the supermarket, who told me not to tell off my youngest son, who was in Year 5, for being placed in time-out two days in a row, because her daughter said that it was the other boy's fault for picking on him. I was dumbstruck. How is it a random parent, who recognises me picking my fruit and veg, is telling me about the school punishing *my* son? What planet was I on?

When I got home, I sat my son down, and he told me about a boy in his class who kept throwing pencils at him, and he got angry so threw one back. He said he was told off and placed in time-out, because the other boy had special needs, so he should have been 'more understanding'. I was fuming!

"What should you do if you are told off by a teacher or placed in time-out?" I asked.

"Tell you," he said contritely.

"You may get in trouble, but you must always be honest," I reminded him. "I am going to contact your teacher, so I can meet with her to have a chat about this, OK?"

"Yes, Mum."

I emailed the school for an appointment, and sat in front of his teacher a day later. She was stuttering. She knew I was also a teacher. The meeting was less than 10 minutes, and I was professional and to the point. If my son misbehaves in her class and has to be punished, I support that, but I want to know about it so I can speak to him and support with his behaviour. I do not want to hear it first from a parent in a supermarket, so I would appreciate a letter in his bag, posted home or an email. I told her that my son enjoys school and his learning, and if something is hindering that, I would like to know about it so I can support.

His teacher looked relieved and relaxed when she realised I was there to support. She admitted there was an issue with the other student, and has asked the senior leaders in the school to intervene. I had no intention of going to war with this woman; she was with my son six hours a day and, right or wrong, it was in my interest that she liked him. At the end of each term, she would get a card and some chocolates from me, and loved my gesture. I'd say that's a fiver well spent.

As I mentioned earlier, it is important you know what is going on when it comes to your child and school. Below, as a starting point, are a few questions you can ask your child when they come home, which should give you a better picture of their day and, if there are concerns, you can pick them up through your developing conversation.

1. What did you enjoy most about your day?
2. Rate your day on a scale from 1-10. Why did you pick that number?
3. Who did you play with today?
4. What was something silly that happened today?
5. What new word did you learn today?
6. Did the teacher ask you to answer a question? What was it?
7. What did you eat for lunch?
8. If you could switch seats with anyone in your class, whom would you trade with? Why?

9. What did you read today? Can you relate to any of the characters?
10. What made you laugh today?
11. Did anyone cry?
12. How did your friends make you feel today? Was anyone not nice to someone?
13. What exciting thing did you learn today?
14. What didn't you like about your day?
15. What did you do that was creative? What made you feel proud?
16. Is there anything that the teacher taught that you don't understand?
17. Did you ever feel unsafe?
18. What made your teacher smile? Did anything make her frown?
19. Were there any guests that came to your class today? What did they do?
20. How do you feel that you did today? Why?

"A nuh ebreeting soak up waata a sponge."

Scrutinise carefully before making decisions.

EPISODE 13

Bunking Off

Our school's whole-school attendance target is 95%. If a child has one day off every week from Years 7 to 11, that is equivalent to missing one academic year of schooling.

After the popular tummy ache, being a translator for their parents comes high on the excuse list as to why a child is not in school, along with - believe it or not - relaxing at home on your birthday, or choosing to stay away for fear of the dreaded birthday beats.

Our attendance figures are broken down into Year groups, and are published every week in our staff newsletter, and the competitiveness is fierce. No one takes losing lightly, so I developed a few methods that have proved successful over the terms, to ensure my students were on the right side of the school gates and on time.

Home visits. Here's the scenario: A child does not want to get up for school. Parents call in, concerned. And I turn up at the house bright and early to wake them up. Unorthodox, yes, but the fear of me revealing to their mates that I've seen them in their pyjamas is incentive enough for them to fix up and get into school on time. However, on one occasion it backfired. Young Adam jumped out of his window when he opened his eyes and realised I was sitting at his bedside. Luckily, his bedroom was on the ground floor.

Gulistan's absence excuse was thankfully not that common. She had been out of school for two days, which was unusual. The receptionist informed me that her father had called in to report she was ill. Not a problem, you may think… Well, yes it is actually, especially when her dad's voice sounds like a 12-year-old!

Busted! I thought it best not to call her mum straight away. Instead, I caught up with Gulli on her mobile, and gave her 30 minutes to report to my office.

She had been with her boyfriend, who had made the call, and was planning to run away because she had just found out she was pregnant and, as a Muslim, was terrified that her dad was going to kill her.

The 'How-could-you-be-so-stupid?' lecture followed. Her response: she was pregnant, but she had never had sex.

I'll clarify for the confused, because I certainly was. Now stay with me, and I'll try to make this as simple as possible.

His 'car' had been in her 'driveway' for about half an hour, but not 'parked' in the 'garage'. However, at some point there was an 'oil leak' that went everywhere. And bang - but not literally - immaculate conception.

I know, I know, some of you may still be confused, just read that bit again. Please don't let me go there. Honestly, this is the best I can do without getting too graphic.

My mind flashed back to the birth of my first child. Twenty-three hours in labour. Gas, air, pethidine and the epidural. Somehow, I couldn't in my wildest dreams imagine what Gulistan had been going through. A baby without sex! It's like paying off your credit card with no goods to show for it! Sorry.

I requested intervention from the school nurse. She confirmed a false alarm. I was relieved. Gulistan was back in class, and my attendance percentage was healthier.

I was concerned about her naivety and, although we do not have to let parents know about incidents like this, I felt it necessary to inform her mother about the absences. I told Gulistan that was what I was going to do, and that it was her responsibility to come up with an explanation. And, in my opinion, honesty was always the best policy.

Surprisingly, a lot of the parents are in cahoots with their children, so I have no sympathy when they are threatened with legal action and if prosecuted a fine of up to £2,500.

Sarbjeet's dad was different. The family were Stage 3. The Educational Welfare Officer (EWO) had completed papers for court action, and he was desperate for support.

I guess I'm a sucker for a man in tears, and tried on two occasions to halt the court case and put systems in place to get his 13-year-old son back into school.

Three-way meetings were conducted. I organised taxis to bring him in; I'd go and collect him from home myself, and I'd even given students canteen vouchers to knock for him at 7.30am each morning, with instructions not to leave his house without him!

Each strategy would work for a fortnight, then we would be back to the drawing board.

Sarbjeet continued to slack; EWO screws would tighten, and Dad would break down in despair. He said he had taken away his Xbox and iPad, and Sarbjeet was grounded until he attended school regularly. I felt so sorry for Dad; it wasn't fair to blame the parents when they were doing all they could. I was determined to up the support.

At Parents' Evening he was at his wits' end. Sarbjeet sat next to him, looking hapless and withdrawn. I sat opposite, with his tutor and the Deputy Head of Year. At the end of the appointment, I told Dad not to worry, and gave him work for Sarbjeet to complete at home, while I worked on a part-time timetable to support.

By seven that evening, only a handful of parents were left, and a group of staff were gathering by the main doors, with the destination being the local pub. Knackered, I declined and headed home for a long soak before I tackled some marking. It was about 8.30pm when my WhatsApp beeped.

It was one of my tutors, Lynn.

OMG! In pub. Just seen in corner, Sarbjeet and Dad. Sarbjeet is drinking a pint!

Shocked, I asked her to go over to the father, and telephone me in front of him.

Mr Patel sounded terrified when I said, "Hello." And so he bloody well should be. Talk about taking the mick!

I was brief. If Sarbjeet wasn't in school **every** day and on time for the rest of the term, not only was I going to make a referral to the Educational Welfare Officer, but I would also make it my personal mission to visit Social Services and report him!

The following day, a contrite father and son were waiting by my office door. It was 7.30am. Before he could speak, I abruptly clarified that last night I had made my position clear. Sarbjeet needed to be in school. Every day and on time!

Nine weeks on, and I was proudly signing certificates for our Rewards Assembly. Sarbjeet Patel: 100% attendance and punctuality.

Now *that* certainly called for a drink. Cheers!

"Man nuh dead, nuh call dem duppy."

Don't underestimate people.

Week Beginning: 11th December

Dress Smart, Think Smart

There are a myriad of reasons why you should dress well every day, no matter what you're doing or where you're going. This essential habit, if embedded at school level, will stay with students throughout their lifetime.

Many people cite a number of reasons why uniform is bad for students: one of their main arguments is that children are individuals, and wearing what they want is a way of expressing that. However, say that to poor little Oliver, who is trying to compete with the other students wearing name brands, and who are teasing him because he is dressed in budget gear.

I have always told students that, when they leave school, most of them will have to adhere to a uniform code: lawyers, doctors, police officers, firefighters, even shop assistants have to conform, so it was good practice for them to start early. I would explain to the unconvinced that dressing well could be so rewarding and really change their day and mood, especially when we live in a society where first impressions count. People make assumptions during a first meeting about someone's professional credibility and potential performance, based upon appearance, and it is difficult to overcome a first impression, regardless of your knowledge and expertise.

For schools, uniform is an excellent way of identifying a cohort; it also supports a level playing field, and ensures at a glance that everyone is equal.

On my journey up the leadership ladder, I was given Uniform as one of my areas of responsibility. Little did I know it was the short straw and, in a matter of months, from holding good ranking positions - either first, second or third - in the popular Year Book categories ('Best Dressed', 'Nicest Smile', 'Who We Will Miss The Most'), I swiftly hit the bottom of the polls, and became the most hated teacher by the fashion-forward girls, who had decided to test me and push the uniform boundaries.

During my first week in power, I sent home a Uniform Policy reminder of what was deemed to be appropriate dress; I created a weekly tutor group checklist, and organised a series of sanctions for those who chose to flagrantly break the rules. Ms B was in the house, and our school was going to be the smartest in the UK. My target? Every student in the school would have a tie, which was tied high (I ordered clip-on ties for the younger students); a school jumper worn appropriately, and not tied around their waist or in their bag; black school shoes, not pumps or trainers, and I was going to tackle the slow but steady rise in piercings; nose, chin, tongue, unnatural hair colours, make-up, fake nails and false eyelashes.

The boys must have breathed a sigh of relief, as most of this did not affect them. The girls, however – well, some of them - were ready for battle.

By week two, I was sending girls as young as 11 to the loos to wash the foundation and eyeliner off their faces. When asked why they were wearing this to school, most answered: "To look pretty, Miss."

By week three, at least four girls had been sent home to cut off or remove their acrylic nails. Most couldn't even hold a pen properly or type during ICT because of the length.

By week four, I had purchased eyelash remover to get rid of the fake eyelashes. They were like spider legs invading the young, innocent faces. Some of the girls couldn't even see properly through the lashes because they were so thick. Oh, please!

By week five, girls were running the other way whenever they saw me in the corridor or playground. One parent complained that she could not stop her child from wearing the piercing in her lip, and another made an appointment to see me to explain that her daughter was refusing to come to school without the false eyelashes, because she suffered from alopecia and needed to wear them for her self-esteem. I asked Mum to bring in a doctor's certificate to confirm this. I'm still waiting.

Jayden's mum was up the school in a flash when I removed his non-uniform hoodie in Assembly. I gave him the choice to sit outside the Hall or wear the replacement school jumper I had in my hand. He stormed out of the school and ran home to report me to his mum.

"How dare you embarrass my son in front of the whole school!" she yelled. She was in the school office, ready for me, in less than 10 minutes. "I'm not working," she yelled, "so I cannot afford to buy him a jumper!" she continued.

Clearly, you're not working, which is why you can fly straight down here to curse me, I thought. Yes, thought. I'm not *that* rude!

"Tell me something, Mum," I asked. "Did you buy Jayden this hoodie?" I held up the Nike hoodie I had removed from Jayden earlier.

"Yes," she snapped.

"How long ago?" I queried.

"I'm not sure!" She began to get agitated at my change of subject.

"Last week? Last month? This half term?" I queried.

"About two weeks ago," she said sharply.

"And how much did it cost?" I asked.

"None of your business!" she yelled. It clicked, where I was going with this.

"Well, let me tell you," I continued firmly. "Not less than thirty quid. I can google JD Sports, if you like?"

Jayden's mum was not happy.

"Our school jumpers, which are available from the school office, are £9.99! I suggest, Ms Hall, that you purchase one, when you can afford it. In the meantime, I am happy to loan you one until then, but I don't want to see Jayden in school until he is wearing a school jumper."

With that, I handed his mum his hoodie and walked away. I could see and feel the steam, which was coming out of her ears, fill the Reception area, but I did not pause from my stride, just in case she decided to jump me! Jayden was back in school that afternoon, wearing a new school jumper his mum bought after I left. Mmmm. I refused to think facety thoughts. He was in school, in uniform, and that was good enough for me.

Consistency is the key to tackling poor uniform and nipping violations in the bud early. If one student gets away with breaking the uniform code, then another will see and think it's OK and join in. It's amazing to see what ridiculous trends catch on and, with every trend, I have to update the policy because if it's not written down, it is assumed by students and parents to be OK.

Update 5. I typed.

- No coloured hair extensions, eg. blue, red, purple.
- No coloured contact lenses, eg. blue, green, purple.
- No white ankle socks over black tights.
- No pink ankle socks over black tights.
- No headscarves… Hmmm.
- No bedscarves.

Can you believe if I challenge students, their parents have the audacity to call up to complain?

"Hilda who?" Laquitha's mum sounded confused.

"Hilda Ogden," I replied. "She was a cleaner, who wore a headscarf on the soap, *Coronation Street.*"

"Are you calling my child a cleaner?" she yelled.

"No. I am saying a headscarf is not appropriate for school. Work, maybe, if she was Hilda Ogden!"

And just when you have quashed one area of concern, up creeps another crazy trend.

"You are kidding me, Ben!" I exclaimed. "Tell me I'm seeing things!"

"My shoes are broken and these are all I had to wear," he responded.

"Flip flops? You are wearing flip flops with socks to school?"

"They're called sliders, Miss," he corrected.

"Well, you need to slide yourself into the Isolation Room right now, and you will be slipping and sliding into a three-hour detention on Saturday. Understood?"

"Yes, Miss."

Most parents were very supportive when it came to our Uniform Policy. When I called home to report Cherelle's skirt length, which was inappropriately short, Mum was shocked. She said when her child had left home in the morning that was not the case. I told Mum Cherelle would be working off timetable with me, until she replaced the skirt with one of an appropriate length.

An hour after my conversation, I got a call from Reception saying that Cherelle's mother was there, and wanted to see me. I left Cherelle in my office and went downstairs. When Mum came face to face with Cherelle, she was fuming. Cherelle stood up and, amazingly, her skirt had gained four inches in length and was past her knees. I was in shock. Did she swap skirts with another student? I felt embarrassed, and did not know what to say to Mum. Cherelle looked at me with a smug smirk. Mum had in her hand a brown paper Primark bag, and began to hit Cherelle with it.

"You tink yuh so clever?" Mum began to shout at Cherelle in a broad Jamaican accent, and continued the hit her daughter with the paper bag.

"Cynthia done seh she see yuh a go school half naked, an mi did tell her, a lie she a tell. But a hitch up, hitch up yuh skirt ina de morning time!"

Oh, I thought, relieved. Cherelle had rolled her skirt up and, when I'd left the room, she'd just rolled it back down again. Cheeky. That was close.

I calmed Mum down and removed the Primark bag from her hand. By this time it was torn, and I removed the navy item that was inside. It was a pair of trousers.

"Mrs Bremmer?"

"Yes, Mum," I replied.

"Beg you hold onto these trousers fi mi, and if you see mi pickney with her legs out a door, jus mek sure she put pon these."

"No problem, Mum," I assured her.

And with that, Cherelle's mum kissed her teeth at Cherelle, and spun out of the office.

When Soli was beaten up by a student's older brother, I was shocked. We were tight on security, so how anyone had got onto the site without being noticed was a mystery. Chanel had run home in tears at lunchtime, and had told big brother Harry, an ex-student, that Soli had wiped Pritt stick on the back of her jumper in Technology. Harry, who was three years older, had told her to go back to school; he would sort it. Somehow, he had walked on site and knocked on the Maths classroom door, and lied to the teacher saying that Miss Bremmer wanted to see Soli and Chanel for five minutes. Once outside the classroom, Harry marched both his sister and Soli around the back of the Science block, and got his sister to punch him.

"Go on, Chanel, hit him." She did.

"Harder." She did again.

"And one for luck," he added. She gave Soli a final whack.

Harry then grabbed Soli by his jumper.

"Now, don't mess with my sister again, or it will be *me* that will buss you up," he threatened, and then left.

When I scanned the CCTV, I immediately realised why Harry had not been picked up by a Mentor or a member of the Office staff. The cheeky boy had walked into school wearing his old school uniform.

I reported this to our on-site Police Officer for him to deal with Harry, and recommended that Chanel be excluded for a week for her part in the incident.

In my role of ensuring the Uniform Policy was adhered to, I had to seek advice from the Head, after a student, who was on the School Council, had provoked my thinking after I had challenged her friend and given them my 'Dress Smart, Think Smart' spiel.

"But, Miss, isn't it contradictory that you keep banging on at us to look smart and all that, and yeah, most of the teachers do dress well… Well, not as well as the Head, cos she wears designer gear," she babbled, "but pardon me if I'm being rude, Miss, but there are a few teachers who look well rough. Some come to school in trainers and they're mash up, or wear *bare* T-shirts and jeans, and some of the garms could do with ironing! It's not a good look, Miss, or example to us students. What you doing about *that*?"

"Hmmm." I had to pause for a second. In fact, I had to pause for a few minutes. Helena definitely had a point.

I decided to speak to the Head about my conversation. The policy around dress was covered in our Staff Handbook, and revised annually to ensure responsibility was taken by staff members to look smarter in the workplace. It even clearly outlined what items of clothing were inappropriate for work, from torn jeans to tight dresses. Although Helena had addressed untidy teachers, the issue stretched both sides of the scale. There were teachers who were scruff pots, and there were even some who dressed like sexpots. I decided to have a conversation with one of the staff members, whose outfits were too provocative for the classroom.

Miriam was young, very pretty and hot in hot pants, but when those pants were being worn to school, and you had horny 15-year-olds on your timetable four times a week... Not good. I decided to approach with caution, not wanting to upset or offend, so began with an analogy.

Miriam was transfixed to my every word. Her big brown eyes opened wider, as she tried to grasp what I was getting at.

"So, imagine this cupboard is your wardrobe," I began. "On the right are all your party clothes. There's a gap in the middle. And on the left are clothes you wear to work."

Miriam nodded.

"The party and school clothes should not mix," I continued. Miriam nodded again. "So on what side of your wardrobe do those very tight leggings you're wearing right now come from?" I asked.

"The party side," Miriam replied innocently.

"Exactly! Not good. Wrong side of the wardrobe," I confirmed. "You need to be wearing to school the clothes from the left side."

"But I don't have any clothes on that side," she responded.

"What?" I replied. "No skirts that go below your knees?"

Miriam shook her head.

"No blouses?"

Miriam shook her head.

"Then you need to buy some. Westfields have lots of shops that sell fabulous workwear. Party wear is a no-no."

On Monday morning, Miriam looked incredible, walking down the corridor in a calf length skirt and formal blouse. Two Year 10s were pretending to faint behind her after she walked past. "Oh boy," I sighed. "I guess some people would look sexy if they wore a bin bag."

Time to tackle the T-shirt-and-jeans crew. I decided to reference the Staff Handbook's dress code to refresh people's memories of what was appropriate attire, and hoped that would be enough for the few to smarten up. I signed the notice off with the Head's name to give the message more gravitas.

Coincidentally, following this, a member of the Art department resigned. She was incredibly talented, but school-famous for her 'very casual' dress. I was sure my dress code notice had nothing to do with her departure but, after listening to her leaving speech, I wasn't so sure.

This normally quiet teacher began to crack jokes about dress, and wanted to give all staff members advice on how to overcome their nerves when in the presence of our immaculately dressed Head. She admonished that we should take a leaf out of her book, and try doing something that worked every time for her when she was nervously face to face with the Boss.

"So…" she confidently began, as she addressed the whole staff, "when she's speaking, just imagine… she's standing there, wearing only her bra and knickers!"

The Hall fell silent and the 150 pairs of eyes either moved to look at the Head, or, like me, awkwardly stared towards the floor.

No. No. No. I began to talk silently to myself. Do not flash up that image in my mind! Ted Baker suit, Ted Baker suit, I kept repeating to myself, believing that being focused was the only way not to have a half naked vision of our leader etched in my brain.

I counted to 10, opened my ears and breathed a sigh of relief. But when I looked at my colleagues, the expression on many of their faces spoke volumes, and I started to chuckle. Clearly their smutty minds were not strong enough!

"Wha de goat du, de kid falla."

Children get their behavioural cues from their parents or other people in their lives. We should set good examples.

EPISODE 15

Week Beginning: 18th December

All Work And No Play

As Senior Management, it's important to support staff social events, but teachers have this tendency, after hours, to let their hair down just a little bit longer than most.

I have an exit strategy worked out before I attend most events, and that usually means I'm there at 7.00pm, one of the first, and gone by 9.00pm, definitely the first!

In the past at one of these dos, I have heard far more than I would have liked about a colleague's personal life, sexual preferences and deep desires, as a result of too much booze. We've had a TA leaving the party with an engaged Maths teacher, and the one night stand resulting in their fiancé breaking it off and ending up with custody of the dog. One staff member even reeled out the different STIs they had contracted in the past year! How do you look someone in the face after a revelation like *that*? Thankfully, they were too drunk to remember - or perhaps too embarrassed to acknowledge the conversation. My lips were sealed.

Believe it or not, staff members have left school as a result of incidents that have occurred after a very merry staff do. Two were caught in the loos one Christmas, with their pants down and in a compromising position, and another woke up the next day, in her bed, naked, with a work colleague who was also starkers, but fast asleep beside her. No big deal, you may think. Well, it is when she couldn't remember how he got there!

My saving grace? I was tucked up in bed by 11pm, and got all the gossip updates the following day.

I love Christmas. I'm one of those people who prefer to give rather than receive, and I get a buzz from seeing folk excited over a gift I have selected. I believed that the genius who invented Secret Santa deserves a knighthood. As a self-confessed shopaholic, I never stick to the £5 budget, and go to great pains to be creative with my random selection.

At school, the end-of-year ritual was the Secret Santa exchange, and I would quietly sit and watch from a distance as a workmate opened my gift. They'd squeal with delight at the voucher that entitled them to a night-time cruise and cocktails on the Thames, and would still be bouncing with excitement five minutes on, passing the token around for all to see. I just love Groupon offers. My money was well spent.

I was due to jet off with my family to spend Christmas in the sun, so I scooped up my two 'secret' boxes, left school promptly, and placed them under my tree until Christmas.

Only when I started to unwrap the first gift did it dawn on me that one of the boxes was very large for a fiver, and the fact that I had two gifts about A4 in size was confusing.

I put the Body Beautiful gift set on the table. Wow! This was lovely. Certainly more than a fiver. Someone must like me, I smiled. I pulled the final piece of wrapping paper off the second box, and placed the gift next to the bath set. Jasper Conran crystal glasses. I was in shock. I photographed the pressies, and sent them via WhatsApp to a workmate.

"You jammy cow. I got a poxy box of Celebrations. And I'd spent seven quid on my gift," she whinged.

"Who do you think they're from?" I said, asking the impossible.

"Someone who wants to bathe you in luxury body milk and then ply you with Dom Pérignon in those fancy champagne glasses," she joked. "It must be the caretaker!"

We burst out laughing.

"What did you tell your old man?" she queried.

"That *you* bought them!"

We burst out laughing again. This time louder. Much louder.

This was going to bug me until I got back to school, I thought. And it did.

On the first day back, I paid Joanie a visit - the Secret Santa coordinator.

"Sorry, Julz, that's why it's called Secret Santa," she stated in her jobsworth tone.

"But I just want to say thank you," I pleaded.

"Then put a message in the staff newsletter," she suggested.

I was not a happy bunny, but decided to let it go and enjoy it for what it was. Lovely gifts from a secret admirer, no, *friend*. Lovely gifts from a secret *friend*. There. I had let it go.

Until Melanie popped her head through my office door.

"Did you like them?" she grinned.

"Like what?" I responded.

"Your Secret Santa pressies!" She was still grinning.

"Awwwww. It was you. Thank you, hon. They were lovely." I got up to give her a big thank you hug.

Melanie was my twin. We were born on the same day, but she was much younger and slimmer.

"Oh no, it wasn't from me," she added. "I was just consulted as to what I thought of the presents."

"So...?" I asked.

She made a zip motion across her lips.

"Arrrrrrrrgh!" I screamed.

"Sorry, but if I tell you, I'd have to kill you," she laughed.

At that point, I gave up.

"OK. OK. I'll drop it if you pass a thank you letter to my Secret Santa?"

"Of course," she replied. "With pleasure."

At lunchtime I penned my thanks.

Dear Secret Santa

I felt compelled to write to express my gratitude at receiving two spectacular Secret Santa gifts from you. Totally unnecessary, but very welcome. I opened my gifts on Christmas Day. They were absolutely fabulous. I am still drinking from my Jasper Conran glasses: rum punch, sorrel, cava, even diet cola, and I've already pampered myself with the gorgeous bath products.

I felt very special and was very excited with my pressies, but also slightly guilty that you went over and above. I want to thank you very much for thinking of me, and doing what you did. I did try and get your name from Joanie to thank you personally, but she is a consummate professional and refused to give anything away.

Anyways, if ever you want to reveal yourself, feel free. I'll have a glass of bubbly waiting, naturally, for you to drink in one of my Jasper Conran glasses.

Thanks again. Very, very much appreciated.

Julz x

As I was scrambling to find an envelope, Melanie came in to collect my note. In haste, I grabbed one from a birthday card pack and placed my letter inside.

"Sorry it's yellow," I apologised for the make-shift envelope.

"No probs," she took the note, laughed and scurried away.

English Club followed Period 5, and an SMT Meeting followed English Club. By 5.30pm, I was knackered. The first day back always left me drained, and I refused to take home any schoolwork, because I knew it would remain in my holdall.

What a day! Walking down the corridor to the car park, I could see Melanie ahead talking to Earl, a hench PE teacher, who was what the kids would describe as peng, but he was incredibly shy. As an English teacher, my metaphor to describe him would be a Galaxy Ripple. Smooth, dark and very tasty. I quickly snapped out of that imagery.

"Have a nice evening, Mel," I smiled.

"You too, Julz," she replied.

"Have a nice evening, Earl," I grinned.

"You too, Miss." He flashed a shy smile and waved.

In his hand was an envelope. A yellow envelope! My eyes were fixated on the bright paper. I then looked at Earl. My Secret Santa! It was the first time I had seen a Black man blush.

Oh my goodness. Say something, Julz. Say anything before the poor guy dies of embarrassment, I thought.

"Cheers," I grinned, gave him a wink and carried on walking.

Oh my God, I whispered to myself, I didn't just say that. And wink! Oh gosh, how pathetic. Is that the best I could do? Oh Julz, you fool. Jasper Conran glasses, so I say 'Cheers'. How corny. I can't believe I said that!

I continued walking. This time at double speed to my car.

How could I have winked? I thought. Oh Julz, you fool. Cheers indeed. Oh man, why did I say that? And I *winked*...!

"Dawg a sweat and long hair hide it."

Things are not always as they seem.

END OF AUTUMN TERM

SPRING TERM

EPISODE 16

Don't Listen To Mother

An attractive but precarious part of my personality is my impulsive nature. It is the one that my mother constantly criticises: "If yuh run too fast, yuh run two time" - one of her pearls - which means you should never make a decision straight away, but always go away and sleep on any proposition. That way, you can be sure you have thought about things carefully and made the right choice.

At the beginning of my teaching career, bravado or stupidity had led me into the Head Teacher's office asking for a pay rise. This was after I had been observed by outside officials, and been given the top grade. His silence and piercing glare made me shiver, and I waited for his traditional bark, which was reserved for cheeky Year 7s. Instead, to my surprise, he calmly responded that he admired my brazenness, and would think about it.

It was a fortnight after our impromptu meet, and I had been summoned to his office. He sat me down; offered me a small bottle of water and also, to my surprise, a promotion, working with a group of disaffected students within Key Stage 4. I was stunned. He said the post was an integral part of moving the school forward, and he was going to take funds from another budget to create this role. He was confident that if there was an effective strategy, it would raise achievement, and this privilege would add an extra £2k onto my salary. I was ecstatic!

As I jumped up to accept the offer, my stride was halted by the words of my mother echoing in my mind: '*Think about it. Think about it. Never respond in haste. Even if it is a Yes, always say you'll think about it!*'

I moved my chair closer to the Head's desk and he smiled widely, anticipating my acceptance. I began to speak cautiously. I told him that the job sounded very attractive and exciting; it was something that fitted my skillset perfectly, and it was also a challenge I would relish, but… I would need some time to think about his proposal. I could still see his surprised expression as I left his office, confused that I had not jumped at the offer. Wow, I smiled to myself, if Mum could see me now, she would be well proud.

That night, I dreamt about my new role, my new office, and creating a department of hundreds, whom I would be in charge of. Well… I *did* say I was dreaming!

The next day, I decided to power dress in my new two-piece and heels, and take the advice of my best mate: just accept the offer, without trying to bump up the salary further.

I made my way to the Head's office during Lesson 3 - first thing in the morning would have looked desperate - but was told by his secretary when I arrived, that the Head was not in school. Disappointed, I made my way back to my classroom. I had looked impressive in my black suit, but decided I would wear my brown outfit (which was just as nice) the next day, and confirm my acceptance then.

Halfway through Period 4, I was handed a memo, which said all students were to go to their tutor rooms straight after the lesson, and would be dismissed home due to a school emergency. All teachers were then to report to the staff room at the beginning of lunch.

Confused, as the radiators were still warm - so it couldn't be an issue with the boiler - I grabbed a cheese bap from the canteen, and made my way to the staff room with two other staff members, Gladys and Debra. Standing at the front of the room was one of the deputies, Mark Crew. Once the room was full, he began to speak, his voice was quivering, and I noticed for the first time, his eyes red and puffy.

"Colleagues," he said forcefully and cleared his throat. "The Head is dead. He collapsed in the night and suffered a massive heart attack."

The filling from my roll fell onto my new skirt, and I look around at others to confirm I had heard correctly. Male staff members bowed their heads awkwardly, and the female teachers, including myself, had tears streaming openly down our faces, as we tried to digest the news and the shock of his sudden departure.

As it sank in, some staff sat in silence, while others began to reminisce on old times and reflect on how life was short.

Mark began working the room with other senior leaders, comforting distressed colleagues.

Grief aside, I swiftly realised that, with the Head no longer with us, my procrastinating had killed my chance of promotion. I wondered if the Head had spoken to anyone about my job offer? Did he leave any documents outlining our conversation? Clearly it was inappropriate to ask "Excuse me, did the Head mention he was in the process of promoting me?" What a joke! What a difference a day makes!

By this time, I was sobbing hard. Thinking of what could have been, if I had only said Yes yesterday. I dusted the grated cheese off my new suit, and put my head in my hands. I must have begun bawling even louder, because Mark came over and placed his hand on my shoulder. "I have arranged counselling for those who feel they may need it. The counsellors are available if you want to get anything off your chest. Talking can be a great way of putting things into perspective," he gently whispered.

Bloody right, I thought, I'm gonna kill my mother!

"Where de goat go, de kid follow."

Children follow the lead of their parents.

EPISODE 17

Inspiring Lives

I'll never forget reading a quote saying: Teaching is a work of 'heart'.

A simple and honest phrase that resonated with me.

We all know that great teachers truly inspire students, and ignite a passion for learning inside a child that reaches far beyond the classroom. And that inspirational teacher will be remembered for life, because they unlock potential; give students the desire to learn, and motivate them to achieve.

My primary school hero was Pamela Robinson. She was my schoolteacher when I was in the Juniors (Years 3 to 6) and instilled within me a love for school. She epitomised the brilliant teacher: organised, motivating, inspiring and fair but firm. My ambition to become a teacher came from being taught by her. She made students feel it was cool to be in school - and even cooler to be a high achiever. My desire to be top of the class stemmed from my eagerness to please her. She was middle class, beautiful and blonde, and I viewed her as my second mother.

By the time I reached secondary school, I was inspired by three more wonderful women, who instilled a love of English, Drama and life into me.

Ann Kyle, who magically made Shakespeare accessible and relevant, had a passion for the literary canon, which rippled through my inner-city mind, and through her I discovered my love of fiction and writing. Growing up on an inner-city estate meant that holidays abroad were wishful thinking, but through her love of literature, which infected my 12-year-old mind, I was able to visit Narnia, Wonderland, Bethlehem and many other fantastic places, without even stepping outside my front door.

Sally Shepherd was my crazy Drama teacher; she was bonkers but brilliant, and she rocked. She was radical, irreverent and bold when it came to her style of teaching. She showed me that you could have a blast in lessons, and that learning could and should be fun. I would race to her classes and even chose the subject as an O Level option, because I loved the way she brought it to life. Drama was one of my top grades when I left school, and I know I owe that to Sally.

Then there was Sandra Bell. She was my first year secondary school tutor and she taught PE. I remember sitting in the crowd of 11-year-olds on Induction Day, and all the first year potential tutors stood at the front of the stage. The students sat quietly waiting for the Head, Miss Tilly, to divide us into one of the four School Houses (which were named after planets), and introduce us to our Head of Year and new tutor.

I was placed in Jupiter, which was looked after by Miss B Ward and, as I looked across at the tutor team, my eyes froze on the young Black woman with the large eyes, tracksuit bottoms and hooped earrings. Wow! I remember thinking. I want the Black teacher. Lord, please put me in the Black teacher's class. Yes! I silently cheered, when my name was read out from a list by Miss Bell. My prayer had been answered. Little did I know that the Black lady was twice as strict, and was going to work me twice as hard as any of the other teachers.

I quickly discovered that, with Ms Bell, there was no let-up. She was a hard taskmaster, and was unfailing in her persistence to ensure I was never complacent and always did my best. She had my mother on speed dial, and was swift to report home if I slacked with my schoolwork or missed homework deadlines. I grew to dislike her *very* quickly.

"What is it with you?" I cheekily challenged one day, as I sat alone with her in yet another detention. "Why can't you just give me a break? You're always on at me *all* the time: grassing me up to my mum; checking up on me in lessons; putting me in detention for no reason… Why are you always picking on me?"

Miss Bell looked up from her desk and gave me a serious stare. Oh boy, I thought, that's another call home and some beats for being facety. She then let out a small laugh that became increasingly louder and louder. The woman's a nutter, was my first thought. Then she stopped suddenly, got up and moved towards the chair next to me and sat down.

"Julz," she said very slowly and quietly. "I'm sorry if you think I'm picking on you…" she began. "It's because I see greatness in you. Great potential, great ability. And I refuse to let it go to waste."

My eyes widened at this revelation. I was stunned into silence.

Sandra Bell ended up being one of my strongest inspirations in my formative years and, interestingly, a lot of the strategies I use to tackle underperformance have been adopted first-hand from her.

It's interesting, when you look back, the connections you make. For me, with Pamela Robinson, Ann Kyle, Sally Shepherd and Sandra Bell, they had one thing in common: they believed in me.

I've been blessed to have had some wonderful mentors, who have shared their wisdom and experience with me; have nurtured me into being great at my job, and shaped me into the person I am today. In my life before teaching, it was Viv Broughton, a wise font of knowledge, whose experience demonstrated he had been here a lifetime before. He was sharp, smart and knew everything about everything, a kind of Wikipedia before the Internet became a staple in our lives. He was generous when it came to sharing his expertise; made me keen to know more, and enthused me to be top of my game, by reminding me that there was always someone in the wings ready to steal your crown. Another mentor was Val McCalla - a canny and ambitious businessman who demanded perfection. I admired his shrewdness and wit - which only a privileged few were permitted to see - and was inspired by a lust for seizing opportunities and taking risks.

When I made the decision to pursue a career in education, the lady who inspired that part of my journey and nurtured my growth was Elizabeth - a remarkable woman affectionately known as Miss Reilly.

My nickname for her was Queen Elizabeth, because she was a queen by name and a queen by nature. She was old-fashioned, honest and, above all, stood for no nonsense. Her attention to detail was second to none, and she was thorough, meticulous and extremely well organised. In meetings, I would glance over at her To Do list and Post-It notes - neatly detailed in her immaculate handwriting - and smile. She was a woman of substance and integrity and, through example, taught theses values without effort. She was the first person I knew who, through personal choice, refused to have a television in her home and who, during the school holidays, would go rambling for pleasure!

When Grandma Bailey died, it left a void I believed could not be even partially filled. I remember sitting in her bedroom on her bed after she had passed away. She was the only person who could make me cry with just a telling off, and her stare alone would make me feel guilty and confess any wrongdoings, even as a grown woman. Elizabeth was also blessed with that unique ability.

A week after Grandma's death, I returned to work still feeling very emotional. The fact she was gone forever was still sinking in. Some of my colleagues did not know what to say, and looked uncomfortable, while others simply looked broken as they awkwardly gave their condolences.

I remember scurrying through the corridor feeling despair, and thinking maybe I had returned to work too soon, when a gentle voice glided down the staircase, calling my name. It was Elizabeth. I stopped in my tracks as she made her way towards me. She stood in front of me, and I moved my gaze to the floor. There was silence. As I slowly looked up, there was still silence and, after a few seconds, I felt her warm embrace, which instantly ignited my heart and, like a boiled kettle, my bottled-up emotions exploded and I began to bawl. I spent ten minutes hidden away in the toilet with Elizabeth after that, but it was exactly what I needed to face the working world again.

Elizabeth was the epitome of good practice, and the model I followed as a Senior Leader. Her trademark cards for all occasions, which she would always date before writing, was an apt example of her thoughtfulness and kindness, and I'll never forget the home-made birthday card (created by Elizabeth on her PC and printed in colour). She would always wish me happiness and health with lots of sunshine, at the beginning, during and end of an academic year. She would apologise for being over-solicitous, because old habits die hard, and politely and gently remind me in May to start planning a summer holiday without school commitments or domestic chores, and to do a review in June of: 1) the things I know, and 2) the things I wish I'd known before the academic year began.

So, taking a leaf out of her book, you would always find a stack of cards and small gifts from the Card Factory in my office cupboard for team members. I'd make it my business to give constructive feedback after Presentations and Assemblies, and always have a kind word of encouragement when I noticed staff wilting or struggling. Even when Elizabeth retired, I would still look forward to her notes arriving in the post, reminding me it was OK to slow down and look after myself.

I would take extra care when writing a memo or email to Elizabeth because, even though she was a Maths specialist, she was a super speller and on the ball when it came to grammar, and I did not want to be caught short. She also loved slogans, and my favourite that was adopted as part of an examination drive was: 'Fail to prepare, prepare to fail'. Elizabeth, the students and I wholeheartedly ran with this notion, and printed posters, using the phrase as our mantra in Assemblies and PSHE.

Teaching is definitely a work of heart, and education - as Nelson Mandela famously put it - is "the most powerful weapon which you can use to change the world."

As teachers, we teach so much more than a subject; we are opening minds, hearts and shaping lives.

And Super Teachers, like the ones I have met on my journey, have done so much more. They have opened the minds and hearts of the teachers themselves, and have supported them into being

confident and responsible in shaping and inspiring the lives of others.
Thank you.

"Mi old but mi no cold."

Do not underestimate the value of your elders.

EPISODE 18

Week Beginning: 22nd January

Like Mother, Like Son

When I retell some of the incidents I have experienced with some of my school children, my mother would often say: "Call me old fashioned, Petal, but I find it strange that, in my day, when I was growing up, children didn't suffer from ADHD; we just used to call as we saw it: damn rude!"

My politically incorrect neighbour, Opal, would take it one step further. "We dress things up too much in this country," she would spout. "Obesity is just kids that are damn greedy; bipolar is people who are bloody moody, and don't tell me about kids with depression. They ain't got to work 24/7, pay bills or live with my old man. Now *that's* a reason to be depressed!"

My grandmother didn't dance around things either. A spade was a spade. If we were rude and the teacher called home, no matter what the circumstance or situation, the teacher was always right. In the Caribbean, if you were naughty and a neighbour or a friend of the family saw you, they would give you a hiding and, if you reported this to your parents, you would also get 'two good lick'! I think, for them, this was what it meant by a village raising a child.

Fast forward to 2018. Parents and kids are buddies, BFFs, mates. Now, don't get me wrong, I love my mum and we get on like a house on fire, but she is my mum, not my pal and, as old as I am and as clever as I think I am, I'm not too old to feel the back of her hand.

Karl and his mum were like husband and wife. The 12-year-old had told me, when his single mother was about to give birth, that she was having a baby for him. When I asked him to clarify, he said that he had always wanted a little sister, and his mum agreed to sort it! To say he was a mummy's boy was an understatement. As my mother would say, he was right under her frock tail. So it was no surprise that when he was in trouble, she was his number one defender.

My role was always to break down and rationalise each incident that was brought to me. Often this could take ages and, on top of my increasing workload, was not always welcome. With Karl, he was often the instigator and troublemaker, and I would have Mum in my office for over an hour, trying to make her see the bigger picture and Karl's role in an incident.

"Now throwing a chair across the room isn't the best way to make sir listen to Karl's point, is it, Miss Martin? What would have happened if it had hit someone?" I pointed out.

"But he was angry," she would defend.

"Yes, but there are ways to express anger that do not involve violence," I would respond.

"But he didn't hit anyone…" she would justify.

"And if Karl came home, and told you another student had thrown a chair across the room while he was in class, how would you feel?" I challenged.

"I'd be vex," she admitted.

"Exactly!"

Miss Martin was silent.

Argument done. I smiled.

"Mmmm," she said, followed by a long pause. She would then address Karl. "Karl, you have to be more sensible. You could have hit someone," she finally admitted.

Ten times out of ten, she would understand. Eventually. And so, until the next time… Which was a week later.

Mrs Barnes called me from her office, very upset. She had just had a meeting with Miss Martin about an incident with Karl, and had been cussed out by the woman. Karl had taken a pair of scissors from a desk, crept up behind a young girl who was busy working, and snipped off two inches from her hair. The young girl was in tears, and Mrs Barnes telephoned Karl's mother and insisted she come into school. In the meeting, Miss Martin refused to admit

Karl was wrong, insisting like Karl that it was an 'accident', and that his hand had 'slipped'. She was not happy with Mrs Barnes' accusations, and insisted on seeing me, but not before she told Mrs Barnes she was picking on her son and she was a 'skinny bitch'!

Mrs Barnes was fuming. More so, I guessed, because she couldn't lick Miss Martin down. What a facety woman! She is damn rude, I thought. Well today, I was not going to waste my time rationalising and pacifying her and her son's behaviour.

"Are you OK to stay in school?" I asked Mrs Barnes.

"Yes," she replied. "That woman!"

"Send her up to me, Mrs Barnes," I said calmly. "I'll take things from here." And with that, Sophia put the phone down.

I could not believe the cheek of Miss Martin. I called the office and asked them to get a Mentor to check on Sophia and bring her some tea, while I awaited Miss Martin's arrival. She was out of order, I thought. If my daughter had come home with part of her hair chopped off by a student, I would be fuming.

There was a loud bang on my office door. "Come in."

In walked Miss Martin, with Karl close behind her. This woman could never be coming to me to justify her son's poor behaviour, I thought. And leaving a member of my staff in tears. No way!

"Miss Bremmer..." Miss Martin began.

"One moment, Miss Martin," I interrupted. "Karl?" I addressed her son. "Did you take a pair of scissors and cut off a piece of Shanice's hair?" I questioned.

"Yes, Miss," Karl responded. There was no remorse in his tone.

"Did Shanice trouble or upset you, Karl?" I continued.

"No, Miss," Karl replied.

"But he was playing..." Miss Martin began.

"One moment," I halted Miss Martin. She was not pleased by that.

"Why did you cut Shanice's hair, Karl?" I asked.

Miss Martin interrupted again. "He was play-"

"Please, Miss Martin, I'm speaking to Karl," I butted in firmly. She was not a happy bunny.

"I was playing," he repeated his mother's line.

"That's what I've been trying to tell you and that Mrs Barnes teacher downstairs," Miss Martin added.

"Well, I'm telling you, Miss Martin and Karl, that is **not** how we play in this school. Karl, I'm suspending you for three days in the first instance, pending further investigation, for taking a pair of scissors and cutting a student's hair."

"What?" The bellow of Miss Martin's voice made the pictures on my wall shake.

"You heard. Shall I repeat myself?" I responded. "Cutting a student's hair is not what we deem as appropriate or safe behaviour in this school. Therefore, I am suspending Karl for three days in the first instance, pending further investigation."

Both Miss Martin and Karl sat in shock.

I walked towards my office door and held it open.

"That will be all," I said professionally and intentionally cold, refusing to entertain a discussion or debate as I had done in the past. "The letter will be in the post."

"But... but..." Miss Martin began.

"That will be all," I said crisply, as I cut her off mid-sentence.

"Who the f**k do you think you are? I'm not going anywhere until you listen to me!" she began. "How dare you f**king suspend my son? Who the hell do you think you are? Just because you wear a suit and weave, you think you're all that?"

"And you think it's OK for your son to go around like Edward Scissorhands in lessons?" I queried. "Get out of my office with your foolishness."

"Don't f**king speak to me like that, you bitch! You teachers are all the same. Looking down on me, picking on my son, who the f**k do you think you are?"

"I'm the teacher who's just suspended your son," I responded. "And, for the record, it's not weave; it's actually all my own hair. Every single strand." I know it was petty, but I could not resist. I then began purposefully flicking my bob from side to side, just to wind her up.

"Arrrrrrrrrrrrrrrrrrrrrrrrrrrrrrrrrrrrrrrrrrrrrrgh!" She ran out of my office into the corridor screaming, and it was at that moment

I noticed Karl standing in the corner of the corridor with his head bowed. He was quietly whispering. I moved towards him. He was repeating the sentence: "Come on, Mum, let's go. Please, Mum, let's go."

I realised it was time to stop this charade but, before I could intervene, an English teacher had come out of her class. "Can we keep the noise down, please?" she innocently interjected. "I have a class full of children trying to sit a trial exam, and they cannot focus."

"What about *my* f**king child?" Miss Martin yelled. "F**k your class! F**k you!" she began to scream at the top of her voice, and twenty-eight 14-year-old faces were suddenly squashed against the classroom window.

Damn! I thought. This is getting out of hand. I glanced over at Karl again, who was at this point weeping.

Why didn't I deal with this differently? I thought. I should have just listened to her, pacified her, and then sent her on her way. What a mess!

Miss Martin was still effing and blinding like a mad woman, when a Learning Mentor and the Music Technician appeared. Thank God, I thought. About time! The Mentor went over to Miss Martin, and began quietly reasoning with her, as he gently escorted her down the stairs. My eyes caught the attention of the Technician, and I signalled for him to deal with Karl, who was still standing forlorn in the corner. He went over and they followed the Mentor and his mother.

The corridor was silent. Just the English teacher and I filled the large space. She gave me a 'What-the-hell-just-happened?' look and, exhausted, I shook my head, walked into my office and shut the door.

As I put my head on my desk, I began to talk to myself. "Oh shit! Oh shit! Oh shit!"

I found out from the Mentor later that Miss Martin had been drinking, which explained her erratic behaviour, something that made me feel even worse, because I hadn't even noticed the smell. As a result of her behaviour, an injunction was taken out against her, and she was banned from the school site and had to nominate a family member or friend to represent her at Parent Meetings and Review days.

Miss Martin had behaved despicably, but I knew I had a role to play in the debacle. My behaviour had contributed to adding fuel to what I knew was an already burning flame. I spoke to Gideon, the Associate Head, and Miss Martin was allowed back on site for a 'making-the-peace' meeting. I sat opposite Miss Martin as Gideon mediated.

Miss Martin began: "I just didn't like the way you looked down on me because I am a single parent," she started.

"What?" I exclaimed.

"Just because I ain't got a man, and I'm bringing up my kid by myself. It's like you look down on me," she continued.

"You are not serious," I responded in shock.

Miss Martin nodded.

"That's a joke!" I began to raise my voice.

Under the table I could feel a kick. It was Gideon.

"You really want to know what my problem is?" I began. "You need to tek your pickney from under your frock tail, and start being a mother and not his mate."

"What?" she responded in shock.

Under the table I felt another kick. Only this time it was harder. Unbelievable! Gideon was actually kicking me. Well, he could kick a little harder, because I was saying what I had to say.

"Miss Martin..." I was ready for her.

I paused. The reason why I was in this situation was because I felt I had to say what I thought was right the last time. But right for whom? My mum would often say: "If you don't have anything good to say, say nothing." Albeit late, but maybe Mum (and Gideon's foot) had a point.

"Miss Martin..." I began again. "I'm sorry if you felt looked down upon. That was never my intention. It's important that we work together to support Karl and ensure he is focused, and that his behaviour does not impede his academic progress. I hope we can move forward from this."

Gideon smiled.

Miss Martin smiled.

Goodness, I thought, as I put on a fake a smile. She looks just like Karl.

Like mother...

"Likkle alligator tun big alligator."

Children invariably adopt all the bad attributes of their parents.

EPISODE 19

Watch Your Daughters

TV documentaries glamorising gymslip mums infuriate me, as most of the girls don't seem to be struggling. In one programme I watched, two sisters under 15 were having babies three months apart, and an 18-year-old had had three for three different men. As if we didn't have enough problems deterring our young girls away from underage sex...

Before I came into teaching, I wondered if there really was a high level of ignorance about sex among our teens, and had this confirmed when I taught my first Sex Education lesson to a group of 13-year-old girls. Horrifically, sitting on a washing machine while having sex topped the poll as an effective contraceptive method, and I found myself literally arguing with a girl during the session, who insisted you couldn't get pregnant if you had your knickers on!

Apparently, some boy had told her that if she kept her knickers above her knees while having sex, she would be OK. Brutally, I had to explain it wasn't where her knickers were that was the problem, but where his penis was, and what it was doing. After a private conversation with her, I had to make a prompt referral to the school nurse.

I found Shabnam, a sweet, 13-year-old Muslim girl, weeping under the main staircase one afternoon, and asked her what the matter was and why she wasn't in lessons. She said that her friends were being mean to her so she did not want to go to her lesson. I discovered, after speaking to her friends, that they had told her they were not going to speak to her until she told her mum that she was pregnant.

"You're pregnant, Shabnam?" I asked when we were alone.

"Yes, Miss," she responded openly. "My period is six weeks late."

"Six weeks!" I exclaimed.

"Yes, Miss," she confirmed. "I was seeing Yusef in the holidays. He said he was my boyfriend and I was his girlfriend, so I should give him head and I did. But it was only once, but that's all it takes, right?"

"And...?" I probed.

"And I haven't had my period since." She bowed her head and started to cry.

"What's 'give him head'?" I asked once she stopped crying. I needed confirmation that she was clear in what she was saying.

"You know, Miss." She looked embarrassed as the tears started to dry.

"No, I don't," I responded gently, waiting for her explanation.

"When you put his privates in your..." Shabnam stopped due to embarrassment.

Damn, I thought when she stopped.

"In your where?" I probed.

"I can't say it," she replied.

Shabnam had now stopped crying, and was giggling like a schoolgirl.

"I'm going to have to get the school nurse to come and have a chat with you, so you can explain to her exactly what happened," I stated. The giggling stopped.

"No, Miss, you can't!" Shabnam shouted. "She'll tell my parents."

"But if you can't tell me, I don't have a choi ..."

"My mouth," she interjected. "I put Yusef's privates in my mouth."

"Anywhere else?" I enquired. "Did his private part go anywhere else?" I asked.

"Eeeeeee. No, Miss. I wouldn't do that. You have to be married to put a man's privates anywhere else."

I was confused.

"Shabnam," I said slowly. "Did Yusef make you do anything you did not want to do?"

"No, Miss," she replied.

"So..." I continued, ever so slowly, because even *I* was getting confused. "Apart from putting his penis in your mouth, did his penis go anywhere else?"

"Eeeeeeeee. I said no, Miss. I just gave him head."

"So why do you think you're pregnant?" I replied, exasperated.

"Because we had oral sex, Miss. And if you have sex, even once, you can get pregnant? Right?"

Oh my days!

"Miss," Shabnam whispered.

"Yes." My head had started to hurt.

"Do different cultures have different colour sperm?"

"What?" I queried.

"Do different cultures have different colour sperm? Yusef's was white but this older boy's that I gave head to sperm was green," she explained innocently.

I was ready to throw up. I handed the incident over to the staff member responsible for child protection. I promptly went back to my office, locked the door and cried.

Note to self: Revamp the Year 8 Sex E ducation PSHE scheme. ASAP.

No matter how long your teaching experience is, there is always a day that can bring an incident or issue to make your hair stand on end or your heart sink.

Listening to a student tell you she has had sex with a boy in the Tesco's toilets on the High Road sank my soul, but seeing social media destroy a reputation at the push of a record button, was even more distressing.

The student grapevine could take the credit for bringing this incident to the fore. All the girls and boys were gossiping: a teacher had overheard what had been said, and had reported it to Endri. I was called on the walkie-talkie to make my way to his office to sit in on a meeting. When I entered, two male students were sitting on the couch, and Endri was pacing the room.

"Miss Bremmer, these boys were caught watching a video on WhatsApp today in their lesson, and were sent to me after the teacher viewed the contents."

"I didn't film it, honest, sir," Billy jumped in.

"No, but you had no problem watching and sharing it!" Endri shouted back.

My eyes widened. This was very unlike Endri; he was the students' favourite, and raising his voice was uncharacteristic unless it was absolutely necessary.

I asked the boys to wait outside.

"What's up, E?" I asked.

"I've got daughters, Julz. I've heard what's on this, and I just can't bring myself to watch. Do you mind?"

I took the phone from his hand and pressed play. There was a naked young couple on a bed having sex. The girl was on top. The boy looked about 16 years old, and it was clear he was video recording the act on his phone without the girl's knowledge. When she moved her hair and I saw her face, my mouth widened in shock. She was one of our students. Lord God Almighty! I looked at Endri.

"It's Charmaine Bryan."

"The boy is from St Paul's Academy down the road," Endri stated. "He forwarded the clip to Billy. Who forwarded it on. It's been shared throughout Year 11."

I felt sick.

"I want him out!" I yelled. "Tell the Head I want Billy out! And I want the Mentors to check every Year 11's phone. Any Year 11 with this on their phone after midday will be joining Billy!"

"I'll meet the parents and recommend Billy stays at home for the rest of the week, if you write up what you saw," Endri compromised. I agreed, and left the room.

The corridor was empty. Fortunately, one of the Mentors had heard me raging in the office, and swiftly removed Billy and his mate from outside the room. Deep down, I knew Billy wasn't being malicious, but children had to understand that their actions had repercussions and consequences.

Fourteen-year-old Adrian was in Year 9 and found himself in trouble. He was a charmer around school and a pleasure to teach. He came to see me because he had a problem. I expected him to pose a homework dilemma but, instead, he asked me where he could get hold of some emergency contraception. He had had sex with a girl in the Year group two days before, and the condom had split and he was worried she may be pregnant. I was proud of his honesty, impressed at his sensibility, but disappointed at the fact he was having sex at such a young age. I passed it over to the school nurse.

As a teacher, you do not have to inform parents if children disclose information about sex and, as a mother, felt sad that another professional could one day be doing the same to my child, without my knowledge.

Adrian came back once things were 'sorted', and thanked me for my help. This was my opportunity for some teacher-to-pupil talk. He confessed to 'doing it' on the balcony in the flats opposite the school. I explained that a woman never forgets her first time, and that is how he would be remembered in her eyes. He was too young, too bright, and had too much of a great future in front of him to mess things up for five minutes of sex. He agreed.

Back at home, my son yelled at the TV with distaste. When I asked him what the matter was, he sneered that this man and lady were kissing with tongues.

"That's nasty!" he shouted, and clicked the off button on the remote before leaving the room.

Secretly I smiled, and wished he would stay 10 forever!

"If fish deh a river bottom an tell yuh seh alligator have gum boil, believe him!"

Listen to the voice of experience.

EPISODE 20

King By Name, King By Nature

On most school days, no amount of money could cover the stress, grief or heartache you go through.

However, a bonus part that my job has afforded me is the privilege of working with some brilliant people, too many to mention, but Martin has definitely got to be someone who is right up there on that list.

Martin King. A former sprint champion who, like most sporting greats, was fit, energetic and possessed an indomitable spirit. He was handsome, incredibly charming, and blessed with a vulnerability that melted most hearts. With all these qualities, ironically he was still a man's man: strong, confident and athletic, but someone who was also sensitive, which was a great characteristic for some of our young men to see.

The fact that he was a graduate from the 'school of hard knocks' made him a magnet as a mentor for our hard-core boys. Most did not have a positive male role model in their lives and, as a result, would gravitate towards Martin who understood the 'streets', and was not afraid to tell the lads that they were talking foolishness or acting like idiots - something, as teaching professionals, we might not get away with.

Our students responded positively to people who had overcome adversity, and Martin King most certainly had. His 15-year-old son was murdered outside of his school. Martin candidly addressed the thousand students who had packed into the Assembly hall and shared his story.

"He loved to laugh. My son loved life, and he was brutally taken away from me. Just like that. I was consumed with anger. I really wanted to kill the boy who murdered my son. He took away a piece of me that day, and I was never gonna be the same."

You could have heard a pin drop.

"But I made a decision. That murderer wasn't gonna get all of me. I needed something for my son. So, with what I've got left, I'm gonna do something good with it. If I have to forgive, I'll forgive. If I have to love, I'll love. I don't wanna hate no more, 'cos that's what killed my boy."

The 25-minute talk ended. The message of forgiveness had resonated. The hall was still and silent. Female staff members were wiping back the tears. Students froze, digesting what they had just heard and trying to comprehend it all. And then, in an instant, applause broke out, and the kids shook off the melancholy emotions, replacing them with cheers and approval screams of 'boi boi boi'. Even when the buzzer sounded, indicating it was time for Period 1, most of them refused to move until they got the chance to spud Martin.

The charisma and sheer magnetism Martin possessed you couldn't bottle. He was certainly a gifted orator but, more importantly, connected with the youth who were on the periphery of becoming disaffected and dropping out.

We had a lot of students who benefited from Martin's skills, and there was certainly a gap in the market for him to work with some of the parents too.

Roger was one of his mentees, and ran rings around his dad. The irony is Roger was a mere 4' 2", his dad a giant 6' 3". Roger was in trouble for swearing at a member of staff.

"Julz, I'm sorry but I wanted to step on him," the Supply Teacher moaned. "Is he on crack? This little shit is telling me to F off and he's shorter than that guy in Austin Powers. I had to get him removed. Please can I not be put to cover that class again if he's in it? I'm begging you."

I looked closely at the Supply teacher. He was deadly serious. Surely not. Roger was a titchy lad. If you took a deep breath, Roger would collapse from your puff.

I checked his file. This was the third time he had sworn at a staff member. Time for another meeting with Dad. They sat side by side in my office. I was looking at little and large. I began to laugh but composed myself and picked up Roger's Progress Report.

"I've noticed that Roger has a reading age of 9 years," I said to Dad. It was coming to the end of the meeting, and I wanted to set some targets. "That's not great, four years below his chronological age."

Dad nodded.

"Do you read with him in the evenings?"

"No," Dad replied. "He's always on his Playstation. Once he goes on it, he won't come off."

"Then take it away," I stated matter-of-factly.

"I can't," Dad said.

"Why not?"

"Well, the last time I did that, he took all my clothes," Dad replied.

"Excuse me?" I was confused.

"The last time I confiscated Roger's Playstation, he took away all my clothes," he repeated. "And I didn't have nothing to wear to work."

I laughed. I looked at Dad. He wasn't joking. I stopped laughing. I looked at Roger. He was smirking.

"Fix your face, Roger," I said firmly. His smirk disappeared.

Exasperated Dad added: "He said if I take away his Playstation again, he will take my phone and I cannot afford for that to happen. I need it for my business."

I'm dead! I couldn't believe what I was hearing.

Roger began to smirk again.

The things children get away with because parents are scared of Social Service intervention. I wanted to tell Dad that he could beat him and not get in trouble if he didn't leave a mark, or better still twist his ears if he didn't listen, but thought I'd better not. Instead, I decided to use the Martin King threat.

"I'm gonna have to tell Martin King about this Roger. It is not on."

Roger sat up and began to plead.

"Please don't, Miss. I'll be good."

"If I call him with negative feedback about any of his students, I hear they get 100 push ups," I added.

Roger was not a happy bunny.

"Dad, this is Martin King's mobile. Roger's mentor." I scribbled the number on a piece of paper. "Feel free to give him a call if Roger's behaviour is a cause for concern. I will be putting Roger in Isolation for swearing at a teacher. And Dad, *you* are the parent. If he refuses to get off the Playstation, take it away. If he takes your clothes, punish him. If he takes your phone, report him to the Police for theft!" Unbelievable!

Martin's Breakfast Boot Camp project was with 15 Year 9s. The boys would be briefed on their focus for the week; have a gruelling 45-minute workout; shower, and then have a group mentoring session over breakfast, which the school would provide. Most were so worn out by the end of the session; they had no capacity for poor behaviour for that whole day. Result.

It was great to see a breakthrough in most of the target group. Martin had connected, and the majority of the boys responded positively, and this had a good impact in lessons and, ultimately, on their Progress Reports. But there was always one.

TJ. He was a miserable sod. Face like a wet weekend. Mouth push up, like he'd overdosed on lemons. He also had a negative influence on his peers. He didn't like school. He didn't like lessons. And he certainly didn't like exercise. He had decided, and expressed his views very vocally with the group, that he was not going to be mentored, and he definitely wasn't going to arrive at school willingly before 8am.

Well, I'd made it clear to his mum that he didn't have a choice, and he had already booked a place at the 'last chance saloon' and was on the list for alternative provision. Therefore, she was happy to support our endeavours to 'turn him around', and ensured he was out the front door by 7am every Thursday morning. TJ was cool with that because, for the second week running, he had purposely left his sports gear at home, so he would definitely not be participating.

"That's a shame, TJ," Martin commented, when TJ strolled in 15 minutes late and was explaining why he had forgotten his kit.

"Looks like you're going to be working up a sweat in your uniform today, mate," was Martin's response. "Get your socks and shoes off and start with three laps round the gym."

Martin continued working on biceps with the rest of the group.

TJ refused to move.

Martin handed over the reins to a student, Tolga, who continued with the upper body exercises.

He slowly walked towards TJ.

Even though TJ was standing tall, Martin towered over him.

"Is there a problem?" Martin asked TJ, with feigned innocence, his deep tones eluding power and dominance. The boys stopped moving their arms, waiting to see the outcome of Martin versus TJ.

"I've got rights," TJ stuttered. "You can't make me."

Martin began to laugh. The rich sound echoed across the sports hall.

"Rights," he repeated in his deep bass tone. "Rights."

He stood in front of TJ, slowly tapping his right hook in the palm of his left hand. His ripe biceps began to bulge. They were thicker than my two thighs. Focus, Julz. Focus!

TJ stood still, trying to big up his chest, but the involuntary shake of his right leg didn't help his fake bravado.

"You've got rights? Rights, TJ? Are you mad, bruv? What rights have you got? I run this show. I've gone through a lot to get here and worked really hard. I've paid my dues. You ain't paid nothing, bruv. And until you do, you need to get those shoes and socks off and start your three laps. You get me?"

I had never seen shoes and socks fly off feet so fast. Martin turned to the group, who quickly began to pick up the pace with their bicep curls.

"You are all examples to somebody. Somebody is going to look up to you. What do you want them to see? Someone who is not ambitious? Someone who is unreliable and lazy? No, you don't, guys. No, you don't! You are just learning. Take it in. You train, you get tired, push yourself harder. You can do it. I'm here as your support. I will not fail you, so don't fail yourself. Can we step up our game, guys?"

A whisper of "Yes, sir" took on the ripple effect, and became a loud ensemble.

"Fall out!" Martin laughed, and the boys followed suit excitedly, cracking up as they slowed down. One by one they slapped Martin's palm and made their way to the showers. TJ, who by this time was sweating buckets in his school jumper, continued running in circles.

"Give me some love, TJ," Martin beamed towards him. Acknowledging this as permission to stop, TJ broke off from his run, and sheepishly walked towards Martin. He raised his hand in expectancy for a high five. Martin grabbed his shoulders, pulled him close and gave him a bear hug.

"I love you, bruv," Martin declared loudly.

I could have sworn I saw TJ give a partial smile.

Hmmm. Yeah. That definitely was some form of smile.

Raaaaaa, I thought. What a ting. Only Martin could rough up the boys like this and they would still listen and smile. Priceless!

"One han' cyaan clap."

You have to work with others to achieve a common goal, you can't do it alone.

HALF TERM BREAK

EPISODE 21

The Race To Deputy

My mum always says: "If it fi yuh, it fe yuh." I used to think that was a loser's way of saying 'Better luck next time'.

My philosophy has always been - go for it! Name it, claim it. Or, in the words of East End philanthropist, Jack Petchey: "If you think you can, you can." But when opportunity knocked, and an opening came up for a Deputy Head Teacher at my school, I was gutted because I felt I couldn't apply. I had just returned from sick leave, with the mind willing but the flesh still being weak, so it did not feel appropriate to put myself forward.

In some schools, 'the whisper' was an informal - OK, OK, unethical - way of telling someone a job vacancy was theirs. If there was a post in the offing, and you were in line as the ideal candidate for that role, someone would take you aside and whisper, 'Apply, it's yours.' You would have had to have mucked up the interview big time to not get selected. However, with this job, the air was still, empty and silent. I could hear a pin drop, as there wasn't even a murmur about this job. So, I guess I was right to assume I should forget about applying.

One likely candidate was Assistant Head Teacher, Anthony Banjo. He had joined the school in a sideways move, and had been told that if he settled into the role, within two years he would definitely be considered for promotion as a Deputy. The other was Toyin Miso. She was ready to move up, and had been applying for Deputy Head positions outside of the school. I had resigned myself to the fact I was out of the picture, but was secretly looking forward to watching this battle unfold, to see who would come out on top.

Then, out of the blue, the Head announced she was looking for two Deputies; you could have knocked me down with a feather. This clearly meant that a post had been created for both Anthony and Toyin, so the process of appointing would now be much easier - or so they thought. I decided to have a chat with my mate, Endri.

Endri was Turkish. He was a charismatic senior member, who was young, popular with staff, and even more popular with the students and parents. He was an outstanding teacher who was committed, hardworking and loyal. He was straight-talking, had a hilarious sense of humour, and was often politically incorrect which, sometimes, I'm ashamed to say, made him even *more* hilarious. We had a great relationship, and had each other's backs. Anything I needed, I would just say the word and it was done. And vice versa.

"Why aren't you going for the job?" I asked.

"I could ask you the same question, Guru," he replied. I smiled. That was the nickname for me.

"You know my situation," I responded. "But you're more than capable of being a Deputy at this school. You would be fantastic! One of those posts has your name on it, and I challenge anyone who thinks otherwise," I said firmly.

"But…" Endri began.

"But nothing," I cut in.

"But I haven't been given 'the whisper,'" he continued.

Endri was also an Assistant Head and, since the Deputy Head vacancy had been announced, he too had been greeted with the wall of silence.

"Not a whisper," he repeated. "It's so out of order. I feel I've been violated without Vaseline," he ranted.

Endri was so out of order.

"Look, mate," I consoled, "I've just appointed myself as your Campaign Manager. One of those jobs is yours, and I am gonna plan the best marketing strategy ever to put you right at the top. So, let the battle commence!"

"There are two jobs, Guru. One for you and one for me," Endri added.

"I'm not ready," I confirmed, "but I'm ready to support you. Are you in?" I questioned. He raised his hand for a high five, and a hug that showed he meant business.

"First, you need to look the part," I said, giving him the once over. "Stop looking like a scruff pot, and go to REISS over the weekend," I ordered. "You need at least three decent suits. You wanna be a Deputy, start looking like one! And get yourself down to Charles Tyrwhitt and get some decent shirts and ties! Asda ain't cutting it!"

When he arrived in school on the Monday, Endri was suited and booted, and looked like a new man. Gwarn, I thought. It was clear he was ready for the challenge ahead.

The next step was to make it obvious he was interested in developing himself professionally, so I signed him up on the National College Leadership Pathways programme, which was a senior management training course, and I even blagged him a place on a pre-Headship study, that was designed for Black senior teachers who were interested in moving into Headship. Endri bragged about being 'the first and only Turk on the course.'

"This would look great on your CV," I advised. "The Head also has to sign off your application, so it will be clear to her that if you are not given the job, you are skilling yourself to move on. Worst case scenario, if you're not selected for the post, the qualification will make you even more marketable!"

Each year, the Leadership team spent a weekend away, strategising and forward planning. The first session was on reflection. We had to work in pairs and reflect, discuss and make notes on our partner's current role. My partner was Toyin.

"Well," I began, "you're doing a great job on Ethos," I said honestly. "Your drive with the pupils, the badges, the Assemblies and the Guinness World Record attempt was incredible."

I had worked on school ethos previously, and had raised the profile around the school dramatically, but had to admit that Toyin, in the past two years, had moved it to another level.

"Well, you know my motivation behind making it so successful," she calmly stated.

"No," I replied.

"To outdo *you!*" she snapped.

I looked up at Toyin. I was waiting for her to burst into laughter. Her face was flint.

Oh my goodness, I thought, as I looked into her eyes. She's serious. No way! She could never be for real! I was silent.

"I know your game," she whispered.

"Excuse me?" I was seeking clarification.

"You're trying to get Endri not to apply for the job, so you can get it yourself."

"Excuse me?" I repeated. This woman is definitely bonkers, I thought.

"You want the job for yourself, so you are trying to get Endri not to apply," she repeated.

Clearly she had her wires crossed. And at that moment, I knew just where I wanted to cross them. Right around her neck! The cheek of the woman. By this point, I was fuming!

I pulled Endri outside.

"Endri," I said, trying hard to stay calm. He was looking worried. Worried and confused. "How would you feel if I put my hat in the ring for the Deputy post?" I asked.

"Yaaaaaaay!" he shouted without hesitation. And began to dance around me.

"Me and you, Guru. Me and you against the world," he chimed. He held out his palm in anticipation of a high five.

"Two posts, Endri. One..." I pointed at him, "Two…" I pointed at me. "Let the race for Deputy begin!" I slapped his palm. "We're getting this job," I said firmly. "Or die trying!"

We both collapsed in fits of laughter.

The fortnight that followed was amusing, to say the least. Four applications had been completed for the Deputy Head post and handed in. The tension between the candidates was fierce. On receipt of the forms, even the Head looked under pressure.

Endri and I were convinced that the other two had got 'the whisper', and they were being secretly schooled or supported. But we both played it cool, and spent most of our time sharing ideas; scanning the net for educational updates; going over probable interview questions, and doing dummy interview practice with each other.

He sent me a card through the post with a pic of Toyin inside, and added a speech bubble next to her mouth, 'To outdo you!' I was in hysterics, and stuck it on my office fridge to ensure I didn't lose my focus. I had read that, when going into 'battle', you should know more about the enemy than they know about you. Work out what distinguishes you from them and, after identifying their weaknesses, create a solid game plan.

Knowledge about Enemy Number 1, Anthony:

- Nice guy
- Likeable
- Great sense of humour
- Always keen to support and help

Key strengths:

- Line Manager for Year 9
- Leader of the Preferences Process
- Creator of Year 9 Graduation

What distinguishes me from him:

- I'm more creative
- I'm better organised
- I'm more experienced with building successful teams

Knowledge about the Enemy Number 2, Toyin:

- Abrupt
- Sharp tongue
- Rude and facety

Key strengths:

- Expert with data

- Hardworking
- Solution-focused

What distinguishes me from her:

- I'm human!

Gideon, the Head's wingman, called a meeting with the four of us. "I thought it would be good for us to meet, so anyone with questions could ask them now before the interview," he started. "I also have a form that I need you all to complete."

The room was silent. I looked at Anthony and Toyin. They looked nervous.

"Why two posts?" I decided to open the floor.

Gideon responded.

"Well, originally we had three Deputies at this school but, with our linear leadership structure, it was felt that was no longer necessary. However, with the expertise we have in this room, we could afford to open up the opportunity to more than one person."

The room fell silent again. I decided to be bold and express my feelings.

"Don't you think it's negative, and very awkward, having four senior members of staff, who are highly talented and highly skilled in their specific roles, going up against each other?"

As Gideon began to faff with a run-of-the-mill answer, I glanced at the two questions on the form he had distributed.

Question 1: If you were successfully appointed, what strategies would you use to build the team?

Question 2: What would you do if you were not successful in this appointment?

That's a bit facety, I thought. Should I be up front and write below question 2 Leave? I didn't realise I had laughed out loud, until Gideon asked me if I was OK.

"You want me to answer these questions before the interview?" I queried.

"Why not?" he replied.

"Well, I would kill myself if I didn't get the job!" Toyin finally spoke.

I looked at her face. It was clear the stress this process had caused. It was replicated on Anthony's face, even Endri's, and no doubt was etched on mine as well. It was in that moment, it dawned on me. None of us had been given 'the whisper'. We were all in the same boat. And, because we had clear strengths in different areas, we saw each other as strong competition, which made us insecure of our own skills and talents.

"You haven't mentioned the pay." Endri decided to focus on what was important.

I couldn't help but laugh.

"But it's true," he added innocently. "None of the documents I received say how much we'll be paid."

I laughed again, and this time Gideon joined in, and added that it would be in line with what Deputies were being offered in the *TES*.

The interview was a week later and went surprisingly smoothly. The panel comprised of the Head, the Associate Head, a Governor and an independent Education Consultant.

"That's all our questions, Ms Bremmer. Is there anything you would like to add?" the Head summed up.

Right. Here goes. I took a deep breath.

"Two things," I began. "Firstly, I would just like to say that I am excited at this opportunity to be a Deputy Head Teacher of this school, and I know I am the perfect candidate for this post. I believe my track record speaks for itself. On a curriculum front, I am an outstanding teacher; I have built successful teams from scratch, and I have also led teams to support the students in making exceptional rates of progress at KS3 and with GCSE results at KS4. Pastorally, my experience as a record-breaking Head of Year would be an asset in supporting existing pastoral leaders, and my knowledge and experience in developing and delivering citizenship, pastoral, careers and mentoring programmes of study would benefit and enhance the confidence and skills of current leaders..."

I continued speaking for at least a further two minutes. I had rehearsed this, and the panel were gonna hear it whether they like it or not.

"Secondly," I continued, "I would just like to leave you with this folder to have a look through. It is something I am very proud of, and speaks for itself."

I placed the A4 lever arch file in the centre of the table. The Education Consultant, who was sitting next to the Head, picked it up and began flicking through the plastic wallets. It was filled with Thank You cards, email printouts, letters and commendations for the work I had done as a senior teacher. There were over 90 documents inside. No big deal, you may think. Well, actually, it was a *very* big deal. All the paperwork in the folder had been given or sent to me from the Head Teacher!

The Head glanced at each page. Her writing was bold and clear: 'fabulous', 'superb', 'great job', 'inspiring' were some of the phrases she had used. Her expression was impassive.

Hmmm. Let's see how you justify not promoting me after the panel have seen this, I thought. I was grinning inside, while on the outside, remained poker-faced.

"Thank you, Julz," the Head said, professionally. "I will be in touch later this evening with the outcome."

My mobile rang as I was getting ready for bed. It was the Head.

"Sorry for calling so late," she apologised, then got straight to the point.

"Congratulations, Julz. I am happy to tell you that from September you have been appointed as Deputy Head Teacher."

"Yeaaaaaaaaaaaaaaaaaaaaaaaaaaaaaaaaah!" I screamed. "Thank you. Thank you. Thank you!" My kids raced into the room, and joined in with the screams and began bouncing on my bed. What a great feeling!

I asked her who the second appointment was, and laughed uncontrollably at her answer.

As soon as I ended the call, I instantly logged onto my email account, clicked Compose, and typed in the subject panel: Congratulations!

In the body of the email I wrote:
Proud of you, Deputy Head Teacher! Well deserved. Julz Bremmer, _Deputy Head_ (Lol)

In the panel that said To, I typed Endri Demir, pressed comma and then typed Anthony Banjo, pressed comma and then typed Toyin Miso. I then pressed the Send button.

All four of us were appointed. It never dawned on me that there was room for everyone.

I felt embarrassed at my desire to crush Toyin and Anthony, in order to get the post. I had let myself down.

Inspirational speaker and teacher, Iyanla Vanzant, affirms: "Accept that what is yours will come to you in the right way at just the right moment."

I knew that. And promised myself that if there was a next time, I would do and be better.

"Bline man se im neighba fault."

Too often we are blind to our own shortcomings but quick to point out those of others.

EPISODE 22

Week Beginning: 26ᵗʰ February

Every Child Matters

Driving the Virgin Group is founder and investor, Sir Richard Branson; founder of SBTV Global is young multi-millionaire Jamal Edwards MBE, and driving, motivating and inspiring our staff, students and local community are the dynamic duo: Head Teacher, Terri Kidney and Associate Head, Gideon Obo.

A *Telegraph* newspaper survey asked 50 chief executives and entrepreneurs to rate what makes a good leader, post-recession. They ranked eight essential skills, and their order of priority included the following:

1. Give a clear sense of direction
2. Communicate clearly - inside and out
3. Be flexible but not floppy
4. Take risks but don't bet the organisation

These are followed by: team building; listening with humility; acting with courage, and building trust.

All of these were the essential skills and make-up of our powerful pair, and it was under their leadership that I quickly realised that the stakeholders were the priority and, as such, the kids came first.

School, for most in our inner-city environment, was a haven from all the additional dramas the students had to deal with, and what we as teachers could do to support was to ensure that all students made progress and left school with excellent GCSE grades. That was the ticket they needed to give them choices.

Our School Development Plan and strategies addressed both academic achievement along with supporting the whole child, and all teaching and support staff worked hard to ensure students received an experience that encompassed not just good results, but supporting students to become well-rounded, responsible human beings.

Terri's philosophy was to reward the positive, and work hard to shift students' attitudes. By ensuring the status quo was to be respectful, enthusiastic, cooperative and worked hard, it would leave pupils with poor behaviour and underachievement in the minority. So, by rewarding excellent attendance, progress, positive attitudes and great standards of work, students quickly realised that to be part of the in crowd, it was cool to be in school and working hard towards being an achiever.

Terri worked with Endri and members of Leadership to create a Commitment Ladder. All students would be given a number between 1 and 5 for effort, behaviour and homework from each teacher that taught them. Each half term, these scores would be tallied up, and pupils in each Year group would be ranked from 1 to 243 according to their final score. So, top of the ladder would be our Platinum students, and at the bottom our Red. All scores were sent home to parents every half term.

Any student who appeared in the Red zone would automatically have to meet the Head of Year and a member of the Leadership team with a parent. I had experienced a more crude form of this in the Caribbean, which was used following academic tests. It formed a list that could be viewed as 'name and shame'. The beauty of our system was that, no matter what your academic ability, you could still be at the top of the ladder if you made great effort in lessons; behaved superbly; completed homework to an excellent standard, and handed it in on time. It focused on a student's commitment to learning, and not on their academic ability.

Terri's motivation went back to her school days. She would often tell the story about her careers advisor, whom she had told she wanted to be a teacher. He laughed at her. The advice she received was that the only realistic option open to her was shop work.

Furious at not being taken seriously, Terri fought against the odds to prove it was possible to achieve your ambitions. She became a History teacher, and was determined to work hard and eventually run her own school. Her dream was to make sure the kids in her care were given the opportunities to do the same.

She secured the top job, and joined our school following the sudden death of the previous Head. I remember her first day: this young, skinny White lady, parking up in her BMW, wearing a Ted Baker suit.

"She can't be more than 40," one staff member commented.

"She was the Deputy at my mate's school, and he says she's 42," another added.

"Well, it'll be interesting to see if she can deal with *our* kids," one piped in.

"Anyone who drives a BM can relate to our kids," chimed in another, and we all burst into fits of laughter.

She worked her way through, personally meeting Senior Leadership, middle management and finally every main-scale teacher and support staff member. She was cautious not to make radical changes too quickly, and kept the current systems in place for the first two terms. So, she continued the school tradition of the Head supervising the three-hour Saturday detention and, like her predecessor, even taught a Year 7 class once a week.

Two months in, I still hadn't made up my mind about her, but I did love the way she dealt with the students.

Terri would make it a point to tell them how great they were, and that nothing was impossible. She encouraged them to dream big, and made them realise that the world was their oyster. Rewards became a big focus, and we had Student of the Week, Reader of the Week, Homework of the Week, School Hero, and prizes for the children who achieved a 100% Attendance and Punctuality record; bicycles, iPads and shopping vouchers would be the annual prize.

My rewards stance was slightly hard-nosed, and I was sceptical of rewarding students for doing what they should do naturally; however, I did see the positive changes that took place, as whole-school attendance improved, and we awarded and recognised more and more students as Heroes, because lost mobile phones, dinner passes, Oyster cards and purses – with the money still inside - would be handed in to the school office.

Our main priority in the early days was behaviour. Getting the students out of the park at the end of lunch and into lessons, and getting them to stay in lessons and on task, was a challenge. Exclusions were at an all-time high. I can remember recommending 18 students be sent home in one day, following a bullying incident. Terri decided to create a Behaviour Working Party (BWP) to resolve this situation, and a group of 25 staff from across the school would meet fortnightly to discuss ideas and initiatives, along with monitoring and evaluating our current provision.

In order to tackle this seriously, the meetings and training venue moved to a local hotel, and would be held over a weekend once a term. The session would start at 5.00pm on a Friday evening until 9.00pm, and resume on the Saturday morning at 9.00am until 1.00pm. Dinner, breakfast and board would be provided. The quality time spent at these meetings gave birth to most of the positive changes at the school, and I was proud to be a part of the fundamental decisions that impacted the school for the better. In less than four years, the name of the group changed to the 'Learning and Teaching Party'. Fixed-term exclusions had dramatically reduced, and permanent exclusions were zero. Poor behaviour was no longer an issue.

After the first Behaviour weekend away training session, I freshened up in my room, and then went down for dinner. There were two spaces left at the table: one next to Sandra, the school gossip, and the other next to Terri. Decisions, decisions. I moved towards the empty chair next to Sandra, and was beaten to it by Andy, who had grabbed the chair from behind me.

Oh boy. What on earth am I going to chat to the Head about for the next hour and a half? #Awkward.

"Loved the school fete you organised last week, Julz," she began. "The children took ownership of their areas and did a great job."

"Thanks," I said.

"I remember early on in my career, when I was teaching History in a Special School, I organised a fete," she began. "The children loved animals, and most of them had hedgehogs as a pet, so I decided to organise a hedgehog race. We asked the students to bring in their hedgehogs and the student, whose hedgehog walked passed the winning line first, would get a cash prize. So they all brought in their hedgehogs, and we put coloured bands around their legs so we could identify them."

By now, the table was silent and all ears were pricked up.

"I brought in one of those starting pistols so it would look professional, and after the count of three fired the pistol," she continued. "And they were off. I noticed that one of the hedgehogs was still in the starting position, so gave it a little shove to get it going, but it would not move. I quickly realised that it was dead. I think the loud sound of the pistol gave it a heart attack!"

Most of the teachers by now had their mouths opened in shock.

"So," Terri continued, "I reached over to pick up the hedgehog as I looked at his owner, a young lad, who was about to burst into tears, and I started to gallop with it along the track as he passed all the other hedgehogs and touched the ribbon first across the finish line. I gave his owner the cash prize and put the hedgehog in his box, and told everyone else to put their hedgehogs away and not to take them out until they went home."

The room was still silent and the teachers still sat with their mouths opened wide.

Terri began to grin cheekily. I could not help myself and burst out laughing. This caught on, and before long, the whole table was in fits of laughter. No one dared to ask if the story was true or not. But I knew it was. I found out later, she had left out the bit where she had given the child's mother twenty quid to replace it without the child knowing.

Terri would never leave a child feeling sad or unhappy. Nor, I would soon discover, a staff member. Staff were regularly recognised for their contribution to school effectiveness with a card or gift; she had everyone's birthday logged on her iPhone, and a box of chocolates or wine would be in your staff tray when you arrived at school. She was a great listener, and would share advice and give practical support to those in need.

When I was frustrated with my heart diagnosis, Terri caught me one morning in tears. I explained that I was not happy with the decision of my Cardiologist, and was searching online for a second opinion. By the afternoon, she had made a few phone calls and had booked me an appointment with a renowned Cardiothoracic Surgeon, who was a friend of a friend and based at a private clinic in Essex.

Ironically, Gideon was very similar to Terri. He was a superb orator and an amusing storyteller. He could hold an audience of both staff and students with his tales of life and experience. You would be sitting with a 1,000-strong crowd and could hear a pin drop. He was loved by all for his logical and pragmatic approach to problems and, as a Scientist, he was very solution-focused. On the days you just wanted to throttle that kid, he would talk you down, step by step, and leave you feeling that the problem wasn't as big a deal as you first thought, or he would swiftly walk ahead while you scuttled behind, ready to solve the problem or get the student to make the peace.

I was enthralled by his Nigerian stories and phrases. His tales would take you as far as a village in Nigeria, and as near as Clapton Park Estate in Hackney.

The academic year was cyclical, and each May you experienced 240 kids exit the school roll and, in September, 240 students would enter. With each new academic year, it afforded an opportunity for Gideon to tell the new Year 11s (who were the old Year 10s) his favourite story about a student called Leo Black…

"Leo was a bright young boy, full of potential but, by Year 11, he'd stopped making an effort and would bunk school. I would go to his house and bring him into school, but he would just sit in the class and not try. He missed most of his exams, and only turned up to the first Maths exam, which he slept through. Surprisingly, he came to school on GCSE results day to see what he had achieved, and was shocked to find that all his grades were Us. I saw Leo two years later, and he told me that he was finding it hard to secure a job or get on the courses he wanted to do at college. He said he wished he had listened when he was at school and not wasted his time."

Gideon would then take the opportunity to dramatically look at the two hundred plus students, making the obvious point that he was trying to see if he could spot a Leo Black amongst them. You could hear their minds ticking away in the silence. It was the way Gideon told his stories that made the children think: 'That's definitely *not* going to be *me*.'

I struggle to remember a time Gideon ever raised his voice or lost his cool. For him, everything was solvable. Not a problem. I asked him once if he'd ever lost it and he laughed aloud. I could feel a Gideon story coming on.

"I was Head of Year," he began. "It was the end of the Summer term and the Year group went to Chessington. We were all having fun in the theme park, and I was stopped by one of the security guards, who asked me to follow him. He took me inside the gift shop, and had about 10 of our kids lined up along the wall. Apparently, a rush of schoolchildren had come into the shop and swiped goods from the shelves and ran off. These were the ones the Security had caught. All 10 were our schoolkids."

"We didn't do anything, sir," one child began.

"Honest, we never," another chimed in.

Then they all began to protest their innocence in what was just a loud ball of noise.

At the top of my voice I yelled for them to put back any stolen items on the counter and the 10 terrified teens, who had never heard me raise my voice before, began to take sweets and toys from their socks, shoes, bras, sleeves and even their pants. I was *seething*. Even the shop staff and Security were shaking. The Security chief said he would let it go, if they went home straight away. Thankfully, the tutors were on hand to lead the children back to the coaches because, Gideon admitted that day would have marked the end of his teaching career, because he was so embarrassed for the school and, if he had caught up with any of them, he would have strangled them.

Oh boy, I thought, not wanting to look at my watch, Gideon was on a roll...

He began. "It was the final school day for Year 11, and this particular tutor group wanted their tutor to remember them always, so decided to create a shrine outside her classroom door. Unfortunately, they had used permanent markers to write their messages on the wall and paintwork. He decided to bang his fist on the table and add a fake roar to get them to realise how outrageous their actions were. The kids froze like rabbits caught in the headlights.

"Get out!" he yelled, and they shot off like mini Usain Bolts. Strangely, Gideon began to hop and howl.

"Thank God they'd gone," he added. "I thought I had broken my hand! I was still in pain days later."

His love for staff was an infectious and beautiful side of his personality and, if you let him know someone was experiencing difficulty, he would be the first to offer a helping hand. I cannot count the number of times he offered to take my son to live with him when he was misbehaving – I'm not sure what his wife would have said, but he did offer.

Even though Gideon was the Associate Head Teacher (first in line to the throne), he was the first to pick up a dustpan and brush if he saw chips on the floor at lunchtime, and he was often the last to leave after Parents' Evening, helping the caretakers to stack the chairs.

I remember a staff member struggling financially when her daughter was hospitalised at short notice. When I called to ask how she was holding up, she openly told me about her struggles. Teaching all day, and rushing to and fro from the hospital in Central London in the evenings, was taking its toll. She explained that she had to wash and dry her daughter's only nightgown every other day, because her financial priority was petrol and parking, along with buying other personal essentials. When I mentioned it to Gideon, his practical brain spun into gear and he ordered me to go to M&S and buy whatever was needed and he would foot the bill.

"If the staff member had one less thing to worry about, that should at least ease some of the pressure she was experiencing," he added.

Gideon did not bat an eyelid when I presented him with the receipt, which totalled close to £300. The staff member's eyes were filled with tears when I handed over the eight bags with goodies. "God told me to trust," she said, overjoyed, "and I did. Blessed be the Name of the Lord." She kissed and cuddled me with excitement. "Save some love for Gideon," I said once I'd caught my breath. "I'm just the messenger."

This type of kindness was not the exception to the rule in our school, but the norm. Our school community was definitely, as Peggy Mitchell *(EastEnders)*, would say: 'Faaaamily!' And in our school, with Terri and Gideon steering the ship, no child was going to be left behind. Every child (and staff member) mattered.

"If yuh nuh mash ants, yuh nuh fine him guts."

It is only when you are closely involved with people are you able to really know them.

Week Beginning: 5th March

Food For Thought

My mother raised my two brothers and me single-handedly - with the support of my grandparents in the background - and, even though I may not have felt it then, looking back and comparing my experience to the students I am in daily contact with, I can honestly say that my mum was the best.

She would juggle work, home and everything else, but always ensured our clothes were immaculately clean and ironed; my two pairs of white school socks were bleached and gleamed daily - our church socks and church clothes were never worn to school – and, although my mum struggled to make ends meet, my siblings and I never experienced hunger. We didn't like soup on a Saturday and, to this day, my brother hates corned beef and white rice, which we had every week and affectionately termed it as 'poor people's food'. Amazingly, one tin always stretched and fed all.

The ice cream van would park outside the flats and play the tune *Oranges and Lemons* on full blast, all the non-Black kids on the estate would yell, "Mummmmmmmmm!" and get thrown over the balcony a 20p coin for a 99 cone and Flake. We knew better, and would head upstairs and take from the freezer a homemade Tree Top orange squash and Jamaican strawberry syrup ice lolly, made in a Tupperware mould.

Mum was an auxiliary nurse at the Royal London Hospital. Her shift would start at 7.00am, so she was out of the house at 6.00am each morning; she had to take my baby brother, who was two at the time, to the childminder's before heading to work.

As latchkey kids, my brother Wayne and I would be woken up by a telephone call from my mum at 7.30 each morning, and our breakfast of cornmeal or oats porridge would be on the cooker, waiting to be reheated and swiftly consumed.

So, unlike today, we did not experience lack of concentration or diminished academic performance because, unlike many of my schoolkids, who leave home without having the first meal of the day, we left home each morning with our belly full.

I was shocked to discover, when I entered teaching, that a third of children regularly start their day without breakfast, or some begin the day with a can of cola and a packet of crisps. I would witness first-hand the impact: these were the students who were more likely than other classmates to be hyperactive and obese.

Research from the European Journal of Clinical Nutrition showed that 32% of pupils do not eat breakfast before leaving home, and only 25% of these sometimes had a morning meal. Surprisingly, boys often blame lack of time, while many girls missed breakfast because they believe doing so would help them lose weight. These findings were of great concern, because these 'skippers' were more likely to develop chronic disease in adulthood, like cancer, heart disease and diabetes.

Most secondary schools contracted out their school meals service, and the catering companies that won the tenders would manage all aspects of the service. My Head Teacher decided to do something radical, and get our school to manage the school meals service ourselves, including the canteen staff, menus, equipment and all the health and safety aspects. We would be the only school in our borough to do this, and Mike, the school's Business Manager, and I were given the task to manage the project together.

Mike was a young, sharp and intelligent young man. He was an ex-student, and had successfully run his own business and other award-winning projects before coming back to the school and taking on the Business Manager role. He took it very seriously and, although his jobsworth approach would sometimes peeve team members, when all was said and done, he was excellent at his job and a pleasure to work with. On the rare occasions when our opinions clashed, I would tell him to keep quiet, and swiftly remind him that, as his former English teacher, I was the person who taught him how to spell and he wouldn't have got an A in English at GCSE without me. "A*," he would always mumble back, just before he gave in.

We were Yin and Yang, but the perfect team for the school canteen project. Our first plan of action was to work out an end goal: look at what we wanted to achieve, assess what we had, and then work out all the bits that went in between. My ultimate aim was for the service to make a profit, so we would be able to fund a series of projects that would benefit the students: a free breakfast club for all who arrived at school before 8am; after-school club snacks; half term, Easter and Summer classes; meals and free lunches for students who attended school trips. All this, along with the purchasing of new kitchen equipment, was accomplished in less than 18 months but, like anything worthwhile, it was hard work.

We ran a competition, where the students renamed the canteen and an ex-student, who owned his own graphic design company, created the new logo, which we used to brand the service around the school. We organised a training programme, new uniform, and hired extra staff to work in the kitchen, along with an experienced second-in-charge. Orders were set up online, and we employed student volunteers to work shifts at lunchtimes for a free meal and food vouchers. Mike and I would meet weekly with the Deputy and Head of Kitchen, and discuss menus and ideas to move the service forward. We would encourage the student body to give us their views, and see how we could put some of these into action.

A regular request from the School Council - but a major challenge for us - was to create additional food outlets to support the large number of students using the service. The Snack Stop was born, with two outlets offering quick and healthy alternatives that were school-safe and sourced by the kitchen staff. A free help-yourself salad bar was also a dinnertime staple, following a comment we received from a group of students who wanted us to be "more like Pizza Hut and Harvester". We introduced monthly Themed Lunches, showcasing food from different cultures or celebrating special events and dates. One of my two favourites was 'Reggae

Reggae Day', where we served jerk chicken, rice and peas, festivals, and black cake with custard. The food sold out in under an hour, so we had to serve the back of the queue nuggets and chips. On my other favourite, 'Roald Dahl Day', the students feasted on BFG Chicken, Fantastic Mr Fox's Fish Fingers, along with Charlie's Chocolate Mud Cake and James' Giant Peach Crumble.

We were approached by different departments for special menu items that could be used as rewards, so the Head of Year 7 offered the students in the Year group who had made the most academic progress, a movie treat during the last lesson of the day, and we provided each child with a healthy packet of popcorn and a drink. The Attendance team went one better, and rewarded the tutor group who achieved the best attendance and punctuality record over a half term period a Pizza Party, and the students worked with the team on the exciting toppings.

The highlight for me was the outcome of an unannounced Environmental Health Service inspection from the Food Standards Agency - 5 stars! Not meaning to brag, but I had eaten out at an Angus Steak House in central London the previous weekend, and the sign in their restaurant window showed a Food Standards rating of only 4 stars!

For the daily smooth running of the service, students, who were entitled to free school meals, were given a plastic photo ID card, and would queue up at lunchtime in the dining hall. Staff would check their passes and issue them with a paper ticket, which they would present at the cash desk, once they had selected their meal. Both free meal and paying students queued on a first come, first served basis, so everyone was treated equally. I was passionate about ensuring no students went unfed. Some of our cohort had travelled from abroad, and lived with family members who were unemployed but, because of the nature of their relative's status (which more often than not was temporary, pending investigation), the families were not entitled to government assistance or to free school meals.

It was important we supported families in this situation but, as with anything, the difficulty was trying to weed out the genuine students who needed to be fed, from the ones who would abuse the service. One strategy was that students with no money would have to wait at the end of the queue before they were fed, but straight away there was a core who felt that was long, and so refused to wait. Couldn't have been *that* hungry then, eh?

Next, I introduced a budget bap lunch for those without money: a bap with cheese, a cookie and a drink. Again, those who pretended to have no money didn't want to eat that, so quickly disappeared from the queue. The hungry few that were left behind ended up being given a hot meal.

One of the great things about my School Dining team was their enthusiasm at catching kids who tried to defraud the system. The most common would be a student who would obtain a free lunch by using a dinner card that was not their own. Lesley, our dinner lady for over 23 years, was an expert. Little Stanley was the latest student to try and fool her, but got caught in the act.

Stanley was in Year 7, and had left his dinner money on the kitchen table. His friend offered to help him out, by giving him his free dinner card to use, but the thing was, it was a *photo* ID dinner card; Stanley was White and strawberry blonde, his mate Ola was dark and African.

I was purposefully gentle, because Stanley was new to the school. I got him a sandwich and a drink, and sat him down in my office.

"Do you realise that it was wrong to try and use Ola's dinner card?"

"Yes, Miss," Stanley replied.

"How do you think you could have dealt with this differently?" I asked.

"Don't know, Miss," he answered.

"Well, you could have told your tutor or the dinner lady that you had forgotten your dinner money, and she would have got you lunch."

"Yes, Miss," he responded.

I launched into my Fraud Speech, but decided to go gentle on Stanley, because he was a newbie that had just made a silly mistake.

"Using Ola's card and trying to obtain a free lunch, which you were not entitled to, can be viewed as fraud, Stanley, so it's important not to do that again. In future, always speak to a teacher."

"Yes, Miss," Stanley replied.

"I am not going to punish you on this occasion, but I'm going to put this down to you making a poor decision, which you know was wrong. I am also going to speak to Ola about this, because he should not, under any circumstances, have given you his card," I added.

"Are you going to tell my dad?" Stanley enquired tentatively.

"No," I replied. "I think you understand where you went wrong, so let's move on from this. Off you go."

Relieved to have escaped a sanction for his actions, Stanley skipped off down the corridor.

I put Ola's card in my in-tray, and scribbled a Post-it reminder to pick him up.

My office phone was ringing as I entered my office the next day. An irate man was on the other end asking for me.

"Speaking," I replied.

It was Stanley's dad, and he wanted to know what had happened yesterday lunchtime. One of the students had told him Stanley had got into trouble at school and, when he questioned Stanley, he said I had called him a fraudster.

I apologised to Dad for not calling him about the incident, but said I felt the matter had been dealt with. I then explained the chain of events. Stanley's dad explained that his issue was with me calling his son a fraudster, and he was not happy with the label I had given his son. I tried my best to be diplomatic, and explained that using someone else's dinner card, which Stanley was not entitled to, *was* a form of unintentional fraud. I was still trying to be diplomatic. Dad was having none of it. He began saying his son was from a good home, and he was not pleased that he'd come to school to have his good name and character trashed by a senior teacher who should know better. It was outrageous. He was going to make it his business that I get into trouble for this, as he would be looking to take this further.

I began to get annoyed.

"Now, let's get something straight here, Mr Bennett." I decided to take back control of this discussion.

"I stand corrected. Your son did not try to commit unintentional fraud yesterday, he tried to commit fraud. Let's make no bones about this. He deliberately tried to deceive the dinner lady, by using someone else's dinner card with the view of obtaining a government-funded meal, which he was not entitled to. That is fraud. Now, I could have made a recommendation that he be excluded for the incident, but he is in Year 7 and made a mistake, which he admitted and has promised not to do it again. You are very welcome to take this further, Mr Bennett. Yes, and I may get into trouble for this…" I added. "Get into trouble for not dealing with your son more harshly!"

There was silence at the end of the phone.

"Are you still there, Mr Bennett?" I queried sharply.

"Yes. But I'm running late for an appointment so I need to go," and with that, the call was terminated.

What a cheek! This is what happens when you are not consistent with sanctions and bend the rules for some. Served me right!

Mike was great at following and sticking to rules and policies, and was keen to bring to account both staff and students who broke them. It wasn't long before this young soul elicited fear among his seniors, along with the boys and girls, and I'm sure Mike secretly enjoyed being Mr Bad Guy. It was just the difficult conversations with parties that did not adhere to the rules that he needed more practice with. That side of things usually fell into *my* lap.

One of the cashiers came to see Mike and me after lunch service, and showed us a few of the paper dinner tickets that had been given to her. At first glance, nothing seemed out of the ordinary but, on closer inspection, you could see they were laminated photocopies. My initial thoughts were, how cheeky. My next thoughts were, how clever this student was, to go to extreme lengths to infiltrate our system. Wow. These kids were something else. Mike was less forgiving, and called a team meeting.

"We have a case of Canteen Fraud on our hands." He switched into Sherlock mode, and was determined to sniff the fraudster out. "How dare they try and abuse our system!"

In less than a week, the perpetrators were in my office, with heads bowed. Mike had scooped up the culprits, three Year 11s: Abdul, Mohammed and Shahid. Three members from our Muslim Prayer group. I was shocked.

Abdul admitted replicating the design. Mohammed copied them in colour, and laminated and cut the tickets out. Shahid was the salesman. Charging £1 per ticket.

I know this sounds bad, but I wanted to laugh. Who'd have thought that my Friday Prayer Boys (whom I gave free pizzas to every Friday!) would be involved in a Dinner Ticket Racket? You couldn't make it up.

They still had heads bowed, and were very contrite.

"You know this is fraud, don't you?" I said purposely.

Each boy began to shake.

"Fraud," I then said slowly: "Fraud. Fraud. Fraud."

These were good boys. Good, intelligent boys. I was going to make a meal of this, pardon the pun, with the hope they would learn their lesson and not do anything like this again.

"Any of you heard of a man called Nick Leeson?"

Abdul and Mohammed shook their heads. Shahid nodded.

"Go on," I said to Shahid, giving him permission to elaborate further.

"He was a banker that did something wrong, and made one of the oldest banks in London collapse."

"Hmmm. Not a bad answer. Close. Very close," I replied. "Can you tell me and your friends what his crime was?" I asked.

Shahid shook his head.

"Fraud!" I shouted. All the boys jumped. "Fraud! He got sent to jail for six years! SIX YEARS!" I shouted louder.

Three pairs of eyes stared at me widely in shock.

"What would the prophet Muhammad say?" I added.

They were silent and stood frozen.

"What would your *fathers* say?" I continued.

Abdul began to cry. The other two were still frozen.

"How much money did you make, Shahid?"

"£6, Miss. I only sold six tickets. I started at break time today."

"I am very disappointed in you all," I frowned. "You have not only let down yourselves, but the school and your families. I'm calling PC Mehmet, the school's Police officer so he can speak to you all about the seriousness of this, and I'm going to place you in Isolation tomorrow. You will all also be on Canteen Duty, clearing plates and tables for a week. Now go and wait in the Isolation Room, while I get hold of PC Mehmet."

"Sorry, Miss," they each mumbled as the exited my office.

"Oi, Shahid!" I called out.

He stopped in his tracks.

"The six quid, please," I reminded him, with my palm outstretched.

He placed the dirty coins into my hand, and mumbled the word 'sorry' again.

"You're £6.00 short, Shahid. Dinner tickets are normally £2.00, so you need to make up the difference."

"Sorry, Miss." He now began to cry.

Hmmm, I thought, as they left. We must add Business Studies to our curriculum offer. Some of these kids would pass with flying colours!

"Lang run, shaat ketch."

It may take a long while for you to get caught and punished for wrongdoing, but you *will* be caught one day.

EPISODE 24

Institutionally Childist

I read a statement once that described teachers as fair people who have no strong preferences or feelings when it comes to their students. Everyone is treated equally, and personal matters do not come into the evaluation of a child.

I wish.

If the truth be told, as much as we try to pretend we are all-loving, all-embracing creatures, in reality, teachers are just people too. And, just like any other person, we have thoughts, feelings, opinions and preferences, and these can roll both ways: negative and positive.

The Macpherson Report brought to light institutional racism, which is a system of inequality based on race. The term was introduced back in the late 1960s, but within the Report, which looked into the murder of Stephen Lawrence, the phrase described the collective failure of the Metropolitan Police to provide an appropriate and professional service to the family, because of their colour, culture or ethnic origin.

Without sounding crass, I coined the phrase 'institutionally childist' to specifically describe teaching staff in the education system, who dislike children.

It's a bit like a baker who hates cakes; a butcher who detests meat; a florist who is allergic to flowers. A teacher who abhors children? A terrifying and scary thought.

However, some can get away with this through the guise of ignorance, which can be a more palatable excuse for education professionals to knock a pupil's confidence, self-esteem and enthusiasm, but hey ho, believe me, it's still a form of being childist.

This is why parents need to be on the ball and keep themselves in the know as to what their children are being taught; what their child thinks about school lessons and their teachers and, if they have concerns, to raise them in an appropriate forum and in a professional way. It's true, a lot of parents can cite their negative school experiences, where a teacher has told them they would amount to nothing, and carry this with them for a long time. This hurt would affect the way they communicate with their children's teachers, the extremes being either aggressively or not at all.

Being a teacher made me more cautious in the way I dealt with my children's teachers. Most did not know I was a senior leader, and more often than not I would let them get on with it, unless they decided to take the mick.

Following a night at the stage show, *Black Heroes in the Hall of Fame*, my daughter went back to her school empowered, and even more proud to be Black. She shared the experience with a few of her school friends, and one raised what she had told them in a History lesson. The teacher also happened to be the Deputy Head.

"Yazmin says that Queen Victoria's grandmother was Black, sir."

"Rubbish!" the teacher replied.

"But she *was*, sir," Yazmin insisted. "She was the wife of King George III, and a direct descendent of the Black Portuguese Royal family. If you look at paintings..."

"Have you lost your mind, child?" he interrupted. "It's not true."

The class of 12 laughed.

Upset and angry, Yazmin relayed the conversation to me at the dinner table that evening.

I was sitting in front of Mr Blakey in his office at 8.00am the following morning.

He confirmed what Yazmin had said.

"It's teachers like you, through your dismissive attitude, that knock the confidence out of young Black children, and they end up disillusioned as a result of one barbed comment or negative jibe," I began.

He then tried to tell me that Queen Charlotte Sophia's colour was 'neither here nor there'.

"Don't contradict what I tell my child, Mr Blakey. Especially when it's to do with her heritage," I responded firmly.

He looked uncomfortable. I decided to change to a softer tack; after all, Yazmin still had two more years at the school.

"If you or your staff need some inset or specific training for your Black History Day in October, I can give you the contact details for Robin Walker, a very credible Black historian."

I then purposely left photocopies of info on Queen Charlotte Sophia and some Google links on his desk before I left.

In my teaching practice school, there was Simon Bryan. He was a character. Warm and funny with staff, but dictatorial, bossy and downright rude to kids. He would patrol the corridors during the winter months, evicting the freezing youngsters, who were clinging to radiators, into the playground and, when they sat in lessons, snuggled in their coats and gritting their chattering teeth, he would insist they remove the outer garment because it was school rules. Similarly, in the summer months, he would not allow students to remove their jumpers and blazers, and they would fry, sweat and smell, due to the intense heat.

Simon was generous in sharing his 'tricks of the trade' with trainee teachers. "Make sure you make a list of all those kids, who have been a pain all term, and then call home, in particular, the day before a long break, to let a parent know that their child was not making progress or needed to reflect on their attitude. The inevitable punishment for the kid, due to the timing of the call, would drag out through the holiday period. That was an excellent way of teaching consequences," he laughed.

He was not a nice person and, where possible, I would avoid being in his presence. The Uniform Policy at that particular school stated that hats should not be worn inside the school buildings, and Simon took pleasure dragging the baseball caps and beenies off the heads of the African Caribbean boys, who had forgotten to remove their headgear once they entered a building. This would automatically create a war of words, and often ended up with one of the boys swearing at him and getting excluded.

Once, a student was excluded for fighting, and his parents were called. His mother was unable to collect him because she was at home looking after a younger sibling, who was ill. She gave permission for the Year 10 to make his way home. I was on duty, and was asked to escort the boy off the premises. As we made our way to the main gate, the student decided he wasn't going home and ran back into the school building. It was 15 minutes before lunch, and if this student was on site when the whole school was dismissed, I knew there would be trouble. As the Beginner Teacher, who should have ensured he left the building, I knew I would end up getting stick for this.

I radioed the Learning Mentor on call for assistance, and received a message back that the student was hiding in the boys' toilets on the ground floor in the main building. As I arrived to reason with the student, Simon Bryan, who had overheard my radio message, was waiting outside the loos.

"Do you want me to provoke him so he hits me?" he asked calmly.

"What?" I asked, incredulously.

"That way, I could get him permanently excluded for hitting a teacher."

That was the first time in my career I was truly shocked. I was also frightened to realise there were teachers in the profession who actually thought like that.

"No way!" I exclaimed, and marched into the boys' toilets, pulled the reluctant student out, and marched him through the corridor and straight out of the main gate.

I reported Simon to the Head, but nothing came of it. I was relieved to get out of that school, but worried for the kids who were left behind and who could not escape as easily as I had. I think it was as a result of this experience that I decided, if I was going to make a difference, I needed to be in a position of power, and needed to work hard as a teacher to get myself onto a School Leadership team.

Thankfully, for every Simon, there was a polar opposite, and I found one in a Deputy Head on my second teaching practice, Mark

Crew. He had been teaching for donkey's years, and was an English specialist of Irish descent, who was a magnificent storyteller and had a genuine love for kids. He was filled with rich and beautiful tales about his experiences within the profession; always had time to share his expertise, and really enjoyed being hands on with his role. One of the jobs he loved doing was supervising the dinner queue at lunchtimes. A short straw for many - and a role he did not have to do - but one he loved because, as he told me, it was a great opportunity to interact with the children, especially those whose families were not well off and received free school meals.

Mark, as a Senior Deputy, displayed no airs and graces and, when other senior staff would reinforce their seniority with the students around the school, by throwing around the classic phrase: "Do you know who I am?", Mark would be standing in the lunch hall daily, checking uniform, keeping order, and revelling in the excitement at such a crucial time of the day.

"Don't you just love 'em?" he would say, as he would banter, laugh and reprimand the hundreds of students as they queued up for lunch.

I remember talking to Mark while he was on lunch duty, and he had spotted a kid trying to jump the queue.

"Oh no you don't, lad," he said in his Irish accent, and told the student to get to the back of the queue. The Year 8 boy began to curse Mark and stormed out of the hall. Shocked at his behaviour, I swiftly followed him.

I stopped him in his tracks. "How dare you speak to sir like that!" I challenged.

"What, Mr Crew? The dinner man?" he replied.

"No. Mr Crew, the Senior Deputy Head of this school," I said.

The young boy looked confused. I collected his details for a Friday detention and went back to Mark.

"He thinks you're a dinner man, sir." I was trying hard not to smile.

"I know, they all do," he laughed. "I love this duty. I get the opportunity to meet and talk to most of the students, and get to know what they really think about the teachers and the lessons."

He took the paper with details of the boy from my hand and tore it up.

"Aren't you going to make sure he's punished?" I said.

"He'll be back. He hasn't had his dinner yet. He can apologise then. The thing about most of these children is they hit out in the heat of the moment, but they're not malicious. They'd have forgotten about it two minutes later and be saying, "Hi sir, how are you today?" You do need to remind them about manners and respect but, at the same time, you need to show them that you care. As teachers, for most of those kiddies, we are the one stable thing most of them have in their lives."

Wow! That certainly was a lesson learned that day. No matter how senior I get, I was going to make sure I always found time to keep in touch with the kids and listen to what they had to say.

Sadly, this was difficult to do, if the child was a thief and a liar.

Ruth was both.

Her photo was displayed in our local Tesco Store Manager's office, with the statement: 'Banned for life. Please report to Security if you see her in the store'.

Last term, she brought into school bags of every brand of crisp under the sun; this term it was a daily box of Krispy Kreme doughnuts - all swiped from the shelves of Tesco's on the High Road.

School equipment needed to be screwed down if she was in the classroom, and most of her class teachers would report expensive pens, money, their purses or handbags missing after teaching her. Naturally, she would deny any wrongdoing - even when the stolen item was removed from her school bag in front of her - swearing blind she didn't know how it got there.

The result of Ruth's kleptomania was becoming exasperating. Her mother was fed up of receiving phone calls to come into school because her daughter was being put into the In-School Suspension Centre, or had been given a fixed-term exclusion. Mum was at the end of her tether, and had had enough. If she received another negative incident report, she would be shipping Ruth out of London to a state boarding school.

Class teachers were on alert and, I'm told, some left their purses and handbags on their desks on purpose, hoping to tempt Ruth into helping herself but, surprisingly, Day 2 had come and gone without incident.

On Day 3, Ruth's best friend, Tina's, iPhone had been stolen out of her jacket pocket. When Tina discovered her phone missing at the end of the lesson, she was inconsolable; it was a birthday gift. Ruth led the classroom search, and insisted the teacher search all the students, including her. After a second search of bags and jackets in front of the Mentors, the class was dismissed and Ruth, Sarah and Abby decided to take Tina home, so she could break the news to her mum.

The Mentors reported the incident to me that afternoon, and I went to find the teacher. This incident had Ruth's sticky palms all over it.

"I felt so bad that it happened on my watch," the teacher said. "We searched the room and the kids, but nothing."

"Did anyone leave the class during the lesson?" I asked.

"Hmmm. Only Ruth. That was about 20 minutes into the lesson. She was back in class within 5 minutes." The teacher paused. "You don't think? Naaah. Not Ruth. She's her mate. She's on a final warning. You don't think...?"

"I think I'll take a drive to Ruth's house." I ended the conversation and left, now 100% convinced Ruth was the thief.

After looking through the letterbox, everything was still. It was clear no one was home. I decided to try Tina's.

I drove over to her block of flats, and pulled at the iron entrance door, but it was locked. I was about to press Tina's door number on the intercom, when a young lady with a child came from behind and swiped her fob against the panel. The lock on the main door released and I pulled it open.

I walked up the stairs to the second floor. Ruth was sitting alone on the concrete stairs.

"Hi, Ruth," I said slowly. Now how was I going to get her to admit she had stolen the phone? I knew if I played this right and got her to confess, she would be out the door, and many of the staff, even students, would be happier for it.

"I guess you want this," she said calmly, pulling the iPhone from her jacket pocket.

I was in shock.

"Thank you." I did not know what else to say.

I swiftly put it into my pocket.

"Am I going straight home, or are you taking me to school to exclude me?" Ruth asked.

"School," I replied. I was still in shock by her straightforwardness, and I was still confused as to the motive. "Why?" I asked. "Tina's your best friend!"

"Yeah," Ruth confirmed, "but I've always wanted an iPhone 6."

Boy! This was too easy. It was not what I was expecting. I began to feel sorry for Ruth. No, not sorry, pity. The situation was pathetic. Coming down hard on a child wasn't a problem for me if they were disrespectful or rude but, to me, Ruth had given in and given up. It was as though she knew everyone expected her to fail and, because she had no one in her corner, she did what was expected.

I felt I was no better than Simon Bryan, the teacher whose behaviour I disliked so much from my student teacher days. Realistically, it was inevitable Ruth was going to trip up, but I felt I should have done more to ensure right to the end that she was supported.

Back at school, Ruth sat waiting for her mother in the Reception area, humming, without a care in the world.

"Can't we give her one more chance?" I pleaded to my Line Manager. "She did give me the phone without me having to ask," I continued.

"This was going to happen again sooner or later, Julz. You know that."

"Yes," I confirmed, "but I'd rather it didn't happen with me sealing her fate!"

There. I'd said it. I didn't like the feeling that it was me who was going to have to sign the form that triggered Ruth's move to another school.

Ruth's mother came and went into the Associate Head's office.

I watched both Mum and Ruth leave 30 minutes later, knowing that would be the last time I would see them again.

"For the greater good," my Line Manager whispered, as I signed the last section of the paperwork. "She still has a chance. A fresh start somewhere else may be the catalyst for change she needs. Doing the right thing doesn't always leave you feeling good, but as long as you know deep inside it's right, then be satisfied with that and let it go. We still have 1,249 kids to love and care about tomorrow." He patted me gently on the shoulder and left.

I began to think about what he had said.

I smiled.

He was right.

The thing that separates the good from the bad, the Mikes from the Simons, is the fact that they love children and truly care.

When all was said and done…

…I do too.

"Book learnin a nuh intelligence."

Not everyone who is educated has common sense.

EPISODE 25

Week Beginning: 19th March

All In A Day's Work

Childhood is often described as the age of innocence, but many of us know this isn't necessarily the case. I have children in my care, who have witnessed family members being brutally murdered in war-torn countries; have experienced loss, due to violence; who are latchkey children, young carers or are looked after and living in foster care... The list is endless. When you work with children from such diverse backgrounds, you hear stories to make the hairs on the back of your neck stand on end, your stomach churn, and your heart break. Perhaps this is because, as an English teacher, I expect the stories of children to begin 'Once upon a time' and end at some point with a 'happily ever after'.

I was sent an email about a student, whose attendance had nosedived since the beginning of term, and I contacted her family who were shocked at the level of absences. Jamelia had been coming home very late every evening, with the excuse she had been catching up with coursework but, as she had not been in school, I wanted to know what catching up she had been doing. Jamelia was a sweet 15-year-old, hardworking and loved school. She had always strived to do her best.

When I received a call to say she was adamant she didn't want to come back to school, I decided to do a home visit. With just the two of us in her living room, between floods of tears, Jamelia reluctantly told me that every time she was working in lessons and it was quiet, she would be reminded of the times she was being abused by her uncle when she was 10 - a disclosure she was making for the first time. I cried at the graphic details. Telling her mother was just as hard.

Back at school, the brief from the top was to clamp down on students who were not wearing full school uniform, and Sade was sent to me because she was wearing trainers, and did not have on her school tie.

As she walked through the door, I instantly went into my 'How-disgraceful-letting-the-team-down' speech, and she stood there silently, with her head bowed.

I continued ranting about how her trainers could buy her at least 10 sensible school shoes and 20 school ties, and that her attire was totally unacceptable.

She said Sorry and began to cry. She told me she had been sitting at home with her family, watching *EastEnders*, when the door knocked. Her father answered it and there was a loud bang. He had been shot. All the family had jumped out the window and ran. What she had on was what she was wearing at the time. She apologised again.

I bowed my head in shame.

Working in an inner-city school comes with challenges, many of which require you to be more than a teacher. A colleague shared a post on my social media page, which I wholeheartedly agreed with. It was created by busyteacher.org and written by Stacey Bonino:

*I am a **counsellor and psychologist** to a problem-filled child,*
*I am a **police officer** that controls a child gone wild.*
*I am a **travel agent** scheduling our trips for the year,*
*I am a **confidante** that wipes a crying child's tear.*
*I am a **banker** collecting money for tons of different things,*
*I am a **librarian** showing adventures that a storybook brings.*
*I am a **custodian** that has to clean certain little messes,*
*I am a **psychic** that learns to know all that everybody only guesses.*
*I am a **photographer** keeping pictures of a child's yearly growth,*
*When **mother and father** are gone for the day, I become both.*
*I am a **doctor** that detects when a child is feeling sick,*

*I am a **politician** that must know the laws and recognise every trick.*
*I am a **party planner** for holidays to celebrate with all,*
*I am a **decorator** of a room, filling every wall.*
*I am a **news reporter** updating on our nation's current events,*
*I am a **detective** solving small mysteries and ending all suspense.*
*I am a **clown and comedian** that makes the children laugh*
*I am a **dietician** assuring they have lunch or from mine I give them half.*
*When we seem to stray from values, I become a **preacher**,*
But I'm proud to have to be these people because...
*I'm proud to say, "**I am a teacher.**"*

At 4.00pm, I began to unwind and decided to tackle some marking. Delroy, who never knocks, excitedly burst into my office. His cheeky grin could forgive any sin. He was at the age when boys have crushes on teachers, which is flattering, but embarrassing. Sadly, they don't teach you in teacher training how to gently let down a lovelorn 14-year-old!

He began his daily ritual of offering me a sweetie from his pack of Love Hearts. "What does it say, Miss? What does it say?" I looked at the yellow sweetie and laughed, "YOLO." He faked a frown and left.

I smiled as I glanced back at the sweet. The manufacturers had clearly been dragged into the 21st century. It was now 4.05pm. Yep, I thought. You Only Live Once. And with that, I packed my Mac, unplugged my charger, scooped up my keys and headed for home.

"Monkey pickney nebba walk pon grung."

Children should be protected until they can identify danger.

EPISODE 26

With Power Comes Great Responsibility

My eldest son when he was upset with me would say: "You're a teacher first and a mother second!"

This is primarily because, whenever he got into trouble at school, I refused to do what his friends' parents would, and support him in his foolishness. More often than not, due to experience, I wouldn't waste time listening to his drawn-out tales of why he got kicked out of a class but, instead, instantly put in place a punishment because he had no business being out of lesson.

When all was said and done, he had a point. I loved my job. I spent too many hours in school - often putting my kids in the staff room to play or amuse themselves on a Saturday, while I caught up with work - and would miss many social gatherings with friends because I was either too busy planning lessons and marking, or was just too knackered.

The nature of teaching and being a teacher means you can't just switch off. When an incident occurs, you have to deal with it and, if you are working with children, you are legally bound to report what has been disclosed. You should never promise confidentiality to the child or to the person reporting it.

I remember holidaying in Florida one Christmas, and was sent a message via social media from an ex-parent. She was concerned about a Year 7 student. She did not have all the details or the child's full name, but she had heard that the girl's family (who were from Pakistan) were concerned about her mixing with boys, so had made plans to send her abroad for an arranged marriage. I sent back a message saying that I would be back in the country in a week and if, after getting more details, she was still concerned, then she was to let me know and I would investigate further.

A week into the new term, I was summoned to the office of the Head of Child Protection, and was reprimanded for not reporting the information. Even though no one had got back to me, the fact that I had even been given the details meant I had a duty of care to report what I knew, because I could have put a vulnerable child at risk.

The stories of what some young people at school have had to go through were sad and sometimes harrowing - from not being fed, to being mentally or physically abused. Suzie was in Year 10, she was articulate, bright and confident, someone you would never expect to hide a nasty secret. Sadly, she was regularly beaten by her father because she looked like her mum. The mother had walked out on the father five years ago to live with another man, and had left the three kids behind. Once I remember noticing a small bruise on her arm and asking her what had happened. She instantly replied she had bumped into a door. When the truth came out, I was shocked but thankful that another colleague had probed the truth out of one of the siblings. Suzie and her two brothers ended up in foster care.

It was not unusual for the children's issues and incidents to spill over into your own life. School problems did not start at 9.00am and end at 3.30pm, so it was not unusual to receive calls, voicemails or text messages from colleagues while you were watching *Coronation Street* or at the weekends. Some teachers have a cut-off point, and real life begins as soon as they step out of the iron gates. For me and many of my colleagues, however, to operate on that basis would be very difficult.

My brain has always been able to compartmentalise things and make judgements on what is a priority: do I work on this at home, should it be dealt with there and then, or should it wait until the next day. The fact that I have remote computer access to students' details is a slight indication as to where my priorities lay.

However, Sundays I set aside as family time: church, everybody present at the dinner table, or catching up with extended family. My kids (and everyone who knows me) have always accepted school as being a part of me. I assumed my husband felt the same. The first indication of his frustration was when our youngest was unwell. It was a school Theme Day and also Tyrone's day off. I decided to attend the morning session to ensure the activities were set up and running smoothly, then come home before lunch and spend the afternoon with my son.

Tyrone's disapproval of me leaving to go to work was obvious, but I was not prepared to enter into an argument. I felt he had a cheek getting upset, especially when I knew it was because his lie-in would be interrupted. This made me even more determined to escape.

Dressed and ready, I paused by the bedroom door. My handbag with my car keys were on the other side of the room. Tyrone dived towards the dresser and grabbed my bag.

"Give it to me," I said calmly.

"Today, you are staying at home, Julz, and looking after your sick son," he stated.

"Give me my bag, please," I requested.

"I said, today you are not leaving this house!" he shouted, and began to rant. "It's always school. Those bloody school kids. Nothing else matters. As long as you can waltz around like Miss Big Shot being so important. Well not today, honey! Today you are staying home to take care of your son!"

I walked towards the door to leave the room, and Tyrone jumped in front of me.

"Sit down!" he demanded.

"Excuse me?" I replied. This man had lost his marbles.

"I said, sit down!" he shouted.

"Are you for real?" I responded. His face was like thunder. Yep, he had definitely lost his marbles, I thought.

"Are you deaf? He was still shouting, but this time shoved me. I fell onto the bed.

I stood up.

"Sit down!" He shoved me harder.

I stood up again.

This time, he pushed me to the floor and began kicking me with great force on my back and legs.

This man was definitely crazy. Our son was asleep across the hallway and he was treating me like a football.

I was still in shock, but this now was coupled with fury. No way, José!

I grabbed his legs and he buckled. Under the dresser were my shoes, and I used the heels to try and dent his bald head. If this is how it was going to go down, I certainly wasn't going quietly.

Tyrone smashed the mirror on the dresser and went for the picture frames next. He progressed to the MacBook and then the television. The bedroom now resembled Afghanistan.

My face was bruised and bleeding from the punches and my body sore from the pain. I crawled across the floor, and mustered the strength to fly through the door and into the kitchen. My destination: the cutlery draw. I opened it and grabbed a carving knife. Tyrone was at my heels. He knocked me on the floor then grabbed my hair and pulled my head back with one hand and, with his other, bent the wrist of my hand, which was holding the knife tightly.

"Oh, so you think you bad, eee? Yes, a bad gyal dis," he taunted.

Holding back the tears, I began to breathe deeply and loudly.

He let go of my hair. Then released my wrist, which was still holding the knife tightly. We stood face to face.

"Go on then, Mrs Bremmer" he said sarcastically. "Stab me if you bad!"

He stepped back and stretched open his arms in a defiant stance. All the time, mocking and jeering.

"Do it J, do it J," I kept whispering to myself, hoping that by saying it, I would have the courage to stab him in the heart.

I eventually opened my palm and the knife clanged to the floor.

Tyrone looked at me, laughed and left the kitchen.

I sat at the kitchen table. I was in shock. I was in denial. I was angry. I was hopeless.

The following day, as I walked through the school gates, I was praying that the thick layers of foundation would hide my shame. The staff in the car park swallowed the story of me walking into a door. I was surprised at how easy the lie rolled off my tongue.

"Good morning, Miss."

I looked up. It was Suzie Reid, smiling brightly and holding open the corridor door.

"Hi, Suzie," I mumbled, and walked swiftly through. I was not in the mood for conversation.

"Are you OK, Miss?" she enquired.

"Fine," I snapped, and walked towards my office door, digging in my bag trying to retrieve my keys.

"Are you sure, Miss?" Suzie's voice startled me from behind.

I stopped fumbling and turned towards her.

"Positive," I replied calmly. Suzie looked worried. "Thanks for asking," I smiled.

She smiled back and hesitated.

"It's just that... you've got a bruise on your eye?" she said cautiously.

So much for expensive make up! I thought.

I replied instinctively, "I walked into..." Then stopped.

Not that long ago, I was annoyed that Suzie had lied about her father physically assaulting her, and there was I, doing the same thing. I wasn't about to tell a fifteen-year-old my business, but the least I could do was be respectful enough not to lie.

"I erm, ermmm, I.., I was involved in an incident... but I'm... but... I'm dealing with it."

That was a crap answer, I thought. But at least it wasn't a lie.

I had spent most of my days telling students to be honest with themselves and to others. I would also go to great pains to tell the girls how crucial it was for them to show respect for themselves, and to expect to be respected by boys. I would also tell the boys how important it was to use the right language and behaviour towards girls.

Values that I have instilled in my own children.

Children learn what they live. A young girl, who witnesses her mother being abused, has an increased chance of being in an abusive relationship as an adult. A young boy, who grows up watching this type of behaviour, is much more likely to become an abusive partner himself.

By not practising what I preached, I knew I was letting them down.

With power comes responsibility. In fact, with power comes *great* responsibility.

That evening when I got home, I picked up the phone and dialled 999.

"Emergency, which service do you require?" the voice announced.

"Police, please," I said calmly. "I'd like to report an assault."

"Wah sweet nanny goat a go run him belly."

Things that seem fine to you can hurt you later.

END OF SPRING TERM

SUMMER TERM

Week Beginning: 16ᵗʰ April

Goodbye, My Friend

As with every family, at school we celebrate life, achievements and successes. But, at some stage, the grim shadow of death will stop in front of our door.

In a school community with close to 1,500 students, it is inevitable at some point we will lose a loved one and, in my time as a teacher, I have had to say an unwelcome goodbye to both colleagues and students, in expected and unexpected circumstances.

I can painfully recall how we lost one student, who was hit by a bus when he was running across a dual carriageway to meet his mother on the other side; another promising pupil was shot in the head at point blank range at a weekend party; a staff member was sadly taken away from us following childbirth, and I have had to say goodbye to many others following fatal health conditions.

The shock waves that send tremors across a school community - and the delicate and sensitive way we have to communicate with and support the students to come to terms with the loss - are always difficult and never get easier, but I am proud of the way we have supported and worked with individuals and groups to deal with tragedy and tried to move forward.

I remember receiving a call from a nurse, breaking the news that a student's condition was terminal, and was stunned at the disclosure, as I had seen the parents the weekend before and their outlook on the prognosis had been positive. When I returned to their home the following week, there was no sign of grief or distress. I realised soon enough, denial had set in, and no matter what the professionals were saying, death was not an option. Their son was going to get better and return to school and complete their studies. And he was just as positive. Always smiling, even when experiencing pain. He asked one of the teachers to print off his lesson timetable so he could create a study plan to ensure he stayed up to date with schoolwork. I admired how brave he was, and his positivity and optimism made me reflective and appreciate the people I had around me.

But my emotions were mixed. As a Christian, I knew the importance of faith and the power of miracles, but it was clear the student was getting weaker and weaker by the day.

I spoke to the Head about my concerns, at this point for the classmates, and how we could prepare them if the worse should happen. We agreed to take the students off timetable to tell them their schoolmate was unwell, and that it would be nice if we could send Get Well messages and drawings, and update him on what was happening in school. It was done, and the gift of messages was received with great joy and lifted the weak spirits of the student. It was so beautiful to see and hear him chuckle in between the readings.

A month passed, and the hospital had discharged the student home to palliative care. We called in the school nurse to talk to the class. The nurse was a familiar figure around the school, and very experienced, professional and caring. She explained that their classmate had a serious health condition, and that we were hoping he would get better, but sometimes people don't recover from that type of illness. I looked around to see if the message had registered with any of the students. Most faces were blank, but three of the girls who were sitting at the back had tears streaming down their little faces. They had got the message.

"Any questions?" the school nurse asked.

Surprisingly, the question we were avoiding came from the mouth of a little Turkish lad. "Is his time up, Miss?" he euphemised.

"What do you mean, Erdi?" the nurse probed, wanting the student to be clear with the question he was asking.

He paused. Looking around at his classmates, whose eyes by this time were all fixated on him, "Is he going to die, Miss?" he asked more clearly. Like at a tennis match, all heads moved to the school nurse, including mine.

"We all hope he will fight this and get better and return to school," the nurse responded. "But this is a terminal illness, so there is a possibility he may die." The students began to look at each other, trying to work out from faces what each other was thinking. At least two more had joined the three girls whose heads were bowed, and began to cry. I told the group that if there was anyone who did not feel up to going to lessons, they were welcome to stay with their tutor, Ms Wilkinson, or if they felt upset during the day, they could come and see me.

A fortnight later, our little Angel passed away. We closed the school as a mark of respect. No matter how strong your faith is, finding a way of explaining the death of a child is one of the most difficult things to do. But I remember the priest at the funeral service attempting to do this through a short story, which I have taken away with me and would like to share with you:

'A little water beetle, in a community of water beetles, lived in a little pond, under the lily pads. They lived a simple and comfortable life in the pond, with few disturbances and interruptions. Once in a while, sadness would come to the community, when one of their fellow beetles would climb the stem of a lily pad and would never be seen again. When this happened, they knew that their friend was dead, gone forever.

One day, one of the little water beetles felt an irresistible urge to climb up that stem. However, he was determined that he would not leave forever; he would come back and tell his friends what he had found at the top. He climbed the stem and, when he reached the top, climbed out of the water onto the surface of the lily pad. He was so tired that he had to take a nap. As the water beetle slept, his body changed, and when he woke up, he had turned into a beautiful blue-tailed dragonfly, with broad wings and a slender body designed for flying.

As he soared the skies, he saw the beauty of a whole new world, and a far superior way of life that he had never known existed. Then he remembered his beetle friends and by now they would be thinking he was dead. He wanted to go back to tell them, and explain that he was now more alive than he had ever been before. His life was now being fulfilled rather than ended. But his new body would not go down into the water. He could not get back to tell his friends the good news. He understood that their time would come, when they, too, would know what he now knew. So, he raised his wings and flew off into his joyous new life.'[1]

I smiled at the analogy, one I have now tailored and used. And whenever I am feeling sad or reflective, and I am on the school grounds, I walk over to the school Memorial Garden, which is in the middle of the playground, and gaze at the beautiful trees and shrubs that were planted in memory of loved ones who have prematurely left our school community. The extraordinary growth and beauty of the greenery I know not only comes from the fact they are diligently tended and cared for by the caretakers, but also helping them to thrive is the special ingredient they absorb and keeps them strong: the inimitable sounds of children's laughter, for 39 weeks of the year.

"Jackass seh di worl nuh level."

Life isn't fair.

---

1   Source: 'The Dragonfly' from the book, *WaterBugs & Dragonflies: Explaining Death to Young Children* (Looking Up) by Doris Stickney

EPISODE 28

The End Result

Often, with the pressure of government inspections and league tables, I find myself so under the cosh, monitoring student levels that, apart from raising achievement, nothing else matters. Often, sadly, it's the numbers and not the children that dominate your thought process, along with the questions around progress and attainment.

How are you going to ensure a particular child or group makes progress? How are you are going to avoid an underachievement trend amongst African Caribbean and White working-class boys? Are the interventions for the children on Pupil Premium effective? What provision has been made for the LAC students? What action points have come out of Learning Walks, Progress Conversations and Self Reviews? All this, in a typical week!

Recently, two incidents made me realise there was, perhaps, more to life than grades.

Alison was at war with a group of girls over a boy. Now I should explain, when boys are locked in battle, they fight and it's over, but the girls... Oh boy, put it this way, some are still carrying 4-year-old grudges and can't even remember what they were about!

Alison's mum, a single parent, was like a lioness when she came down the school to slap the ringleader who was making her daughter unhappy. She also wanted to stress her point that she was going to report the Head Teacher and me to the education authority for negligence. We parted with her, happy that we had the incident in hand, and I promised to keep an even closer eye on her 'baby' - a promise that became all too real just over a month later. Alison's mum collapsed at home while Alison was at school doing her trial exams, and I had to escort Alison to the Intensive Care Unit. I sat with her, holding her hand while the Consultant delivered the fatal prognosis. For someone so young to lose a parent so suddenly was heartbreaking.

Jeremy's experience was different. I stood by his hospital bed while he slept, staring at the bandages neatly taped around his left wrist. He was a Grade 9 student, gentle, sweet natured, naturally gifted and highly intelligent. His mother had been in my office an hour before, crying on my shoulder. He had swallowed bleach, a bottle of *Paracetemol, and* slit his wrist.

Three thoughts flashed through my head:

1. Boy, he really wanted to end his life!
2. Why?
3. My GCSE results are going to go down!

Shit! I couldn't believe I had thought about exam results at a time like this. Oh Lord, that's bad. Really bad. Oh God, what kind of person does that make me?

Jeremy looked so vulnerable, asleep in the hospital bed. I knew suicide is the biggest killer of men under 45, but I never imagined teenage boys in that statistic. The image of the life-size sculptures standing at the edge of the roof on the ITV building in London flashed through my mind. It was a campaign to raise awareness of the men who die through suicide each week. I tried to shake it off.

He had such a big future ahead of him. So much to look forward to. So much to experience. How could he throw that all away? How could he be so selfish?

He slowly opened his eyes. He looked up at me and Gideon, the senior teacher who had driven me to the hospital. He looked embarrassed.

In my role, I have to make quick decisions as to how I handle situations. Do I tread softly, softly? Do I play good cop? Do I play bad cop? Oh God, I didn't want to make things worse, but I was vexed. Jeremy was a smart lad. He knew better. How could things have got so bad to end up like this? Why didn't he talk to someone?

214

I decided to take the bull by the horns and speak to him straight. No beating around the bush.

"Well, well, well. Glad to see you've decided to wake up," I began sarcastically.

Gideon stared at me in shock. "Errrr, Julz," he began.

I ignored him.

"So, did you just decide you were going to end it all today, or was this planned?" I probed.

"Julz!" Gideon exclaimed.

Jeremy spoke. "I'm sorry, Miss," he said softly.

"Sorry you're here? Sorry your mum found you? Sorry I'm not going to have to tell your mates you're gone? Sorry we're not all lighting candles in Assembly for you next week?"

"Stop it, Julz!" Gideon said sharply. "Jeremy, we're glad you're OK. Aren't we, Miss?" Gideon looked over at me, waiting for me to turn back into an adult. I was silent. I was too mad, too angry to respond.

"I'm sorry, Miss," Jeremy repeated. "You're right. What I did was selfish. I didn't think about anyone else and I should have." Tears began to fall from his face.

I walked over to his bed and gave him a hug.

"I'm really sorry, Miss," he repeated for the third time.

"I'm sorry, too," I replied.

Once the nurse had checked his vitals, Gideon went to get a coffee and we talked. I told him in five years' time, he would have his A Levels and degree under his belt; be in a great job, and in a position to make choices that would significantly improve his life. I wanted to know why he tried to kill himself but was too scared to ask.

I didn't need to. He opened up and explained the reason for his dramatic course of action.

He said he felt isolated because he had found it really hard coming to terms with his feelings. He felt he was a girl, even though he'd been brought up a boy. He said he had tried to fight against his feelings for a long time, because he knew how upset his mother and family would be, but he wished he could change his body to look more like the way he was feeling inside.

I was gobsmacked! This was a first for me. However, I realised that more important than my shock was this tormented, scared, young man. I held his hand and told him not to worry; we would work this out and get support for both him and his family, but his priority was to get better and out of hospital.

I had attended Transgender Identity training some time back. The course materials were filed in my office. Information I needed to look at again.

We spent the rest of the afternoon talking openly. I searched for Transgender support on my phone, and we found an organisation called Mermaids that offered support for young people up to the age of 19, who felt at odds with their birth gender, and also helped and advised parents. Good old Google! I admitted I was out of my depth, but there were more experienced teachers at school who could help him to explore support networks in order for him to feel positive about himself and his emotions.

They would also be able to prepare him on how he could tell his mother.

He leaned forward, hugged me and whispered, "Thanks, Miss."

That night, I lay in bed and thought about the many pressures students faced - even without the burden and stress of examinations - and how I shouldn't take that for granted.

I leaned over to my bedside table, and picked up the stapled data pack.

Trial exam results. I began to highlight the students who were working below a grade 5, and those who had not met their expected levels of progress.

Hmmm. OK now, let me have a look and see... Who do I need to pick up and deal with tomorrow?

"Fowl im no pray fe feather, im pray fe life."

Don't be discouraged by setbacks,
concentrate on your main goal.

EPISODE 29

Week Beginning: 30ᵗʰ April

New Kids On The Block

One of the areas of my job I love is visiting Year 6s in their primary schools; telling them about how great our school is, and filling them in on the secondary school experience. I carefully select Year 7 students who attended that primary school previously; do an exciting video and Prezi presentation, and get the Year 7s to lead the Q and A session, only intervening if they are stuck.

Every year, the same questions are asked by the wide-eyed prospective pupils, and I'm always left amused.

"Will I get lost? Do you get loads of homework? How many children are in the school? Do you get detention if you don't do your homework?" and the classic killer question: "Will I get my head flushed down the toilet?" When you consider that these students are the big kids in a school of 600, joining a school of 1200-plus as the babies must be a daunting experience.

Our school has a fantastic induction programme prior to the Year 6s joining us in September, which includes: National Curriculum testing, Reading Age tests, a Taster Day (where they get to experience five subjects in the school setting), a Parent and Child meeting, a Saturday school meeting, and a two-week Summer school programme, along with starting school in September before the rest of the Year groups, so that they are the only students in school for a couple of days before the rest of the cohort begin the term.

During the Taster Day and Summer school programme, staff members are allocated to a group of students, and get the opportunity to observe student behaviour and also how they interact with each other. This gives us an opportunity to make changes to groups and/or provide extra support where needed. And, believe me, some *do* need the support.

A memo sent to Senior Management after a History teacher's first lesson with a Year 7 group confirmed this.

Dear Ms Atille,

Today was my first encounter with Barry!

In the course of the lesson, we had a series of incidents, which would ordinarily result in him being removed from the class:

He called me a 'fat pig' – I did not immediately remove him from the lesson, because I wanted to clarify with his TA, the precise nature of his AEN (I did not have the information). I did not want to remove him if this was Tourette's – the students seemed to treat this outburst as if it were relatively normal.

He faked injuries, and falsely claimed that other members of the class had hurt him.

He walked out of the class without permission - three times.

He was rude and uncooperative to the people on his table.

He threw his book across the table and onto the floor - at least three times.

He banged the table during student presentations.

He stapled his finger.

He argued with his TA when his TA took a staple extractor from him.

He repeatedly sang during teacher explanation: "Boom, boom, boom."

Clearly his behaviour is a long way from being normal. I would appreciate some guidance. Looking forward to hearing from you at your earliest.

Miss Markham

Well, she was better than me. He would have gone after the 'fat pig' comment. You still think working with new kids is a piece of cake? When Kerriane got rude, and decided to shout abuse at a member of staff, she got more than she'd bargained for. Her primary school records showed she was confrontational to teachers, and many of our secondary staff had been tip-toeing around her, because they did not want to be at the other end if she blew. She was loud, an attention seeker, but that had been put down to her mother travelling to and from the Caribbean, trying to sort out the family's stay in the UK. Her mother was away in Jamaica when I called home to discuss the incident, so her heavily pregnant aunt came to school in her place.

I explained that a male member of staff was walking to the station after school and Kerriane, who was with three of her friends, decided to shout 'Batty Man' repeatedly at the staff member, and laughed loudly when he stopped and turned around.

"What?!" the aunt screamed loudly. "What?!" She stood up and dragged the 12-year-old from her seat.

I decided to get in the middle for two reasons. The first: she looked like she was going to knock out Kerriane, and the second: she was close to nine months pregnant, and the excitement could just cause her to drop that baby any minute.

"You tink seh yuh can call someone a juju man ina England and get away wid it? Dem will lock you up! Pickney, yuh outa order! Lawd a mercy, pickney yuh mad?"

Kerriane's aunt was trying to grab her school jumper, but I continued to stand in between, trying to keep the peace.

"I will be recommending a five-day exclusion for her behaviour, and would like her to write the teacher an apology letter while she is at home. I'll also organise some work for her to complete over that period."

"Lawd! What me going to tell her mudder when she get back?!" Kerriane's aunt continued to wail. "Kerry, yuh see dem skirting board? Yuh goin' 'crub dem whiter than white from top to bottom!"

It was only after her aunt mentioned cleaning the skirting boards that tears began to roll down Kerriane's face.

"And yuh see my foot bottom, and how mi cyaan ben' down cos a prignant mi prignant? Yuh goin' 'crape off di hard bits until sarf mi foot bottom sarf!"

By now, Kerriane began to wail.

I wanted to laugh but had to hold it down. I was confirming in my head whether cleaning skirting boards and removing calluses and dry skin from your aunt's feet was a Child Protection issue. Naaaaaah, I think it could be termed 'alternative discipline'!

"Miss," Kerriane tried to speak between the sobs. Her nose was running, and the tears refused to stop. "Miss, will I be able to go with my sister to Chessington?" She had paid to go on the May Day Year trip.

"Well..." I began, but was swiftly interrupted by her aunt.

"Chessington? Chessington? Did you think about Chessington when you were calling that teacher a Batty Man? Get out of mi sight and get in di car! Chessington...!" her aunt continued. "Chessington, mi backfoot!"

I'll take that as a No then, I thought. Boy, I couldn't make this up. Sometimes families had better sanctions than schools. I wish I could get some of these naughty kids to 'crub my skirting boards and 'crape my foot bottom as a sanction. Wouldn't *that* be wonderful!

I'm sometimes left wondering why the age of innocence ends so abruptly these days. During my secondary school years I was a tomboy, and there would have been hell to pay if a boy attempted to kiss me. Some people would say the kids nowadays are just too 'prime' or 'bright', but I have to put a lot of it down to naivety.

Kofi was 12, handsome and confident. When most of the Year 7 girls had their noses in their books, there was still a significant number whose eyes were on boys. I'm told at least five of the confident 11-year-olds had asked Kofi out.

Pleeeeease. Where on earth were they going to take him? Late night cinema at Lea Valley?

For a young man who seemed to have it all, Kofi was incredibly naïve, and would usually follow what his mates said and, by doing so, stayed in with the popular crew.

Nadia had a crush and would constantly Snapchat, FaceTime or WhatsApp Kofi, begging for a date. How the world had changed. I'd deal with my daughter if I ever found out she was begging a man to take her out - and she's 25!

One of the Assistant Heads had asked me to sit in on a meeting with Nadia and her mum. They had turned up at the school without an appointment, and were very distressed. When I walked into the office, Nadia's mum was crying; Nadia's head was bowed, and she was looking embarrassed.

"To get you up to speed," Sophia, the Assistant Head began, "Nadia's mum has come in this morning very upset. She was going through Nadia's phone and found this picture, which was sent to Kofi in Year 7."

To my shock, it was a photo of Nadia with her breasts exposed. I scrolled up the WhatsApp message and scanned the message trail.

Nadia: ur peng
Kofi: den proof it
Nadia: ????
Kofi: let me see your breasts
Nadia: :-O
Kofi: Go on...
Nadia sends picture
Kofi: nice nice

I was stunned. I also noticed the messages were sent between 12.30am and 1.00am in the morning.

Nadia's head was still bowed.

"Nadia. Why did you send Kofi this photo?" I asked gently.

Nadia shrugged her shoulders.

"Did you send this photo to anyone else?" I asked.

"No," she said quietly.

"Did you send Kofi any other photos of yourself apart from this one?"

"No," said Nadia.

"OK. Can you wait outside for a few minutes, while Miss and I have a brief chat with Mum, please?"

"Yes, Miss," she replied. And left the room.

"Mum," I said firmly, "the first thing we need to do is to get Kofi in here with his phone, and hope he hasn't sent it to anyone else."

"Oh no!" cried Mum. She hadn't realised this pic could go viral.

"We need to get Kofi's mum down here too. ASAP."

"On it," Sophia, replied.

"Without preaching, Mum, you need to confiscate her phone. Why she is chatting to boys after midnight is beyond me."

Mum began to speak between the tears. "Ever since she started secondary school she's a different person. Rebellious, into boys, more conscious of her body, appearance, sexuality... I can't cope with it."

"And what do you think you should do about it?" I put the ball back into Mum's court.

"I don't know. I thought about sending her to a girls' school," Mum continued.

"Well, that's something I would certainly consider, if I were in your shoes," I confirmed.

"Take Nadia home today, while Miss and I speak to Kofi and his mother. I'll get some work organised."

She thanked us and left.

Kofi's mum came into school straight away.

"He mentioned it to me, but I told him to be careful around girls like that. Lots of girls call him because he is good looking," she said, nonchalantly.

Is it me, I thought, or is there something different about mothers who have sons and not daughters?

"He asked a Year 7 girl to send him a picture of her breasts," I clarified.

"But he said he deleted it straight away," she continued.

This wasn't getting anywhere. I turned to Kofi, who was sitting next to Mum.

"Kofi, why did you ask Nadia to send you a picture of her breasts?" I asked.

He shrugged his shoulders.

"Was that an appropriate thing to do?" I continued.

"No, Miss," he replied.

"Do you know you could get into a lot of trouble for what you did?" Kofi nodded his head.

"Young boys or older men should never be involved in anything like this. If Nadia or anyone else is bothering you, what should you do?"

"Tell a teacher," he replied.

"That's right. Or your mum, so she can tell us. Kofi, you did the right thing by deleting the photo, but you should never have asked a student to send you a photograph like that in the first place. Mum..." I directed the next part of the conversation to her. "I'm going to recommend Kofi stays at home today, while I investigate whether he is telling the truth about deleting the image. I will organise work for him to do. However, if anything like this happens again, in or outside of school, I will not hesitate to recommend Kofi is excluded for his behaviour."

Mum was fine with this outcome, and left with Kofi.

It is so much easier when you are dealing with students who are honest and upfront - no matter how naughty they appear to be. It's the students who want to go head to head with you, and challenge your will and staying power, ignorantly unaware that most of us have been there and done that, way before their time. However, most of the things some of the kids get up to nowadays, I would never have dreamed of doing in my day.

Carter was one of those smarty-pants students that knew who and who not to mess with. He was a cover teacher's nightmare, and would purposely play up or play the innocent, so they did not know whether they were coming or going. Young new teachers were also a good target for Carter and his mind games, which he more often than not got away with.

His new English teacher, Miss Ben, came to see me to voice her concerns.

"Can I have a quick word?" she asked, as she popped her head around the door.

"Sure, grab a seat," I replied and stopped typing.

"It's little Carter," she began, and started to shudder. She placed his open exercise book on my desk. "Homework last week was a descriptive piece of writing, using SOAPAMS and a minimum of four paragraphs. Start reading from paragraph 2," she said.

"Paragraph 2. OK… '*He places both of her hands in a tight grip above her head, and presses her to the wall using his lips. His other hand grabs her hair and brings her face up, and his lips touch hers. His tongue slowly and softly strokes her…*'"

Whooooooooah! I stopped suddenly and looked at Miss Ben.

"Exactly. Carter keeps grinning at me, asking if I've marked it yet," Miss Ben said, agitated.

"Did he write it?"

"Hell, no! He's done this to make me feel uncomfortable, and has certainly succeeded."

"Are you sure this is not something he's seen or heard?"

"Well, not unless he's got a subscription to the Fantasy channel."

"Read the first line to me again." I requested.

"What?"

"Just read it."

I opened Google and began to type.

"What are you doing?"

"What would your lecturer at uni do first, if they thought your work was plagiarised?

"Check it through Google."

"Exactly. Read on."

Miss Ben reluctantly continued reading, and I then joined in.

"You're joking!" Miss Ben yelled.

"Nope." I burst into a fit of laughter. That little sod had pulled this text from *50 Shades of Grey*!

"You're joking!" Miss Ben was furious.

"So, what we going to do about it?" I grinned.

Miss Ben stood in front of her Year 7 English group. Carter was sitting up straight, with that smug smile on his face.

"We're starting with DIRT time, with your creative writing homework," Miss Ben announced. "You have 10 minutes to respond to my feedback. Oh, and Ms Bremmer took one book from this class pack to monitor my marking, so if yours is missing, you will need to collect it from her in her office."

Miss Ben gave the exercise books to two students to distribute. Carter began to look agitated, as the pile began to reduce and he still hadn't got his book. Tonia handed the last book in her pile to Martell, then went back to her seat.

"Off you go," said Miss Ben. The students began to respond to the marking with their green pens. Carter sat quietly in his seat.

"Carter," Miss Ben called across the classroom. "Why aren't you writing?" she asked, knowing full well the answer.

"I don't have my book, Miss Ben," he said hesitantly.

"Oh, Miss Bremmer must have picked yours to check my marking and your progress. Go and collect it from her in her office."

Carter froze in his seat.

"Hurry up, Carter, you're missing DIRT time." Miss Ben went up to his desk, and shooed him towards the door.

I could see Carter hovering outside my office, but not making a move to knock my door.

"Come in!" I shouted, although there was no knock on the door. Carter sheepishly entered.

"Hello, Carter," I said slowly, without looking up from my desk. "Sit down."

Carter slowly sat on the seat. I could cut the fear oozing from his pores with a knife.

Without looking up I said: "I've left your exercise book with someone in Reception. Please can you collect it and come straight back to me."

Carter flew out of the seat, relieved to get out of my office.

Out of the frying pan, I thought. Yes, I had left his book in Reception. In the Reception area with his mother.

Three minutes later, Carter and his mother both entered my office.

"Thank you for being so patient, Miss Barrett," I said when they had both sat down. "As I explained earlier, I have two concerns: The first, the content of his creative writing homework, which he was set last week. Would you like to read this to your mum, starting from paragraph 2?"

"No, Miss," Carter said sharply. He was visibly embarrassed.

"Why not, Carter?" I queried.

"Because... Because... Erm, because it's a bit naughty," he stuttered.

"But it's alright for Miss Ben to read your naughty writing, Carter?"

"No, Miss," Carter whispered quietly.

"I have told your mum that writing like this from a schoolchild is a concern, and will have to be referred to our Child Protection officer, who may inform Social Services, who may want to investigate you and your family."

Mum was silent. I had told her when we met earlier how this meeting was going to pan out, and that she and Carter would have to have a conversation with our CP officer because of the content of the writing. She was furious with Carter, but kept quiet.

Carter then piped up, "But it was a joke, Miss!"

"You see anyone laughing?" I animatedly began looking around the room.

"No, Miss," he answered.

"My second concern is plagiarism - a lazy person's way of completing homework or research. When you cut and paste something from the net, or copy something wholesale from a book or document, it's called plagiarism. Like your creative writing homework, Carter. Students fail exams for committing plagiarism; it's cheating. Carter, you will be spending lunchtime all this week with Miss Ben, completing your creative writing homework. Properly. Understood?"

"Yes, Miss," Carter replied.

These newbies, I smiled, they can be more of a handful than the older ones.

Carter's mum finally spoke. "Thank you, Miss Bremmer."

She then turned to Carter as she was about to leave the office and whispered,

"Chile, you have Social Services to thank why you're still in one piece. Because right now, I just wanna knock your block off!"

"How did it go with Mum?" Miss Ben queried. "Carter came in 10 minutes before the end of the lesson and looked very flushed, hot and bothered," she added.

"Well, let's put it this way," I stated confidently, "Carter's in a whole heap of hot water right now, and that cheeky chappy has good reason to be very, very bothered!"

"Quatti buy chubble, hunjed poun' cyaan pay farri."

Little blunders can cause us to find ourselves in situations so complex that we cannot extricate ourselves.

EPISODE 30

Protect Our Children

Early in my teaching career, I was asked to set cover for a Year 8 class whose teacher was absent. I gave them a timed descriptive writing task, 'A Day at the Seaside', and started the on-line timer.

Five minutes in and over half the class had either the tip of the pen in their mouths or were just sitting, staring into space.

One child put up their hand and asked the question most had on their minds: "What does a seaside look like, Miss?"

I was gobsmacked!

"Put your hand up if you've been to a seaside?" I asked. Two out of twenty-eight raised their hand.

My eyes widened.

"Put your hand up if you've been to Chessington?" I continued. Twenty-eight out of twenty eight raised their hand.

"Thorpe Park?" Twenty-eight out of twenty-eight raised their hand.

"Margate?" I continued. Not one hand went up.

Wow! I loved my trips to the seaside as a kid. Clacton-on-Sea, Great Yarmouth, Southend and especially Margate. The Dreamland funfair was awesome: the arcades by the seafront, with brightly lit penny machines, real fish and chips and the yellow sand. I would sit on the beach with my bucket and spade, and play for hours. These kids didn't know what they were missing.

I felt a lot of my students needed to be exposed to things that could widen their understanding of the world - opportunities that lay outside their postcodes and that built their cultural capital through a variety of experiences and adventures. This would most certainly help them when they were trying to access the reading components of examination texts but, most importantly, as citizens operating in society.

To partially address this, I introduced with my Year 11s a Monday News Quiz as a lesson starter once a week, covering local, national and international news stories, along with questions about music, theatre, literature, television and sport. Confirmation that this was needed was given when I asked the question: Who is the Mayor of London? And a student replied: "Chaka Khan!"

I knew I shouldn't have, but ended up rolling on the floor like a 'Mash Get Smash' Martian.

I invested in a set of the Steven Covey book '*7 Habits of Highly Effective Teenagers*'; it was a success guide of how students can learn to navigate through their teenage years, and come out the other side as highly effective adults, and shared excerpts from our class reader, Paul Lawrence's '*101 Lessons I Taught My Son*' - insightful tips and hints around a variety of topics including love, money, goals and education. For twenty minutes, three times a week, I would comb through each book with the students, and have lively discussions about habits, personal development, them as individuals, their qualities, their values, and getting them to see that they were the creators and in control of their destinies.

The benefits of adding our 'reading time and news quiz discussions' to the curriculum were apparent through their interaction with me, other teachers and their peers. They would excitedly want to discuss a wide range of topics, including the impact of President Trump's latest tweet, Brexit, that 'Coolest Monkey in the Jungle' hoodie, or their view on the latest BBC documentary.

One news story that resonated with the boys was a tragedy that received international coverage, but for me was too close to home.

My son had called me early one Saturday to say that his mate, Rashan, had been killed. The news of a youth death or near-death experience sadly was commonplace in our area, and my heart sank at the news that Rash - or Rashman, as he was affectionately known - had died. They had been friends since Primary, and Rash would often knock for him. Most of my son's mates knew I was a teacher, and it was clear that mark of authority unnerved them. So I would play on this when they came knocking. I'd open the front door and they would be standing outside the front gate yelling: "Is he in?" Purposely, I'd scowl, then go back inside giggling to myself, and my son would tut: "Mum, stop that!" as he walked through the door.

I was on edge that whole morning thinking about Rash's family, and my prayers were interrupted when Shelly, a good friend, telephoned me that afternoon. She was close to the family, and said he had died following an altercation with the Police. She said he had been pursued into a shop, pinned down by a Policeman and subsequently died. All afternoon, I couldn't shake the fog and fear that dominated my mood. I don't know if it's an emotion that just mothers with Black sons feel, but the fear, sense of foreboding, coupled with depression is an ugly, damp cloud that is very hard to shake off when you hear a young Black male has died in unnatural circumstances.

That evening I visited Rash's gran's house with Shelly to pay my respects. The pain and anger amongst family and friends was evident, even before I entered the front door. Outside were a large number of young boys, a few annoyed, some agitated and most angry. It was like a precursor of the calm before the storm. Inside, family and friends were scattered through the house - serious, sombre and silent.

Rash's gran's face was etched with pain, and tension began to bubble, as a mobile phone began to be passed from person to person. Each time it changed hands, the person looking at the phone screen began to curse, and this got louder and louder with each exchange.

Shelly took the phone and I peered over her shoulder, horrified at what I was watching. It was CCTV footage that had been placed on Instagram of Rash's altercation with two men in a shop. One was clearly a Police Officer, as he was wearing a bulletproof vest with the words POLICE printed on the back. He had followed Rash into a shop and then wrestled him to the ground. The Policeman's arm appeared to be around Rash's neck and, from nowhere, another man appears and is on top of him with his knee in the small of

Rash's back. Rash is struggling and eventually becomes still. It's at that point it dawns on me he is either unconscious, or dead.

I was stunned. It was like a movie or worse-case scenario - one of those Police brutality videos from the States that you'd find in your Facebook newsfeed. The difference being, this was a young man that *I knew*. Jesus! Father! Was this for real? I replayed the footage. I was numb. No one. No one deserved to die like this!

Why was nothing being done? It had been 18 hours since Rash had died, and the family and friends had contacted all the TV channels and news outlets to tell their story, but they had faced a wall of silence. I stood on the porch and watched the frustration of friends and loved ones begin to bubble. The anger amongst the group gathered was clearly felt, but wanting to show respect for Rash's family, tempered any flares of outrage.

In my job, I have always had positive relationships with the Police and found (bar two incidents) the officers I had encountered very positive. My niece was a DCI, and I was very proud of her achievements, but tonight I wasn't a Teacher. Tonight I was a mother. A mother of two young Black boys, and I could not stand aside and do nothing.

I downloaded the CCTV footage from the phone and forwarded it to three people: a news journalist, a Black community activist and Peter, a videographer who had over five thousand followers on Facebook.

He was the first to call.

"What the f**k!" was Peter's opening statement.

"We need your help," I pleaded. "I knew that boy in the video. This happened early this morning, and the family are struggling to come to terms with it. No one has picked this up. It needs to go viral."

"Is this for real?" Peter asked incredulously. "Jesus. This is serious shit!"

"We need your help?" I pleaded.

"This is serious shit," he repeated.

"They can't get away with it!" I stressed.

"I'll call you back," Peter cut in. The line went dead.

I left the house with Shelly and headed home.

That night I cried. Cried for Rash. Cried for his friends. Cried for the boys in my class, and cried for my sons who had to grow up in this society. And that was if they were lucky enough to make it past 21!

My WhatsApp pinged. It was Peter.

"Done. 8k views" was the message.

"????" was my reply.

"FB" he responded.

I swiftly logged on to Facebook. The CCTV footage had been posted less than an hour ago and comments were firing, people were tagging friends, MPs, activists and news outlets into the clip. The comments towards the Police were less than favourable, but blame the bad apple was my justification. The views had soured to 10k, and by 8am Sunday morning 40k people had watched the clip with over 1k shares. The BBC, Sky News, ITN and the IPC had all finally reached out to the family.

"Thank you, thank you, thank you," I whispered, with eyes closed and palms pressed together. "Dear Lord, please let justice be served."

A week later, masked youths set up barricades, lit fires and pelted riot police with bottles, bricks and fireworks in protest.

"Serves them right!" one of my Year 11s yelled, when we picked up the discussion at the beginning of the Autumn term.

"Who is 'them'?" I queried.

"The Police, Miss. They lied about the boy swallowing drugs. The officer who killed him hasn't been sacked. So of course people will be angry and want to riot and mash up the place."

"But what about the community?" I added.

"But we don't own or control the community, Miss." Isaiah, one of my AG&T boys, chipped in. "It ain't ours," he continued. "Gentrification isn't for 'our' benefit. The boroughs are commissioning new builds in the inner cities, and committing a small portion to social housing, but they are placing those homes at the back of properties with no access to the posh reception areas. The Council want us out. The young people who were rioting weren't mashing up anything that belonged to us, so they ain't gonna feel no way. My dad said there is no love for young people in the community, so for them to feel warmth they will burn it down!"

A large portion of the class began to clap excitedly.

Isaiah's nonchalant attitude and the support it received made my heart sink. I was sad at the fact that this was the feeling of doom from our youth.

"Well, as far as I'm aware, the area where Rashan died *is* a community," I countered firmly. "Don't you think that the shopkeeper, by giving the CCTV to the family and not the Police, is an example of that?"

"He better watch it. They'll be after *him* next!" a student jumped in.

I continued: "Most of the rioters were clad in balaclavas, and they often are people that come from outside the area to make trouble and their presence felt. Smashing up shops, destroying cars and public spaces is not what *I* consider to be positive action. To ensure that Black people gained equal rights under US law, the Civil Rights Movement in the '50s and '60s chose to stage non-violent protests and civil disobedience through sit-ins and boycotts, which crippled the establishment economically."

"But Miss, if we refused to get off the 149 bus, the driver would call the Police and we would be back to square one," a student responded.

"Boycotting was in the olden days, Miss," another student continued. "The reality is, CCTV or no CCTV, young Black boys don't stand a chance when it comes to the Feds."

"We have to have faith in the criminal justice system," I interjected. "Rashan's family have been quoted as saying what they are looking for is a fair and transparent investigation, where the people involved are accountable for their actions. With the CCTV evidence that we have all seen, I can't see how this will not happen," I confidently ended.

Six months later, the news reported that the CPS confirmed that the Police officer in Rash's CCTV would not face charges for his death. They had considered a common assault charge, but felt 'the evidential test for a prosecution was not met'. Therefore, they would not be taking further action.

"You said that boy's family would get justice!" Mushid directed the comment at me. I was organising Poetry worksheets at my desk.

"The Police can never be held to account," Isaiah answered. "My dad said if you prosecute one officer the rest will argue that they do not feel confident to do their jobs for fear of prosecution, so it's well known within the Police that nothing can happen to them. They can behave like they are untouchable - even kill people - and get away with it."

"That's not true!" I yelled.

The class went silent.

It wasn't fair to shout at a bunch of 15-year-olds just because I didn't have answers to their questions. When I read the news the night before about the Police Officer not being prosecuted, I was horrified. How could that be? I was angry and frustrated, because I wasn't able to honestly quell the boys' fears. I stopped the lesson five minutes before the end, and spoke to the class.

"I apologise for raising my voice earlier. The truth is, I don't have the answers that you may be looking for. There are, most likely, things we don't know about the case, and also areas of the law that we are not familiar with. But I have an idea of how we can explore this further, so if you are interested, meet me outside my office at the beginning of lunch.

"Are you sorting food, Miss?" cheeky Adrian piped in.

"Why not?" I laughed, and they left for their next lesson.

At lunchtime, five boys showed up.

"I want you to hold onto your questions, thoughts and feelings about this case, and put all that energy into a piece of writing. Each of you are going to write a letter and address it to the Commissioner of the Metropolitan Police in London, Cressida Dick, and the Mayor of London, Sadiq Khan."

Their eyes lit up.

"Are they really going to read it, Miss?" Nathaniel asked.

"I'm going to make sure your feelings about this are read by as many people as possible," I promised.

Below is an amalgamation of writing from five 15-year-old boys. They are excerpts of their thoughts and feelings on what they deem to be an injustice. At the time they wrote these letters, the Rashan Charles' Inquest had not yet occurred:

Dear Cressida Dick & Sadiq Khan

Adrian:
Can you feel at peace when you hear the following names? Rashan Charles, Edson DaCosta, Sarah Reed, Sheku Bayoh, Mzee Mohammed, Sean Rigg, Julian Cole, Kingsley Burrell, Christopher Alder, Jimmy Mubenga? Can you *honestly say you have ensured measures are in place so members of the public feel safe? Have you done enough to ensure justice is served for victims of police brutality? Have you supported the families, loved ones and the communities of these victims?*

Nathaniel:
I am 15 years old and angry. Too many of my brothers are dying at the hands of the organisation that has been created to protect me – the Police. Mr Khan, you have been telling young people that London needs us alive. Why? To be suffocated by white men with badges with a licence to kill? I'm not shocked that the officer we saw on the CCTV was not charged. Even one of your ex-Superintendent's Mr Leroy Logan has criticised the decision not to charge the officer. This is not the first time excessive force has been used on a Black man, and no one held accountable, and I'm sure it won't be the last!

Bradley:
You don't have to be an expert to question the force that was used. It was way too excessive. The boy was in handcuffs when the officer's arm was around his neck, and there was even someone sitting on his back. How's a man supposed to breathe? I don't believe the Police were trying to prevent him harming himself after he had swallowed something. I read that he should have been given urgent medical attention, I didn't see no CPR being carried out or did I miss that bit? I feel the

Feds and the Press demonise victims as drug dealers or gang members so the public can blame them for their own deaths. When Mark Duggan was shot by Police in Tottenham, the press put out stories that he shot at the Police first. That was lies. It's disgusting. When lies are published, the public believe it and it's hard to take it back.

Isaiah:

I've been stopped and searched 3 times and I'm only 15! I was with my friends and we were spoken to rudely, our school books were thrown out of our rucksacks and one officer asked my mate where the money came from to buy his Nike TNs. Another officer asked us where we had hidden our knives! I just shut my mouth because I just wanted get home safely and if that makes me moist then whatever. I can hold my anger, but it's hard. That officer getting away with Rashan's murder is a joke. It's like there is one rule for Black people and another for the Police. Black lives don't matter. My faith in the justice system is zero, and I can say this is the same for all my mates. I've been mugged but never reported it, what's the point? If I felt my life was in danger, calling 999 would be the last thing I'd do. I do not trust the Police, neither does my father or my grandfather.

Levi:

This is a Mash Up of the first verse of the poem, Education for Leisure, *by Carol Ann Duffy.*

Carol's words are in plain text. Mine are in bold:

*"Today I am going to kill **a Black man**. Any **Black man**.*

***They'll be an initial fuss in the community but eventually** ignored and today*

*I am going to play God **and do it again**. It is an ordinary day,*

A sort of grey with boredom stirring in the streets."

Yours sincerely

On 20th June 2018 at St Pancras Coroner's Court in London, a jury found the death of Rashan Charles was an accident, following a justified use of force. They believed he died of a cardiac arrest caused by upper airway obstruction by a foreign body while being restrained. They said the Police Officer did not follow Metropolitan Police protocol by taking "immediate and appropriate action in the face of a medical emergency", and they recognised he had not managed the involvement of a civilian bystander, but concluded these factors were not significant and Rashan's life was not salvageable in any event.

When the Rashan Charles Inquest started, my Year 11 Boys group were on GCSE study leave. When the verdict was decided 11 days later, the students had left secondary education. I felt relieved that I did not have to continue the discourse with the boys around the jury's judgment, because it would have been very difficult for me to remain professional.

Sleep In Peace, Rashan Charles.

"Duppy know who fi fright'n."

People will take advantage of those who are vulnerable.

Week Beginning: 14th May

The Sins Of The Father

It's not uncommon for a motivated Year 7 lad to metamorphosise into a disaffected teen. Fatherless homes are where the blame has often been placed and, sadly, in my experience, this is the case. No matter how strong, positive or driven a mother can be, she cannot take the place of the strong male role model a teenage boy craves. I have seen brothers, uncles, even cousins step in and fill the gap, and this has sometimes proved sufficient, but as ex-President Barack Obama confirms, we need fathers to realise that responsibility does not end at conception; what makes a man is not the ability to have a child — it's the courage to raise one.

As a female from a single parent family, my experience was positive. I never met my father, but was blessed to have had a great role model in the form of my grandfather, Gramps Bailey - a simple and honest man, with integrity, pride and a formidable love for the Lord. He could pray for England, and would openly weep during those moments of intercession, especially when he was asking God to help those less fortunate than us.

He was emotional, traditional, old fashioned and uncompromising. He could cook and bake - better than my gran - and his sewing skills went beyond fixing loose buttons. He would make dresses and suits from scratch, and knit jumpers and cardigans better than M&S. No one could style my hair better. He would scrape up the messy bits with the comb and, without Dax, create the neatest ponytails you'd ever seen. He would plait the ends, and make sure my silky ribbons shone brightly, and all the girl children in the family would sport the whitest socks, which were two to three years old, but you would never guess, because they were soaked and handwashed by Gramps.

In the Caribbean, he had a good standard of living, and worked as a chef in a top hotel in Kingston. When he emigrated to England in the early 60s, he ended up living in a pre-war estate and he hated it. Gramps vowed he would take his family out of the inner city and buy a house in suburbia. He worked the night shift for London Transport and, even though he was diabetic, he never had a day off due to sickness because that, in his books, was a sign of tardiness.

He saved his pennies, never making unnecessary purchases, and he would take a packed lunch to work every evening. We would take turns to make his Hovis sandwiches; pack some fruit in a Tupperware container, and pour tea into his Thermos flask. He never took out hire purchase or owned a store card, because he didn't believe in unnecessary credit, and never ate out - God forbid - because he believed that the English people who worked in restaurants were nasty, a judgement made after witnessing first-hand a commis chef not washing the meat or rice, and a waitress shining the silver cutlery by *breathing* all over it!

I remember Gramps coming home beaming one afternoon with a new set of door keys, and the family driving down the A13 to see our new home. The property had five bedrooms, a massive front and back garden, and was located in the countryside. Well, in comparison to east London, at that time, Essex *was* the countryside! His next vow was to pay off the house before he died. He came close. After suffering from renal failure at 65, his death-in-service benefit cleared the mortgage debt, ensuring he rested in peace.

Because of my relationship with Gramps, and his positive influence on my life, I never thought about not knowing my biological father. Any void that would have been left by my father was never apparent, because my Gramps was so great and naturally bridged any gap. His influence was so strong that I named my first son after him, in the hope that a fraction of his superior qualities would be passed down.

For some of my school kids, they were in a Catch 22 situation. Either there was no father figure in their lives, or the one they *did* have was such a poor parent. Many knew they would have to work extra hard to break the cycle, and it was my business as their teacher to ensure they did. In Assemblies, I would emphasise how education was the key to being the catalyst for change in their lives, and the biggest thing it could offer them was choice. This would be reinforced in mentoring sessions and PSHE. It was important to make the boys feel like they were men of merit, and could do great things if they focused and grabbed the opportunities that had been afforded to them.

When Gramps died suddenly, my world stopped. He had been experiencing severe pains as a result of his dialysis treatment, and an ambulance came to take him to St Bart's Hospital. The pain was unbearable. It was *peritonitis*. Gramps begged for God to take him.

The following day, he was in a coma and, by Friday, we were told he had gone, and that it was just the machine that was keeping him alive. My grandmother gathered us around his hospital bed and began to pray. Everyone's head was bowed and eyes closed as she spoke. She thanked God for being so merciful. My eyes were on the doctor, who was standing by the machine. Grandma went on to give God praise for blessing us, by allowing Gramps to be part of our lives.

By this time, my aunt's and uncle's eyes had joined mine, and were fixated on the doctor by the machine. His hand was now close to the on/off switch. Grandma began to recite the 23rd Psalm, and we all instinctively joined in. All eyes were now on the doctor, who by this time, had turned down the sound on the machine as the heartbeat signal began to flatline, everyone who was reciting the Scripture got louder:

"Surely goodness and mercy shall follow me, all the days of my life, and I will dwell in the house of the Lord forever."

The doctor pressed the switch to off. We all broke down.

That night, for the first time, I wondered where my birth father was. Did he care that I existed? Why did he never come to find me? I began to understand the feelings of rejection that some of my friends expressed that they felt, because of never knowing their fathers. I must admit I did feel like a fraud jumping on that bandwagon because, with Gramps, I had a fantastic 'dad' but, with the void his death had left, why couldn't I have it all - a relationship with my birth father as well?

My mate Sonia felt I was being dramatic, and should leave the past in the past. She said I was a grown-arse woman and should move on with my life. Louise, who had recently connected with her biological father, thought it was exciting and I should go for it.

I hired a private detective and the search took him to Jamaica, Florida, London with the final stop, Crowthorne in Berkshire.

He was alive and, at the age of 35, for the first time in my life, I sat face to face with my father. A man, who I was biologically connected to, but did not have any real bond with.

He was handsome. He was tall, chunky, fair-skinned and with a full head of jet black, coolie hair. When he smiled, gold beamed from every part of his mouth. His fingers, wrists and neck were weighed down with bling. So that's where I get my swagger from, I smirked. We talked.

He spoke about his life, and my mum. I was fixated on his appearance, trying to work out what similarities we had. Did we have the same eyes or was it the nose? He smiled a lot. Maybe that's where I get that from. It was a surreal experience. He was nice. Open, warm, witty. In fact he was more than witty, he had an incredible sense of humour. Again, very similar to mine. I liked him. If things were different, we could have really got along. But this was the real world, and maintaining a relationship would be difficult.

An hour and a half passed and in the background, a bell rang.

"Times up!"

I looked up at the middle-aged man and thanked him for the reminder.

We both stood up and for the first time in my life, my father gave me a long, warm hug and a kiss on the cheek.

"See you soon," he probed.

"Sure," I lied.

He grinned and walked toward the door at the far end of the room. His orange fluorescent waistcoat fading into the distance.

I made my way to the electric gate, which clanged shut after the final visitor, and rescanned my fingertip on the ID box. As I drove out of the car park I glanced back at the iconic brown building, an image I'd seen only on the national news. Broadmoor Hospital. It had been my father's home for 15 years and would continue to be, for the rest of his life.

Ironically, I realised that by growing up without my father had a positive impact on my life. Having Gramps step in and influence my beliefs and values made me who I am today. Don't get me wrong: as a youngster, at times I hated my strict upbringing, but have since come to realise, it saved me.

Without my father in my life, I guess I had actually broken a cycle. And, like me, I believe many of my students would too.

"Blood ticka dan waata."

The bond between blood relatives is strong.

Week Beginning: 21ˢᵗ May

Dying To Make
A Difference

Many of my friends envy the fact that, as a teacher, I get 13 weeks' holiday a year but, in reality, for the majority of that period most teachers are working: teaching catch-up classes, marking books, updating Assessments, reorganising classrooms… The list is endless.

Many of my colleagues suffer from stress as a result of the job, and I have known a few - too many for my liking - who have reached the point of retirement and ended up with a terminal illness, or have died before they could enjoy the fruits of their labour.

Once the term sets in, it's all systems go and, as a Senior Leader, you are juggling so many balls and trying to be ever so careful not to drop any.

Personally, I've always loved being busy and felt I thrived on stress. It's kept me on my toes: arriving at school just before 7am and, more often than not, leaving the site 11 hours later. Sadly, this is the norm for a lot of teachers, and those who *do* leave early are either setting work, marking assessments or catching up on general admin at home. This scenario in teaching is commonplace. However, the fact that we love what we do, and see it as a vocation, is what keeps us going, ensuring we do nothing but the best for the children.

On this particular day, I left school at 5.00pm, because I had felt nauseated and slightly breathless all day. My marking and some data analysis were packed in my bag and, once in the car, I began to feel a pain down my left arm. I did a detour because I needed to pick up some papers from a friend before I headed home and, to my despair, ended up in traffic - hot, bothered and frustrated.

I was feeling sicker by the minute, and had to get out of the car. I swiftly pulled over at the earliest opportunity - upsetting the driver behind - and immediately opened all the windows while I tried to catch my breath. Just in the nick of time, I jumped out and began to vomit uncontrollably onto the pavement. I felt flushed, and the pain in my arm was increasing.

From nowhere, my mind flashed to a television commercial: Stroke Act F.A.S.T.

Oh my God! Think, Julz! What does F.A.S.T. stand for? *Think!*"

F, Face. Can I smile? Yep, sort of.

A, Arm. Can I lift it? No. No. It was aching. Oh no, oh no. I've got a pain in my arm.

S. Oh my God, what did S stand for? Oh my God, I'm having a stroke.

Images of Patrick Trueman, collapsing in the square on EastEnders, flashed through my mind.

T, what was T for? Telephone an ambulance. No. Oh God, why couldn't I remember?

Calm down, J, calm down. I began to breathe slowly and purposefully. If you were having a stroke, girl, you would have collapsed by now, I was telling myself. Stop being so dramatic. I needed some water. I had to have some water.

I scanned my surroundings, and made my way across the road into a chicken shop, and asked the guy behind the counter for some water. The friendly assistant began to try and sell me one of their chicken meals.

"Just water!" I yelled, and the shocked young man rushed to the fridge and picked up a small bottle. As I drank the fluid, my head began to feel heavy. I was still having difficulty breathing, and my legs began to feel weak.

I began to pray.

"Dear God, whatever happens, please don't let me die in this chicken shop!"

There was no way I was going to die in a chicken shop. Especially since I was overweight! Imagine the talk of me collapsing after eating two pieces and chips! My family would never live it down.

I mustered all my strength to get out of there, and inhaled and exhaled deeply as I made my way back to the car. I needed to get home. Once I was home I would be OK.

"Come on, Lord, don't fail me now. We can do this!" I shouted to myself, and sped towards the A12 repeating the 23rd Psalm until I pulled up outside my front door.

Once inside, I headed straight to the bathroom and began to vomit profusely, and then dragged myself to my bedroom and flopped across my bed. The pain in my arm and the breathlessness instantly disappeared. As I lay still, I felt assured that everything was going to be alright.

I slept off the madness of the evening, and was back at work the next day.

The nausea had disappeared, but I was still feeling slightly breathless, so my mother insisted I go to my GP to get checked out. I had a couple of important meetings I was leading on and, to be honest, couldn't be bothered with the fuss.

I typed my symptoms into Google, which confirmed I was going through the menopause.

By Day 5, breathlessness and hot flushes had not subsided, and walking up a flight of stairs was like an Everest expedition. I was ordered to go and get checked out, so I reluctantly agreed to go to A&E.

My Aunt drove and we walked into the Reception area. There were over 40 people waiting, leftovers from Saturday night.

"I'm not waiting behind all of these people. I'll still be waiting tomorrow!" I was exhausted.

"Just get seen by triage and, if it doesn't seem serious, we can leave," she compromised.

I told the receptionist my symptoms and, for the first time in my life, I was fast-tracked to the front of the queue. The nurse took my blood pressure, temperature, and put me on an ECG machine. A series of blood tests followed, and I was placed in a cubicle while they processed the results. Less than half an hour later, a doctor was breaking the news that I was going to be kept in for monitoring. The blood tests had shown that I had suffered a heart attack.

I was stunned.

"Come again?" My Aunt was the first to speak.

"Mrs Bremmer has had a heart attack. She is going to need an angiogram to ascertain how bad it was, but we will have to keep her in so we can closely monitor her." He handed me a cup of dissolvable aspirin to drink, and informed me that a porter would be coming to take me to a ward.

I was gobsmacked. My friends were shocked. My workmates were astounded. My family were frightened.

The next day the angiogram was conducted under local anaesthetic, so I was awake throughout the thirty minutes.

"Mrs Bremmer, the procedure showed you have triple vessel disease," one of the Consultants confirmed.

"Which means...?" I probed.

"Which means," he continued, "there are significant blockages in three coronary arteries. Unfortunately, they are too damaged to stent."

Tears began to well up in my eyes. I hadn't made a will. I had the forms at home, but had never bothered completing them. The kitchen skirting boards needed cleaning. I was supposed to do them this weekend. What if people came round and noticed the skirting boards?

The things you think about at poignant moments in your life.

"What do you do for a living?" the main Consultant asked.

"I'm a teacher," I replied.

The four professionals in the room looked at each other and in unison chimed: "Stress."

I decided to take the bull by the horns.

"Am I going to die?"

"I jolly well hope not," he replied. "We can start with managing the disease with medication, but if that fails, we'll have to look at the possibility of having to perform a coronary bypass procedure."

How could I have let this happen to me? My family are going to be mortified at the prospect of me being operated on. Why hadn't I taken better care of myself? How did I let things get so bad? I knew if I were to have some quality of life, I needed to revisit my priorities, slow down, and look after myself.

Back at home, I began scrolling through my social media newsfeed on my laptop. Five minutes in, I came across a status from a mother about her daughter. It was someone I had never met:

"Today, Neveah had an MRI scan in the hospital. She had to be put to sleep and to see her distressed, coming round from the anaesthetic, broke my heart. She endures so much and still carries on. I will celebrate her life always, as she has taught me so much in her four years of life so far. I type this with tears, as this up-and-down journey of life can be so hard sometimes with what is thrown at you, and nothing like you would or could imagine. Yes, there are people worse off and going through things I and we would never know about. LIFE is what you make it, and God will never give you more than you can bear. To my Neveah: We are here for you and right by your side always. <3"

There were pictures of little Neveah: always smiling, with beautiful eyes as bright as new buttons. Her mother had captured so many precious heavenly moments that most of us take for granted: singing in the car; dancing with a wiggle; posing outdoors; saying bedtime prayers…

Sometimes we need reminding how blessed we are, and the courage and beauty in others is sometimes the inspiration we need to move forward and fulfil our purpose.

Staying in bed was not going to heal my heart, but spending beautiful moments with loved ones and doing what I loved and, believe it or not, that included my work. Creating the balance would be key.

My mobile was ringing. It was my mum. Even though I was a fully-grown, hard-back woman, if I told her I was planning to go back to work, if the heart attack didn't kill me, she most certainly would!

Maybe I'll follow the doctors' orders and rest for the next four weeks, and then sit her down and broach the subject…

"Di daakes' part a di night, a when diay soon light."

When things and times are the hardest, brighter times are near.

HALF TERM BREAK

Week Beginning: 4th June

Mama Can't Raise No Man

Growing up with just my mum and brothers was hard. It could have been harder, but Grandma and Grandad Bailey were there in the background as support.

Looking back, as a child, I never saw the positives of what I had - food, clean clothes, my own room - selfishly preferring to focus on what I *didn't* have.

As part of a single-parent family, we were entitled to a uniform grant, so my plimsolls were from Woolworths: black, with the arch shape elastic at the front and, when I graduated to trainers, they were the Whizz Kid brand. We were also entitled to free school meals, which allowed concessions on school trips and, in my first year of secondary, there was a trip to Barry Island in Wales. I was excited at the prospect or going with all my new friends. It was the talk of the 1st Year, so when my mum sat me down one evening to say I couldn't go, I was gutted.

"But it's not expensive!" I cried. "We get a discount!"

"You went to Marchants Hill last year," she explained. "I cannot afford to buy you a new set of clothes for this trip."

"Then I'll wear what I've got," I counteracted.

"Over my dead body!" she flew back. "No child of mine is taking old clothes with them on a trip. You're not going, and that's the end of it!" And, as far as she was concerned, it was.

I cried in the lead-up to the trip. I cried when I sat in the half empty classroom - the trip had been scheduled during term time - and I promised myself that when I grew up, my kids would have what I didn't, and never feel what I described as my 'Butlins pain'.

I grew up in an era where Caribbean parents did not spare the rod and spoil the child, but gave you 'two lick' if you stepped out of line. In our household, if we misbehaved outside the house, we would get our hand or mouth squeezed and, if we were *really* out of order 'on road', my mum would pinch us. Hard! When we went to birthday parties, my mum would feed us before we left the house, and we were warned not to hover around the food table - something my brother would often forget, and would get beats when we got home for embarrassing the family. When I slipped up I, however, mastered the art of bawling *before* my mum slapped me, so my punishment was always over before it began.

I remember my brother and I waiting for my mum at a neighbour's house. In Caribbean networks, all older men were your uncles, and the ladies your aunties. 'Aunty' Tulip was our two-doors-down neighbour. She was a kind, old fashioned and devout Christian. Her husband had died early in her marriage, so she had raised six children on her own. She was admirable, very traditional, and lived on a diet of healing herbs, cerise tea and callaloo. As a result, she was as strong as an ox. She always had pure love, hugs and kisses for me and my brother, but ruled with an iron fist when it came to her offspring. To this day, I don't know what Steven had done but, as we sat on the settee watching *Grange Hill*, Aunty Tulip entered her front room with a thick leather strip in her hand. We were told it was given to her by her brother, Uncle Rupie. It was from his Singer sewing machine wheel. She charged towards her middle son Steven, and let off a lash.

"No mummy, no mummy, sorry mummy," he yelled, as she started thrashing him and he began to dive behind the sofa and around the glass cabinets.

"The Lord is my light and my salvation," Aunty Tulip chanted, as she continued to chase him. Steven darted up the stairs, swiftly followed by Aunty T. "Whom shall I fear?" she continued, not a bit out of breath as she closed in on Steven.

My brother and I looked at each other in shock. And then he voiced what we both were thinking. "I'm never getting beats by Mum again, J," he confidently stated. "Bwoy, can you believe we don't have to stand there waiting for the lickings…" he added, "we can actually *run!*"

"The Lord is the strength of my life…" Aunty Tulip carried on yelling from upstairs. It was clear Steven was too fast for her. Me and my brother looked at each other, and burst out laughing.

I realised swiftly that, as a single parent myself, raising a son and daughter is a totally different experience. I split with my children's father when they were young, because he was a serial cheater and a champion liar. The fact he was DJ in a Sound didn't help. I was so determined not to repeat the cycle and bring up children on my own, but my self-respect told me to leave; the kids and I would be better off without him.

Author Robyn Travis' second novel had the apt title '*Mama Can't Raise No Man*' - something I would have poo pooed if someone had said this to me 10 years ago, because *this* mama was mother, father, breadwinner, disciplinarian and a kick-ass independent woman!

Raising my boy pre-teens was smooth sailing. Theo was named after his great-grandfather, who died before he was born and, like his great-granddad, he was charming, thoughtful, sensitive, caring, loved people and was God-fearing. At eight years old, he could pray for England and, at mealtimes when saying the Grace, he would never forget the less fortunate and name them one by one. Five minutes on, I would have to intervene before we all starved!

By the time Theo hit Secondary school age, I decided to pay to educate him privately, because I believed the opportunity would be highly beneficial in the long run.

My experience growing up taught me to study hard and work harder, and the financial benefits would follow. I was determined my children would want for nothing and, if hard work offered the privileges of a nice home, quality clothing, opportunities to travel around the world and a first class education, then the six-day weeks and late nights I was experiencing would be worth it.

It was week four at Private school, and the Principal called. Theo had been beaten up on the way to school by thugs from the local area, because he was wearing a 'posh' uniform.

It wasn't the first time. He hated being different, and begged me to send him somewhere 'normal' like his friends. It broke my heart seeing my boy broken, so I gave in and issued the private school notice, and enrolled him in the local comprehensive.

In Year 8, Theo came home with a black eye and an injured leg. Frightened he was being bullied, I called his mate's mum, who told me her son had told her that Theo and some friends had arranged to meet a girl at her mum's flat at lunchtime, and they had bunked school for the tryst. Unknown to them, it was a honey trap, and all three boys ended up jumping off a second-floor balcony, after been set upon by a gang of eight.

Theo had an entrepreneurial streak. He loved money, and set up a car wash enterprise and, by the summer holidays, business was booming. I spent the first four weeks of the break working, while his sister spent time with her Nan, and Theo developed his business.

I arrived home early one afternoon, and was in the kitchen preparing the evening meal, when my neighbour Opal called. Her cousin had been arrested for robbing a house. Apparently, he had entered through the back door, not knowing that the homeowner was in. The youth was chased, caught red-handed and arrested by the Police.

Stupid boy, I thought. How could he do that? Serves him right.

"Are you sitting down?" she continued.

"Why?" I put the phone on loudspeaker and took out the Dutch pot from the cupboard.

"Theo was with him but got away," she continued.

In shock, I flopped onto one of my kitchen chairs.

An hour later, I heard Theo's key in the front door. I was still sitting in the same chair.

"Hi Mum," Theo waltzed in with a grin on his face, and gave me a kiss on the cheek.

"Sit down," I said calmly. Perhaps *too* calmly, because he instantly sat opposite looking worried.

"Did you try and rob someone's house today?" I asked.

Shock was his first facial expression, then embarrassment.

"Yes, Mum."

"Why!" I screamed.

"Because I needed the money," was his reply.

"You 'needed the money'? You 'needed the money'? If you want money, you just have to ask!" I continued to yell.

"I wanted my *own* money," he defended.

"You mean someone else's. Robbing someone doesn't make their stuff yours. It's theft. It's stealing. It's a crime!'

Theo sat silent and bowed his head.

"I've told your gran."

"No!" he yelled. He began to show signs of anxiety.

"And I've told Nanny." By now he was distressed.

"Why did you do that!?" he shouted. He stood up and banged the glass table.

The doorbell rang.

"And I called your dad."

Theo kissed his teeth and went to his room.

I opened the front door.

"Where is he?" Theo's dad stood on the doorstep, fuming.

"Hello, Charles. He's in his room."

He paused outside Theo's bedroom door. "I think you should wait downstairs. This may take a while," he stated seriously.

As I waited, the silence was broken by shouting and furniture been knocked over. I raced upstairs and stood outside the door.

"You think you can take your belt to me? You're 10 years too late, mate," Theo cursed.

"Shut the f**k up, you little shit!" was his dad's reply.

Oh my God, they were fighting. I was going to enter the room, but thought against it and went back downstairs. What have I done? I shouldn't have called Charles to intervene. For years I have set the standard for my children, and disciplined them when they have fallen short. Why did I hand this over to his absent father and give him permission to batter my boy?

After 10 minutes Charles appeared. He was flushed, out of breath, and sweat was falling from his forehead. If this weren't so serious I would have laughed.

"We'll talk tomorrow," he said and left.

The next day I told Theo to get dressed, we were going out.

He got into the car and I drove for 10 minutes and pulled over on the High Street.

"I've been doing a lot of thinking," I started. "Actions have consequences, and I'm reporting what you did to the Police."

Theo looked out the window and realised we were parked outside the Police station.

"No, Mum, you can't!" Theo yelled.

"Yes, I can. And I am. You trespassed into someone's house to steal from them. Knowing that, how can I *not* do the right thing? Let's go."

I opened the car door.

"No, Mum, NO!" Theo began to cry.

"Come on. Let's go." I stepped outside the car and shut the door. Theo climbed out of the car and ran.

"Theo!" I shouted, as he disappeared in the crowd. "I'm still reporting you!" I yelled.

I locked the doors and went into the station. There was no one at the desk. I stood and waited. After five minutes, I began banging on the desk, trying to get someone's attention, and an officer came out of a door at the back.

"I'd like to report a robbery," I stated.

"One moment," the officer replied, and went back out the door.

Ten minutes passed. I sat down and waited. Twenty minutes passed.

If they charged him, his ambitions to go into law would be squashed. I began to question if I was doing the right thing.

I went back to the desk and again knocked loudly on the surface. The same officer came back. This time he was clearly irritated.

"We're very busy at the moment, can you be patient, please? I will be with you shortly," he snapped and disappeared.

I'd had enough. I called Theo from the car.

"Where are you?"

"Are you with the Police?" he asked.

"No. Where are you?"

It took me five minutes to pick him up. I was shocked at what faced me. Theo's face was battered: left eye black and blue, cheek bruised and lip bloody.

"What happened?" I asked.

He explained. When he left the car, he ran into some flats and came face to face with a local gang. They battered him with bricks and pieces of wood, because he wasn't from the area.

As I cleaned the wounds, my conscience in a warped way reconciled that Theo had got his comeuppance, and hopefully he had learnt his lesson. And *my* lesson? Less time spent at work, and more time keeping a closer eye on my child.

How could I be investing so much time in other people's children and not enough on my own? Things were going to change.

I gave up my Master's course, and made sure I was at home by 6pm the latest each evening to eat dinner as a family. Theo's progress at school was positive; he was meeting all his targets, but he had the potential to do better. His Head of Year, Joe, a friendly Ghanaian man, called me.

"What time does Theo get home in the evenings?" he enquired.

"It depends. But before 7pm," I replied. "Why'd you ask?"

"Well, I've been told that Theo is 'on road' until way after midnight. Sometimes he comes into school very tired."

"No way," I stated. "Theo's at home by 6pm and in bed by 10pm."

"Are you sure?" Joe questioned.

"Positive," I confirmed. I felt annoyed at being challenged.

A few days after that conversation, while watering my plants, I noticed one of my stools sitting on top of the garden shed. What on earth was it doing *there*? Later that day, I had the light bulb moment. The shed was located under Theo's bedroom window.

I entered his room at 11.30pm that night. The pillow trick was in place. Both tucked under the duvet in the shape of a sleeping body. Theo was gone. The stool was a handy tool to aid in an escape from his window to garden, then over the garden wall to the lures of the night.

I locked his bedroom window and waited.

The doorbell rang at 6am. It was Theo looking contrite. Unbelievable.

"Really?" was my one-word statement. "Where have you been all night?" I continued.

"The Snooker Hall, Mum," he replied.

"Doing what?" I demanded.

"Playing snooker."

As I was trying to work out if he was just being honest, or playing the smart alec, Theo headed towards his room with head bowed.

"Oh no, you don't!" I stepped past him and stood in front of his door. "Bedtime is over, mate. It's bath and school."

I called in late, and ensured Theo was school-ready and out the house by 8am, then ventured into the shed and pulled out my toolbox. It took less than five minutes to permanently seal the window frame with nails. If Theo was going to make a great escape, from now on it would have to be through the front door - and I had the key!

I got fed up of updating his father, because his input was zero. I don't relish being negative towards the opposite sex, but you have to call a spade a spade, and Charles was useless. Yes, more fool me for getting involved, but being young and naive was my excuse. Charles was great at talking the talk, but fell dramatically short when it came to walking the walk.

His mother was a great support, and Theo adored his gran. She was a strong matriarch - the mother of six boys, and the only person on the planet who could make Charles see sense. She was Theo's champion, and stood by him through the good, bad and ugly. In her presence, no one could say a bad word about him and, when he slipped up, she defended and supported Theo. She couldn't see the forest for the trees when it came to that boy. She criticised me for spending too much time with 'other people's pickney' and often suggested I leave education and get a part-time job in Tesco, so I could be a 'proper mother'.

It was just after 9am, and I had just finished Assembly. Opal, my neighbour, was calling my mobile.

"Julz, you need to get home. The Police have just kicked down your front door and they are manhandling Theo."

I called Gideon to let him know I was off site and, in less than two minutes, I was driving out the school gate. The drive home took 15 minutes and, as I walked though my front door, which was hanging by its hinges, I could hear Opal effing and blinding.

Theo was face down on my settee and his arms were twisted high behind his back. He was being held in place by a 6' 3" policeman. In addition, there were four officers scattered in my living room. One was wearing plain clothes; he looked like the boss.

Theo was shouting and swearing and yelling he couldn't breathe. I garnered composure from God knows where, and coolly told Theo to calm down. I thanked Opal, and told her I would take it from here (she was still cursing and recording the incident on her mobile). I asked the officer who was manhandling my son if he could ease the pressure; I was Theo's mum, and he would listen to me. All this was said in a measured and even tone. The plain clothes officer looked at me, reinforced my request, and Theo was released.

"Are you in charge, sir?" I directed my obvious question to the guy in the suit.

"Yes," he said with authority.

"May I have your name, please?" I waited, ready to type it in my telephone.

"DCI Andy Gaines."

"May I see your warrant, Detective Chief Inspector?" I asked.

I knew watching those police dramas would come in handy one day. Just not in my house.

"Here you go." He handed me a piece of A4 paper. "If Theo had just opened the door, things would have been so much easier. And, if your gobby neighbour didn't put her tuppence in."

The warrant was to enter and search my premises for Class A drugs. Seriously. These people were *mad*!

"We heard a phone vibrate, but it stopped, and Theo won't tell us where it is," he added.

"Theo?'

"Yes, Mum."

"Are you hiding a phone from the Police?" I questioned.

"No, Mum," he replied. "These fools are crazy."

"Theo. Show some respect," I responded. "They're doing their job."

DCI Gaines was impressed. Black folk with manners. I smiled inside. I'd been around long enough to know how to play the game.

"You are welcome to search my home, Detective. Let me know when you want me to unlock the garden door."

In bounced an English Spaniel, who sniffed my house room by room. After 10 minutes the dog and handler left.

"Can I have a word outside, Mum?" the DCI requested.

"Sure."

"You do know Theo's in a gang?" he began.

"Excuse me?" I exclaimed.

"Theo's on our matrix. In fact, we have intelligence that tells us he's top dog. He's still young, and can be saved if he's ready to leave that lifestyle. I have a team that can provide support when he's ready. Here's my number."

He scribbled on a piece of paper, and handed it to me just before he and his entourage left.

Theo in a *gang*? Is this man on crack? I thought, as I put the paper on the side and googled a carpenter.

Growing up in the inner city, the Grim Reaper was more likely to visit a young healthy Black teen, as opposed to an older lady with a chronic illness. I would hear stories weekly about Theo's mates being rushed or beaten up and, when Theo refused to visit his grandparents because they lived in the 'wrong postcode', I began to take what DCI Gaines had said more seriously. I was not the type of parent to have my children's friends in my house, especially if I did not know their parents, but the ones who did knock for him were respectful, offered to carry my shopping from the car, and always had a warm good morning or afternoon greeting whenever we met.

I was horrified when I heard that Theo's mate Jay had been stabbed two minutes from his home, and that was followed by Theo being threatened in our local park by two boys with knives. At 4 o'clock in the afternoon! I called his father immediately.

"Charles, you need to take your son for a while," I pleaded. "I'm still recovering from surgery, and just haven't got the energy right now. He's going to get killed if he stays around here." Footage of our son being threatened at knifepoint had been posted online, and I sent him the link. I hated to beg, but my son's safety was more important than my pride. "He was rushed in the park by two boys with knives. If he is not away from here, we're gonna be burying him."

The other end of the phone was silent. Charles finally spoke.

"What's he gonna do if he stays with me?"

What a bloody stupid question, I thought. I'm telling him his son's life is in danger, and that's his lame response. What a flipping joker!

"Well, I'm looking into an Apprenticeship," I calmly responded. "He got good GCSE grades, so it won't be hard for him to get a placement. I can make a few calls and sort."

"Well, I'm due to go to holiday next week," he stated.

Really? I was struggling not to curse, but had to keep it together for Theo's sake.

"How about when you get back?" I suggested nicely.

"OK," Charles agreed. "I'll take him then."

The weight that had been pressing on my shoulders instantly lifted. I felt relieved. All I had to do was put Theo on lockdown until his dad came back, oh yeah, and convince him to stay with him for a bit. When I spoke to Theo he wasn't keen.

"It's only for a while," I promised. "You can't stay here. It's not safe. It will be a great opportunity for you to bond with your dad. Please, Theo."

He reluctantly agreed.

A week after Charles returned from Turkey, I called.

"Can't do it this week. I'll pick him up next," he stated.

"OK." What else could I say?

The following week he did not show up. I called again.

"It's a bit difficult at work at the moment, I'll collect him next week," he said. I was starting to lose my patience, but for the sake of my son I held it down.

I called again the following week when Charles did not show. I was furious, but refused to lose my dignity by cursing. By now, it was clear he never had any intention of taking his son. I decided to stop pussy footing around.

"Charles, this is the first time I have asked you for anything, and it wasn't for me but for our *son*. If anything happens to Theo, I will make sure you never forget it. You're are dead to us!" And with that, I clicked off the phone.

Six months later, Jay was fighting for his life. He had been stabbed again. This time Theo was with him. Jay was ambushed outside a newsagent's by three teenagers, and stabbed 10 times while Theo had popped into the shop. Jay had to be airlifted to the Royal London Hospital. Furious, Theo with some friends, tooled themselves up with knives and poles, and went searching for the perpetrators. They were caught on CCTV. A warrant was out for Theo's arrest, and he went on the run.

I couldn't sleep. His phone was off but every other day I would get a text saying 'Don't worry mum, I'm safe.' I received a call from Theo a week later.

"Mum, I'm in Scrubs. Please don't worry. I'll be OK." He sounded like he was crying.

He was caught by Police, arrested and placed on remand without bail. They had found a knife in his rucksack.

For the next week, I carried on as if everything was normal. Painted a smile on my face, and threw myself into my work. I spoke to Theo daily, but refused to visit. He had no business being in a big man's jail. I loved my son, but there was a line and he had crossed it. After a long day, I sat with my head on my desk. Gideon walked in.

"I did knock, but you were sleeping," he laughed, as he sat in my 'Parent' chair.

"Theo's been arrested. He's in Wormwood Scrubs."

"No! No!' His voice boomed. "No! What happened?"

I told him the story.

"I'm not going to visit him," I said firmly. "I can't. He knows right from wrong, Gideon. God knows I've tried. How does it get to this? My boy living in a 6 by 6? We spend all our time teaching, talking and investing in other people's children, telling them about doing the right thing, and my boy can't. What does that say about *me*? How can I be an example when my own back yard is full of shit!"

"No, Julz, no!" Gideon repeated. "You must go and see him. He's your child. He needs you. I'm gonna go. Book me a visit. I'm going."

I laughed. Typical Gideon. His first point of call was always to look out for others.

"Who else knows?" he enquired.

"Only family and Ade," I confirmed. "She's also begging to go."

"Then we'll go together."

"What about his dad?" Gideon enquired. I kissed my teeth, and with that Gideon changed the subject. "He's your boy, Julz. No matter what he's done, he's your child. Right now, he needs you. If he was a schoolkid, you wouldn't turn your back, so why dig your heels in when it's your own?"

For the first time in seven days I cried. The floodgates opened, and I sobbed. In fact, I *bawled*. Bawled for putting my work before my family; bawled for allowing myself to get sick, and bawled for failing my son.

Gideon gave me an 'it's-gonna-be-alright' hug.

"Theo can come and live with me when he comes out," Gideon grinned.

"I'm sure your wife will love *that*," I replied, and we both laughed.

I walked towards the yellow tabard and Theo's wide smile. This was not the first time I had been in a prison, but it was most certainly my worst. I gave him a hug, and the tears began to flow.

"Please don't cry, Mum. Please," Theo begged.

"I'm sorry," I apologised. "I promised myself I wouldn't, but you know our side of the family are big softies." Theo smiled.

His face was bruised. It was obvious he had been in a fight or been beaten up. My inside sunk. Someone had wounded my boy. My child was hurt. My heart was crushed. I didn't comment, because I knew he felt awkward. Just by the way he had positioned his body and head, it was clear he was trying to hide it. In two weeks his hair had grown, and it made him look rough. He looked grimy and smelt frowsy. My illness had created a divide in my relationship with Theo. After my heart attack, I could feel the distance growing. He thought I was going to die, so he spent less time in the home and more with his friends. I felt guilty.

"You stink." There, I said it. I couldn't help it.

"Sorry, Mum, but I'm not showering in this place. I could stink a little more," he responded.

"Jesus." The prison shower stories I'd heard came flooding back, and I began to worry.

"What are you eating?" I instinctively asked.

"Food. I sometimes make noodles in my kettle," he replied.

"Yuk," I responded, and we both laughed.

"I don't want you to come back, Mum. You can email me and I'll write. This place is not for you. Don't worry about me. I'll be home soon, and everything will be cool."

I sat and watched as he walked away. Because of the knife crime epidemic that was staining London, my prayers had slightly changed. Rather than beg the Lord to release him from jail, I now asked God to have mercy, and protect and guide him. Protect him from the trauma he had already experienced and would still experience in this dog-eat-dog situation.

As parents, we need to hold onto our children, and not allow the outside influences to be greater than the ones at home. A child spends on average 35 hours a week at school and, for some, that is more time than they spend with family. *We* have to teach our children right from wrong, and not leave it to 'professionals'. We must also ensure that our children take responsibility for their decisions and actions. If a child has the right foundation, no matter what path they take, deep down, they know what the right way is and, more often than not, will find themselves back on the right track.

Yes, I believe that 'Mama Can't Raise No Man', but if the alternative is a useless father - then we damn well just have to try!

"Ben' di tree while it young, cause when it old it a go bruk."

Discipline your children and teach them the right way when they are young, because trying to do it when they are older might be too late for them and for you.

EPISODE 34

Week Beginning: 11th June

You Can't Save Them All

I don't know of any Black teacher who didn't come into teaching with the view they were going to save the world, in particular Black boys. The inner city reality is, a lot of the Black boys are damn rude and, as a teacher - Black or White - you have to make a choice. Not everyone can be saved, and sometimes you have to lose one in order to save the many - something I had to learn quickly, but still find difficult to deal with.

I'll be blunt; some boys are just rotten and, like a bad apple, if you keep them with the bunch, all become contaminated. And, as a teacher, where you are accountable for the well-being and achievement of so many, you cannot afford for this to happen.

Take John. Popular, good-looking, worshipped by the boys and loved by the girls. The young pretenders want to be him, and all the female students wanted to date him. However, when one unattractive student had the gall to say she was dating him, she was told to get down on her knees and was slapped in the face - in front of a crowd. He was excluded for a week for his behaviour, but couldn't understand why. After all, she'd asked for it; how dare she say he was her boyfriend!

John was close to being permanently excluded after he was accused of letting off a firework in the school hall. A riot ensued and one student, who tried to escape, was taken to hospital after they had smashed their face into a glass door. Witnesses came forward and identified John, but he vehemently denied the charges. I was summoned to the Head's office to discuss the incident.

Although all fingers pointed to John, I wasn't comfortable with the circumstantial evidence, and told the Head Teacher I couldn't support the decision of permanent exclusion.

Despite the fact John had previously been involved in instances of poor behaviour, if he hadn't committed *this* offence, permanent exclusion would be the beginning of the end for him.

I wasn't happy being party to this, and I spoke off the record to his mother, whom I had a good relationship with, and told her to bring representation with her to the school and challenge areas of the incident, in order to keep John in school. She did and he stayed.

This victory seemed to make him more cocky and arrogant. When reprimanded by classroom teachers about his poor behaviour in class or the corridor, he would challenge and answer back.

Our relationship broke down when a full-scale argument ensued, after he refused to sit outside my office because, at 14, I couldn't tell him what to do; he was not a boy.

My Line Manager requested mediation, and I was forced to sit across a table from this 14-year-old I had helped and supported for three years, and given two minutes to say why his behaviour was a cause for concern, and he was given two minutes to express his feelings. This went on for an hour and, by the end, I was angry, pissed off and ready to blow.

To hear a child that you have supported, cared for and 'had their back' since they joined the school, say you hated them and had it in for them was more than hurtful. John was given an in-class support learning mentor, anger management, an off-site mentor; he was part of a motivational programme, and took part in a residential boot camp programme. What more could a teacher or school do?

The crunch came when the mini clique John moved with began to openly display poor attitude and behaviour in the classroom, and these were boys who had the potential to leave school with good GCSE grades.

They were beginning to spend more time out of the classroom than in.

The incidents continued. An 11-year-old Turkish boy identified John as the boy who had been forcing him to use his £2.00 dinner money to buy him a hot dog and ice cream at lunchtimes.

After a Sports Rewards Assembly, John had forced three award winners to give him their medals, and was parading them around his neck in the playground. He hadn't even attempted to take part in any of the sporting challenges, but was happy to bully winners into handing over their hard-earned prizes. Two of the boys, who had given John their medals, were in tears. This incident was followed by three students being 'rushed' behind the Science block by John and his mates, and another group being 'jacked' in the boys' loos.

It was at this point that I met with senior staff, who insisted Alternative Educational Provision was sought for John off site, before permanent exclusion became the only option.

I telephoned his mother, and left a message for her to call me urgently.

As I escorted John off the school premises, he continued to curse and swear. The school was racist; I had it in for him, and he was going to take the school to court.

I am still waiting for his mother to return my call.

Politicians, activists and concerned community members can say schools are failing Black boys, but my response is - you can't save them all!

"Every pot hav fe sit pon it own batty."

We have to take responsibility for our own life and actions.

Week Beginning: 18th June

I Run Tings

It never ceases to amaze me, how children think they know everything and that, as adults, we have never lived life.

As a school with ICT specialist status, all our classrooms are kitted out with state-of-the-art technology. Every room has a top spec interactive whiteboard, a projector and surround sound, which resulted in lessons jazzed up at the touch of a keyboard. Teachers have the option of showing videos or web resources and, better still, students have the opportunity to get up and participate in lessons by activating an app.

As a teacher, in-class technology is your pride and joy - the tool that supports engaging learning and teaching - so you can imagine the pandemonium that broke out in the ICT suite, when a student had written graffiti *in permanent black marker* on the £2k screen.

I surveyed the damage with four senior teachers, then turned to address twenty-seven pairs of anxious eyes.

"I'm giving the person an opportunity to do the right thing and own up," I said calmly. "I'll be waiting outside."

The Head of ICT, Miss Lee, was hysterical. Why hadn't I bollocked the children? The damage was a criminal offence, and I was not taking this seriously.

Three minutes passed, and the Head of ICT was still pacing her office and I was still waiting in the corridor — alone.

I re-entered the suite and asked Kevin O' Dane to come outside. The students were in shock, as I fed him to Miss Lee and completed the exclusion form. I clarified the period would have been shorter if he had had the guts to come clean and not wasted people's time.

If I had received a £1 for the number of staff and students who had asked me how I knew, I would have been rich. I kept the secret close to my chest but, in all honesty, it didn't take a CSI team to figure out who 'KOD SWAG' was. If you were going to leave your tag on school equipment, at least avoid using your initials!

Chris Simpson was just as stupid. He had the gall to remove two £1 coins from my desk and deny any knowledge of it.

I discovered the money missing five minutes before the end of the lesson, and was furious that someone could be so brazen to take something that did not belong to them.

I was a nice teacher. Taught fun lessons. Had a great relationship with my students. What a cheek!

Now, if there's anything I loathe more than a thief or a liar, it is someone trying to make a fool out of me, and if I had to turn every kid upside down and shake my two quid out of them, I was going to.

I quietly asked the class to take their seats, because I had an announcement to make. They faced me in silence, and I put on my 'you-have-been-sentenced-to-the-death-penalty' expression.

I stood in front of the board and slowly closed my eyes. The room was silent. I then began to rock gently from side to side, and placed my palms on the side of each temple. You could have heard a pin drop. I then began to sway faster and moan. My audience was mesmerised. Then, when they least expected, I began to speak loudly and rapidly in a different tongue. And after 45 seconds, without warning, suddenly stopped. The pupils were in awe.

Then, as if nothing had happened, I walked back to my desk, sat down and dismissed the children. No one moved. The students were glued to their seats.

A brave student broke the silence.

"Miss, Miss, what was all that about?"

I explained that if I did not get my money back, a curse would be on the person who had stolen the money on my desk.

I glanced over to Chris who, at this point, was beginning to sweat.

I dismissed the class again; this time, I stood by the door. The students got up to leave.

"Miss, Miss, look what I've found!" It was Chris Simpson. He was the last to leave. He put into my hand my shiny bright coins.

"Wow, thank you, Chris," I enthused with fake excitement, and quickly closed my palm over his sweaty fingers. He was shaking and, as he looked into my face, I widened my eyeballs, like those horror film characters. I had never seen a kid run so fast.

Damn teef, I laughed. Served him right.

I expected him to bunk my lessons after that, but no, he was there every week like clockwork. The difference being, he'd changed his seating position to right at the back!

Some children just need to be taught a lesson. Although you are the adult and, as such, should know better, sometimes, just sometimes, you can't resist.

David was a stirrer. He viewed himself as a 'Don'. By Year 9, he had made it clear that teachers could not tell him what to do.

He knew his rights. He was an intelligent soul, and he spent most of his time spreading his philosophy to the other students, careful to ensure he was never in a position to test his theory.

But, as fate as would have it, he slipped up. And guess who was waiting in the wings? Me!

With school out and exams in full swing, David was careless. He scribbled all over a new exam desk, and refused to clean it. When asked nicely, his response was he had officially left school and I couldn't make him.

Oh yeah? Well, I was determined come hell or high water that desk was gonna get scrubbed - and not by the caretakers.

Stage 1: He was kept behind after his GCSE History exam.

Surprisingly, he was cool with that.

Stage 2: He would do his assessments in isolation.

No big ting.

Time to step things up a level.

Stage 3: His mum was called.

Arrangements were made for him to collect the Flash Multi-Surface Cleaner after Wednesday's exam. He did not show.

By Day 4, it was time to end the charade.

Stage 4: 1-2-1 chat.

Pre-empting my speech, David made it clear that he knew his rights and, if I stopped him from taking the rest of his GCSE exams because of the incident, I would be infringing his human rights. I was impressed.

I explained that stopping him from taking his exams would be very stupid, in light of the fact he was predicted to get 9 A* to C grades in his GCSEs, and that figure was important for the school's overall league results.

However, what I *had* planned to do, if the desk was not sparkling, was to prevent him from *getting his results*.

Oh, if only I had my iPhone to capture his expression, I thought, as I left the room. Mine was that of a Cheshire cat.

At 4 o'clock, David arrived at my door. His hands were loaded with cleaning materials.

I grabbed my bag and whizzed past him, saying he would have to come back another time because I was late for a meeting. Hiding in the office downstairs, I was now the Cheshire cat - with a large bowl of cream.

By Friday evening, the desk looked spanking new. I telephoned David's mother, and thanked her for her support.

"No problem," she laughed, as she relayed how he had confided that I was 'dark', and admitted the whole thing seemed stupid now, and he should have just rubbed the scribble out in the first place.

I felt slightly guilty, knowing I had always held the upper hand. More so, I remember being similar to David in my youth, challenging and holding out because nobody could tell me what to do.

Hopefully, David, like myself back then, had learnt a valuable life lesson, which was not to 'test' his seniors because, believe it or not, like it or not — I run tings!

"We run tings, tings no run we!"

I am in control of the situation.

Week Beginning: 25th June

My Darkest Day

For every great half term in teaching, you can guarantee there'll be a crap day.

A day when, at the end of it, you just want to curl under your desk and scream, or simply scrape your nails down the chalkboard and piss off the world.

My darkest day came close to the end of a term, which was fortunate, because I would have resigned, if I'd had to continue.

The mobile phone is a deadly weapon.

In school, so much crap surrounds the mobile: kids jacked on the High Road or in the park for their smartphone or iPhone and, as a result, threatened, beaten and often humiliated.

One of my boys was told to hand his over and, when he did, the muggers made him take off his clothes. To date, it is still difficult for him to look me in the eye, because the dutty criminals made him walk back to school naked.

Another girl was in a mad panic and hysterical when someone stole hers from her bag during a Drama lesson. Her mother was in hospital, convalescing from a brain tumour, and the mobile was their daily means of communication. I decided that no one was leaving the studio until I had that phone. I was fuming and, in a deadly tone, addressed the fearful class.

"Someone's taken it; I don't care who, I don't care why, I want it back. Today!"

It took 15 minutes for the phone to end up outside my door. Result.

The grapevine leaked Simon Thomas as the culprit. Registered. Not today, maybe not tomorrow, but I *would* deal with him for this, when he least expected.

An old Trident campaign featured a Nokia with the implicit message: 'Phone Beats Gun' but, in my reality, a simple thing like a phone can lead to gang warfare, which involves a gun.

Delroy's mobile was taken during his GCSE exam. By the time he realised it was gone, the majority of the students had left.

I checked the seating plan, and headed to my office to investigate, unaware furious Delroy and his crew were determined to make someone pay for him being 'mugged off'.

Innocent students were roughed up, slapped and searched, and a group were rushed and attacked by Delroy and his mates in pursuit of the culprit.

What followed was World War IV, and knives had to be removed from two fifteen-year-olds, and a teacher was viciously punched for trying to stop the street brawl. The outside troublemakers finally fled when the shouts of '5-0' were heard over police sirens.

By the time the news hit my desk, the full extent of the madness was revealed.

Prior to the arrival of the boys in blue, WhatsApp group messages ensured Delroy and his schoolmates had back-up, and swarms of guys were present in less than ten minutes, 'tooled' up for action.

A member of staff bravely (or foolishly, depending on how you viewed it) intervened, and came face to face with a boy no older than 20, whose right hand was in front of his stomach and moulded around a weapon, the size and shape of a hand gun.

Shocked, the teacher mouthed, "Why?" and the child replied matter-of-factly, "I'm backing my manz, dem."

With each detail retold, I lay my head on my desk in despair. You spend a lifetime working with kids, trying to reinforce what's right from wrong, and what is the right way to deal with a situation and, in an instant, it's wiped out, with external pressures taking charge.

What frightened me most was how events could have worsened, and none of the students had the foresight to see this. I envisaged the headline on the front of the local rag: School Bloodbath.

I was fuming.

Never in my career had I wanted to lash out, shake to death, or knock the teeth out of a group of children.

I was angry.

How dare they behave like animals, hooligans and gangsters outside the school premises?

I was hurt.

Five years of blood, sweat and tears had been invested in these boys, and they behave like this.

I was MAD!

The seven boys were lined up outside my door, and I called them in one by one. Calmly, I explained to each that we all had choices, and today they had seriously blundered by making a poor one. A choice of death over life. A choice that could have just cost them their GCSEs.

Jeremy and Trevor were repentant. Lennox, Dennis and David couldn't give a shit.

Later that afternoon, I was going to have to sit with Senior Management, trying to resolve the mess.

I had worked my butt off to support my boys; begged for funding for mentoring; put gun and knife crime and drugs education on the curriculum and, most importantly, made sure they had opportunities to ensure they achieved the highest GCSE grades, which would give them a good start in life and allow them options and choices.

But, today, they had crossed the line, and I was ready to support the decision in favour of permanent exclusion.

Sometimes we spend so much time protecting our children, they don't learn the reality of consequences.

Delroy, whose stolen phone was the catalyst of these events, I left until last. His mother was at school within half an hour. I had briefly explained what had happened over the telephone. It was so sad to see a mother look to her son for an explanation for his disgraceful behaviour, and receive an 'I-don't-business', blank expression in return.

Delroy was a good kid - smart, charming, hardworking and consistent with coursework. He was the type that could easily mingle with both the geeks and the lads, and still retain respect. Even when he was moving with the hard-core crew, his homework was always complete, and he was in school every day and on time. I had purposely moved him away from a poor influence back in Year 7, and placed him into a high-achieving group in Year 8 to keep him on track. By Key Stage 4, there were concerns that he was 'puffing', which we discussed, and I enrolled him onto a mentoring programme to ensure he remained focused. Sadly, the course was dissed by his mates, and he promptly dropped out to gain approval.

Without declaring favourites, I'd have to admit I had a soft spot for Delroy. He had manners and was respectful. He would come into my office every lunchtime offering sweets, bad jokes and corny charm and, in between confiscating his baseball cap, we would have a laugh and chat.

Throughout, his mother was supportive and worked with the school. I would update her with praise and concerns and, with his back in sight, I would pull him into my office on a regular basis to chat, catch up and monitor.

I outlined to his mother, in detail, the violence that ensued following the mobile phone going missing, and couldn't stop the tears welling up my eyes. Delroy's mum began to weep openly.

Clearly uncomfortable, Delroy sat in silence with his head bowed.

I made my position clear. This was my Darkest Day.

"Today, Delroy, I feel so empty. You know something…" I exhaled deeply and paused. "This situation has just left me with nothing more to say." I got up, hugged his mother and left the office.

All the boys involved in the brawl were banned from the school premises.

It was agreed they would do their exams externally at an off-site venue in the borough.

I've never saw Delroy again.

"If yuh nah hear, yuh muss feel."

If you do not listen to advice, you will suffer the consequences.

EPISODE 37

The Death Of
The School Trip

The tragic stories in the news - of students plunging to their deaths on ski trips, or drowning on residentials - have made school trips for teachers and parents a living nightmare.

No one is brave enough to venture past the High Road with a group of pupils and, if we do, red tape makes things even more difficult. If you want to organise an outing, you have to complete a Risk Assessment (20 pages that include you having to explain how you plan to cross the road!). You then need to collect a Risk Assessment from the venue you are visiting; complete and purchase fully comprehensive insurance, and also get parents to complete a two-page consent document - all of this being a journey in itself!

Naturally, kids can be very excitable when they are off-site. Being in a theme park, for some, is comparable to Willy Wonka's factory. As a trainee teacher, I can remember venturing with a group of Year 10s to Chessington. Home time was at 4pm and, at 5pm, 15 staff were running around - literally - collecting students and depositing them onto the empty coaches. I was not pleased having to play hide-and-seek with over a hundred 15-year-olds. We were ready to leave three hours later than scheduled, and didn't get back to London until 10pm that night. It was an experience that made me determined in future: *only to take the 'good' kids out on trips.*

However, in reality, it's not that easy.

It was the end of the academic year, and all roads were leading to Margate's Dreamland in Kent. I wanted everyone to have an opportunity to go, but was not prepared to deal with behaviour issues at the seaside. My inspiration for a solution came from football. It was the simple 'two strikes and then out'.

The trip was open to all students; however, those who misbehaved in lessons would be issued with a yellow card. If it was a second offence, a red card would be given and, as a result, they would be off the trip.

I had hired a luxury coach with TV, video, drinks machine and toilet to add to the incentive. The other Year groups were travelling by double decker! It worked a dream. I was so proud of my naughties; they were trying so hard.

With only a fortnight to go, student talk was only about Margate: how much spending money they were bringing; what outfits they were wearing, and whether it would be white Adidas or Prada. I didn't have the heart to tell them how dirty the sand was!

I left staff instructions to freely hand out yellow cards, but to report any 'red' incidents to me. I would then make the decision whether or not to allow them to issue a red card and remove the student from the day out.

Jesse was being a prat in Languages, and getting on Miss Thomas' wick. She had warned him twice, and he continued to ignore her. The crunch came when he mumbled, "Shut your mouth," and, furious, she went into her desk and pulled out a red card. I'm told, the class gasped in shock, as Jesse realised he was off the trip. His eyeballs mirrored the colour of the card, and what followed was a scene from the movie, *The Incredible Hulk*.

"Noooooooooooo!" Jesse rose, picked up the desk, and threw it across the room. Children began to scream and run out of the classroom.

When I arrived, Jesse was collapsed on the floor, sobbing his heart out. As I knelt beside him, he began to blub into my lap.

"Miss, I got a red card. She gave me a red card. I've tried to be good. I've tried to be good. I *have* been good. Honest, Miss, honest. Miss, I got a red card!" He began to wail.

I had no choice but to send Jesse home for putting staff and students' safety at risk, but I did not feel good about myself. It was apparent that my two-strikes idea, which I thought was sheer genius, was not that clever after all. I had 'bigged up' the trip so much in letters home, in Assemblies and in tutor time, that everyone wanted to be a part of it. The benchmark I had set (a yellow and red card) was accessible for most but, for some, different criteria or consideration perhaps should have been made for those who may have struggled.

In Jesse's case, before he blew, he had done incredibly well not to have been involved in any incidents for six weeks and, for that, credit where credit was due. I had made the mistake of looking at the Year group as one entity, and not making allowances for those who may have needed it.

I sat with Miss Thomas and explained how I felt. There was no doubt that Jesse was out of order in her classroom and, for that, he had been punished. However, I did not want to stop him from going to Margate.

Home time was at 4pm and, at 5pm, staff were – again - running around Margate, looking for three students. I gave instructions for four of the five coaches to head home. The last one waited while we hunted around Dreamland. Jesse and his mates casually showed up around 6pm, amused they'd had two hours more fun time than the rest of the kids. We arrived back in London close to 10pm, and I had to face a large number of irate parents.

You know something, I silently fumed, *I am definitely, only going to take 'good' kids out on trips.*

Frustrated at the level of exclusions among my Black boys, I was determined to do something about it. Don't get me wrong, I was the person making the recommendations for them to stay at home, and felt perfectly justified with my actions. Fighting with weapons, carrying knives, assaulting teachers and members of the public were just a few of the incidents I have had to deal with. However, it didn't mean I was content with the situation.

Inspired by US talk show host, Sally Jesse Rafael, I organised my own boot camp in south Wales, tailor-made for my excluded boys. I handpicked 12 of the worst (two were White) and designed a programme that would build on social skills, self-esteem and teamwork. It was up at 7, breakfast at 8, clean-up 'til 9, and the daytime was activity-based. Dinner was at 5, and lessons in a converted classroom would run daily from 6. Recreation was from 8 to 9, and it was lights out by 10. The instructors were fierce, and there was no let-up. Spending three hours in a pitch-black cave, sliding on their tummies under deep water to progress to the next stage, was too much for some - along with working together to canoe along a river. Most ended up in the canal, because they couldn't work as a team.

If I had collected all the tears that had been shed over the week, I would have filled *buckets*. They were a bunch of hard-core babies. One boy refused to get out of bed by Day 4, and at least three wanted their mums. Some boys relished the opportunity of being away from home, and thought it amusing to get up to mischief and create havoc - two of whom decided it would be fun to set off the fire alarm during a thunderstorm. Aware that it was a false alarm, all the boys were clearly amused that the instructors and myself were in a panic, and everyone got soaked lining up outside.

Keith and Jevon were heroes following their prank but, clearly, they hadn't heard the phrase 'He who laughs last'.

It was 3am, pouring with rain, and the boys were sound asleep. However, the staff and I were wide awake, and fully dressed in our waterproofs. With fingers linked - we all wanted the credit for this - all four of us intentionally hit the fire alarm. Shocked, vexed, oh, and wet, twelve tired boys waited outside in the cold, soaking in their pyjamas, while we took our time checking the annexe for a fire that we knew did not exist.

Twenty minutes later, it became clear to the boys we had set them up and, inside the lounge, I gave a ten-minute lecture on health and safety, stupid pranks, and told the story of '*The Boy Who Cried Wolf*'. This proved a risky lesson, for me especially, when one boy suffered badly from the flu after being soaked.

There goes another reason why *I should only take 'good' kids out on trips!*

Boot camp was the longest week of my life. Being in a different environment with the boys meant I had built better relationships;

working, eating, talking, laughing, sharing and socialising together had created a bond. It was a turning point for the majority – and for me - but I was drained, and grateful I could finally relax when we were on the motorway heading home.

As I shut my eyes and stretched out at the front of the minibus, I couldn't believe my ears. I had only been napping for 10 minutes, when a cussing battle had ensued at the back of the bus: John and Isaac. The two top dogs were sizing each other up. It was clear this was going to escalate and, as expected, blows began to fly; students on the periphery jumped up and down with excitement, and I was bloody tired and annoyed.

One of my professionals had the belief that some children would not fight if they knew teachers would not separate them. A teacher getting involved often helped the soldiers save face by not battling till the end.

Knackered, I felt this an ideal moment to risk testing this theory, and to see how this would be resolved, if I did not intervene. From the aisle, I shouted over that I was not going to break them up, so if they wanted to bust each other's heads, that was their business. I leaned back into my seat and, within seconds, the boys stopped fighting, and silence - or shock - enveloped the atmosphere.

Wow! The number of nail infills I've had to have after breaking up fights. This showed me I should definitely be revising my stopping-a-fight strategy.

The journey home was bliss. Thankfully, they all slept right through to our destination. As I gazed towards the dozen, peacefully snoozing, I was not fooled by the melodic breathing and their angelic expressions... My head began to pulse, and I could feel a migraine coming on.

I know, I know, I'd said it before, but I bloody well meant it this time: *I'm only going to take 'good' kids out on trips!*

"Mischief come by de pound an go by de ounce."

It's easier to get into trouble, but harder to get yourself out of it.

EPISODE 38

Week Beginning: 9th July

Graduating In Style

Five years is a long time to be in one place, even as a student. I made a promise that, if I was still a Head of Year when my Year group were in Year 11, I would make sure they would have a send-off that was unprecedented. These kids were going to 'Graduate in Style'.

I had been to a wedding at a posh venue called The Palace Suites, and it was a classy affair. I decided there and then: this would be the ideal place for my students' Graduation and Prom. Previous Year 11s had had their ceremony in the school sports hall, and the Prom Party on an old boat on the Thames.

I recruited a Graduation Committee, which was led by Jo-Anne; she had excellent knowledge of US proms and enthusiasm galore. As a team, we put together a proposal for Leadership and crossed our fingers. We needed to raise £10k to cover venue hire, buffet, DJ and a guest speaker, which meant we would have to charge parents to attend the Ceremony; students would have to buy a ticket to attend the Prom, and we would have some serious fundraising to do to make up any shortfall.

The news came back from the Leadership team, and it was not positive. They felt the idea sounded great, but the overheads were steep and they weren't convinced the costs would be covered for such an ambitious venture. The Graduation Committee were not happy; they had already spread the news to the rest of the Year group that they were organising a Graduation and 'Glitz & Glam' Prom, and excitement among the kids had been bubbling. Jo-Anne had been researching Graduation rings and ribbons; had already secured a national Radio DJ to play the music, and was in the process of conducting a poll on who the kids wanted as the guest speaker for the event. She was certainly in her flow.

There was no way I was going to disappoint the children. This event was going to happen by hook or by crook. And I had an idea.

At our weekly Assembly, I broke the news that Graduation and Prom were not going to happen. Disappointment filled all four corners of the hall. However, if we could show the Head and Deputies that this was what we really wanted, we had a good chance of changing their minds. So I was setting a challenge. I needed all the students to bring in their ticket deposit of £10 by the following Friday and, if we could collect at least £1,000, it would be a good sign that we meant business.

The next day, the tenners began to roll in. The day after, the money was still flowing in thick and fast. By day three, I had collected over a grand and handed it into the office with a massive grin. We swiftly got the go ahead, and we pulled out all the stops for our final showcase.

Lunchtime fundraising activities were in full swing: raffles, guess the number of sweets in the jar, drinks hoopla... The students were going fundraising crazy.

Comedian, actor and TV presenter, Richard Blackwood, was secured as our special guest, even the staff were excited because he was *fit*!

Caribbean buffet ordered. Check. Balloons ordered. Check. Graduation teddies ordered. Check. And kids, who did not bring in PE kit, were recruited to making table favours from scratch. Prom wear ideas were showcased weekly in Assembly, and a local tuxedo company was invited into school to measure the boys for suits.

Tutors were so excited by the event that they paid for the tickets for some of their students, who were having difficulty with the cost.

The Graduation in the morning was a moving event. Watching the students collect their Progress Files in such a beautiful venue was sublime. Richard took photographs with every student, and staff members hung around at the end for his autograph.

Students, who had attended our Alternative Education provision placement, the Boxing Academy, were kitted out in new tracksuits, and collected their Files as well. A very proud moment.

Radio presenter, Eddie Nestor, always used to end his radio show with the saying: 'You can be what you want to be, the only limits to what you can achieve are the limits of your imagination', and I truly believed that for each and every one of the students.

By six that evening, uniform had been replaced with ball gowns, heels, tuxedos and bow ties. I glanced around at these young adults, dressed to the nines: the young ladies struggling to walk in stilettos, and the young men fidgeting with their ties and cravats. They had made a magnificent effort with their outfits, and many had arrived at the venue in stretch limos. They looked so grown and beautiful, as they danced to the sounds of Martin Jay. Staff members beamed at the incredible sight of our boys and girls.

Wow! I thought. Just look at these children. They have their whole lives ahead of them. Memories of the past five years came rolling back:

Dean, in his tux and bow tie. His dad had insisted on taking him to school for three years, and would sit in the main hall until the buzzer went.

Raquel, in her black and white gown with matching stole. She had lost her mother just before she started school in Year 7, but was always positive with a smile on her face.

Musa, in his grey suit and pink-and-blue-striped tie. An 'A' grade student, who hadn't said boo to a goose for four years, until a younger student provoked him and he knocked him out with one power punch.

Andrew, classically suited and booted. He was put on the register in Year 7 as Audrey, so kept being called that throughout the first term.

Lynne, in her fitted red dress with sequins. She had lost her mother suddenly in Year 11, but she still kept her focus and sat all her GCSEs.

Sharm, in her beautiful silk blue sari. Shy, with such a lovely, sweet temperament.

Fran, in a black dress with a pink ribbon on the waist. Our mathematical genius, who was destined for Cambridge.

Elle, in pink and Seray, wearing white. Like superglue since Year 7. Clearly friends for life.

And the Animators, our Year group music stars. Half of them dressed in black suits with white shirts, the rest in white suits with black shirts, plus shades.

And beautiful Aliyah. Gold gown. Gold shawl. A true princess.

So many memories. After tonight, they would be flying solo.

Oprah once said that when she looked at the future, it was so bright it burned her eyes. That encapsulated what I hoped for each and every one of these students.

I looked forward to hearing their life stories, and hoped that, as their teacher, I had made an impact along their journey, and made some form of a contribution to their many, many incredible successes that lay ahead.

"Hog say, 'De first dutty water mi ketch, mi wash.'"

Make use of the first opportunities that come your way.

EPISODE 39

Week Beginning: 16th July

So Hard To Say Goodbye

One way of making Year 11 students realise how quickly time flies in their final year was the creation of 'The Countdown'. One savvy SLT member posted the remaining days the Year 11s had left in school in the weekly Staff Bulletin, and that ammunition was communicated in Assemblies and in lessons.

As the days flew by, more and more of the students became either focused or stressed. My office window faced the playground - a prime advertising spot - so I used the opportunity to share the Countdown with the whole school. I stuck 144 on the window. Triple digits reduced to double, double moved into teens and, with the final week, as I changed the numbers from 4 to 0, the hole in my heart grew wider.

I am a self-confessed softie, so I surprised myself with the cool, calm and composed way in which I was dealing with the Year group's impending departure. The Year 11s would just hang in my office or chill on my sofa, with tears flowing from their eyes, as they reminisced at how time had flown by. I would smile and pass the Kleenex, surprising myself that I hadn't joined in the weeping fest.

"I want to stay, Miss. I don't ever wanna leave," Janine bawled. Funny, I thought. This was a student, whose parent had been fined for her poor attendance to school! My mouth curved upwards with amusement, as she draped herself over any willing student who would listen to her statement, waiting for them to reply with words of comfort.

I sat at my desk, and walked through the academic year in my head. It was like a conveyor belt. Every year, a set of 15/16-year-olds would leave your care and move on to the next stage of their journey. Most were ready. Some were not. You would hope that the time spent on the hidden curriculum would have equipped them to become successful citizens, and also the time and efforts invested would drive them to accomplish great things. Not just sport, music and television successes, like many of our ex-students had previously achieved, but you clung onto the hope that someone in that Year group would discover a cure for cancer; move and shake in corporate industry; be an innovator or a great inventor, or even take up residence at 10 Downing Street.

I entered my office on the Year 11s' final Thursday, looked at the window, and instinctively removed the number 1 sheet and searched the pile for the paper with zero written on it. As I blu-tacked it into position, the reality hit: after five years together, my 'babies' were leaving today. And with that thought in mind, the floodgates opened and I began to blub.

All day, tears streamed down my face, and boy, did I look ugly. A red-eyed panda with a runny nose. My only comfort was that this image was also mirrored by most of the girls, who would intermittently wail as they walked the corridors, hugging teachers and friends, as they got their books and shirts signed.

The school cycle was indeed a treadmill; however the outcomes would always be varied, because of the content of the characters we deal with on a day-to-day basis. I always viewed the opportunity to work with children as a privilege, because I knew that not only did I help to shape young intellects, but those young people also shaped me.

A government campaign succinctly put it: 'Those who can – teach'. I was blessed with that gift and skill, and tried to use it to the best of my ability to make a positive difference. My gran's favourite refrain would often echo in my head, confirming my vocation: *'If I can help somebody as I walk along, then my living shall not be in vain.'*

With the Year 11s gone; examinations over; new prefects in post; internal and external assessments complete; Sports Day finished, and the annual Student Awards event and Year group trips done and dusted, I paused and breathed a sigh of relief. After 39 long weeks, I could sit back, stretch out and chill.

I locked my office door, and looked back down the corridor at the remnants of the classroom clear-outs: old exercise books, broken resources and general rubbish... The space was deadly quiet. All the schoolchildren had gone home a couple of hours earlier (as it was a half day), and the majority of staff had rushed out the gates, ready to begin their summer break. Most of my mates had already updated their Facebook status: 'Schools Out' or simply tweeted: 'Holiday!'

As I walked through the school gates, I checked my bag for the essential item I needed to survive the next six weeks. I had printed the e-ticket from my email earlier: London Gatwick to Montego Bay, Jamaica, Saturday 21st July to Saturday 1st September.

42 days, lazing in the Caribbean sun to refresh, revive and revitalise...

...and prepare for the next 39 weeks that lay ahead.

"Good, Better, Best."
You think you may have something good, but something better for you is around the corner; in fact, the BEST is yet to come...

END OF ACADEMIC YEAR

EPILOGUE

1.
Out Of The Mouth of Babes

Dear Miss

I am typing this letter to you rather than writing it, because I wanted to be sure that when you receive it, no words are lost due to my sometimes bad handwriting.

I am sitting in Halls at University, and wanted to let you know that words alone cannot capture the level of gratitude and appreciation I feel for everything you have done for me. I would go as far as to say I truly love you. Yes, very much, because you saw something in me that many teachers failed to see and, because of you, I have the audacity to dream and believe that I can make something of myself, and believe me, Miss, when I say that I will, I will make you and my family proud of me.

Forgive me if I am rambling but, as I am writing, the memories of school life come flooding back. I will never forget my time there. When teachers complained, you stood up and gave us a chance. Most importantly, you taught us to aim high. To say you inspired me would be an understatement; you are the teacher that broke the bar. You drive your students to use that inspiration, and to turn a dream or vision into reality.

You made me believe that I could be the best, and I still hold that belief to this day. Seven of our crew are in our second year at Uni, and Andrew is doing a business apprenticeship. He's got his eye on becoming a Black Richard Branson, so make sure he gives you some of his money for the work you put into his lazy self to get him where he is now!

Thank you again for everything you have done for me and for all the other kids. We, especially I, love you very much.

Your student/son

Stevie R x

Steve Richards

PS

I've signed this letter too, coz you know this signature is going to be worth a lot in the future!

2.

My Dear John Letter

Dear John

One of the reasons I have taken so long to publish this book is you. Your episode, '*You Can't Save Them All*', was one of the hardest to write. Not just because you come across unfavourably, but also because it was an indication of how I had failed as a Head of Year.

I know I said in the book 'You can't save them all' but, from the get-go, I came into education to give to kids what I didn't get at school: confidence, self-belief, ambition, drive, and also to make sure students - especially Black boys - left school with opportunities and options, so they would succeed in life, and not end up being permanently excluded with a one-way ticket to Feltham.

Your exit from school was swift and harsh and, although I told myself repeatedly that it was for the best, it never sat comfortably with me, and I would often wonder how you were and what you were up to.

The old crew, your peers, would update me on their progress and what was going on with the rest of the Year group. Who was at Uni? Who was doing resits? Who was working? Who'd had a baby? Who was doing time for bad behaviour? So far, two of our boys have been incarcerated, and a third got off a lengthy sentence after I wrote a glowing character reference. The shock had settled him, and he was now successfully running a car hire firm just outside London with two of the boys from the Year group. He had promised me a massive discount, but if I needed to hire a Benz, I was getting that for free. Discount, my back foot! Only joking.☺

Strangely, your name never came up in any of the conversations, and I never asked for an update on you, for fear things hadn't turned out well. But, deep down, I knew that your pride and skills would not have allowed you to do anything but the best.

It was only when one of our Angels from the Year group died suddenly, your name surfaced.

"John was looking for you, Miss," one of the kids told me the next day.

I wasn't sure if I was relieved or disappointed that I had not seen you after all these years.

"How was he?" I cautiously replied.

"Cool," they responded. "We chat all the time on social media."

That evening, I logged onto Facebook and typed your name in the search panel to see if I could get a peek at what you'd got up to after all this time.

I wasn't disappointed. Your profile picture instantly brought me back to Year 9. There you were in the photograph: glasses, beard, still very handsome, meticulous with your designer style and appearance, and posing with a bottle of bubbly in your hand. Cristal, methinks! Still the same John! I smiled. Your employment status said you worked for an international architectural practice in the West End. I smiled wider. Only you could turn such a negative into a positive. I felt relieved you had made something of your life but, more importantly, you looked happy.

Keep rising and following your dreams. If anyone can…

Miss J Bremmer

About a week later I got a message in my Facebook inbox.

"How are we, Miss Bremmer?" It was John.

Oh wow!

I instantly replied: "Well, well, well." ;) I pressed Send.

"I've got so much to tell you, Miss! I think it's best I come in one day for a catch up ☺, John continued.

I paused.

"I've written a book about school and you're in it. I didn't want to publish it until I had a chat with you first. I hear you're doing really well." I paused. "I expected nothing less." I pressed Send.

"I would love to read your book, Miss. Definitely be supporting," John replied.

I smiled and continued typing. "Proud of you." I pressed Send.

After what felt like a lifetime in thought, I got up and went over to my chest of drawers and pulled out my thick folder labelled '39 Weeks', and went straight to Episode 34. After re-reading it, I sat back, deep in thought.

"Yeah, John," I said aloud. "You certainly turned it around, and I am very, very proud."

GLOSSARY

Teaching Terminology

AEN: Additional Educational Needs.

Analyse School Performance (ASP System): The organisation that analyses school performance, replacing RAISE online.

Baseline: The starting grade of your child, which all other grades are measured against.

CAMHS: Child and Adolescent Mental Health Service.

Child Protection: The protection of a child from violence, exploitation, abuse and neglect.

Commitment Ladder: The measure of a child's commitment to school, specifically their Effort, Behaviour and Homework.

Coursework Component: An area of the GCSE specification that measures subject-specific skills that cannot always be assessed by timed, written exam papers.

Cover: Lessons that a support teacher takes in a teacher's absence.

Data and Evidence Folder: Folder with analysis of a subject's policies and data of all their students.

Detention: A sanction that has been put in place if a child breaks school rules or the behaviour policy.

DIRT: Direct Improvement & Reflection Time, where students look at the work marked and respond to comments made by the teacher.

Exclude/Exclusion/Fixed-Term Exclusion: Also known as a suspension, it is an exclusion from school for a specified amount of time.

Extra Curricular Clubs: Lessons/curriculum sessions that occur after school hours.

Free School: A non-profit making, independent, state-funded school, which is free to attend, but is not wholly controlled by a local authority.

GCSE Specification: Detailed information on the criteria students have to meet in a subject, in order to successfully pass a

GCSE subject.

GCSE Study Leave: The period just before GCSEs, when a student leaves school.

Head of Faculty: The leader of a number of subject areas.

Isolation Room: A sanction room, where students are placed during school hours for breaking school rules or the behaviour policy.

LAC: A Looked-After Child, whom the local authority has responsibility for.

Learning Walks: When an observer goes into a classroom and observes a session for 10-15 minutes, and focuses on a specific aspect or theme.

Macbeth: A Shakespeare play.

Managed Move: An arrangement made between two schools to move a student.

Ofsted: The Office for Standards in Education, Children's Services and Skills. They inspect and regulate services that care for children and young people, and services that provide education and skills for learners of all ages.

Pen Portraits: A detailed analysis of data on a class, and strategies for support to ensure achievement.

Pritt Stick: Solid glue stick.

Progress Conversations: Conversations with subject Postholders and staff about their teaching groups, progress, strategies, support and intervention needed for achievement.

Progress Report: A report written by class teachers every half term, outlining a student's progress and areas of concern.

PSHE: Personal, Social and Health Education.

Pupil Premium: Additional funding to help schools close the attainment gap between children from low-income and other disadvantaged families and their peers.

RAISE: System that analyses school performance using Year 11 GCSE data

S Block: The Science area of the school.

Saturday Detention: A three-hour sanction on a Saturday.

Saturday Supplementary School: Academic learning that happens on a Saturday, and run by the local community.

Schemes of Work: An overview and breakdown of a topic that students are studying in each subject area.

School-to-prison Pipeline: The disproportionate tendency of young adults from disadvantaged backgrounds to become incarcerated, because of harsh school policies.

SDP: School Development Plan.

Seating Plans: A diagram of where the children in your class sit.

SEF: Self-Improvement Form.

SEN: Special Educational Needs now termed as AEN – Additional Educational Needs.

Self Reviews: A document created termly to monitor progress and record updates of subject areas.

SIMS: Administration computer application that schools use to take the register, store student contact details, rewards and sanctions and academic data.

SMSC: Spiritual, moral, social and cultural development. All schools in England must show how well their pupils develop in this area.

SMT Meeting: Senior Management Team meeting.

SOAPAM: Description language devices: Simile, Onomatopoeia, Adjective, Personification, Alliteration and Metaphor.

Starter: The first activity that happens at the beginning of a lesson.

Student Set Lists: The names and data of all the students in your class.

TA: Teaching Assistant.

Teaching Practice School: The school where a trainee teacher does their placement.

Teaching Set: The class a child is placed in, according to academic ability.

TES: *Times Education Supplement*, education newspaper.

Theme Day: A special school day, where lessons are suspended and students do project-based activities.

Year 6 Results: End of primary school test results.

UK Street/Caribbean Slang

A&E: *Accident and Emergency department in a hospital*
A hitch up yuh skirt: *Make your skirt shorter*
Backing my manz dem: *Supporting your friends*
Bad: *Contradictory slang, meaning good*
Bang: *Highly attractive*
BFF: *Best Friend Forever*
Birthday beats: *When you are hit by a group of children, because it is your birthday*
Blighty: *England*
Callaloo: *Caribbean green vegetable (from the spinach family)*
Clapped: *Ugly*
Corrie: *Coronation Street, UK television soap opera*
Cosh: *Under pressure, or in a difficult situation*
Cracking up: *In a fit of laughter*
Dutty: *Dirty*
EastEnders: *BBC1 television soap opera in the UK*
Facety: *cheeky, rude*
FB: *Facebook*
Garms: *Clothes*
Gob: *Spit with phlegm*
Good lick: *A beating*
Gwarn: *Go on*
Hard: *To be cool*
Hard–back: *Mature, grown-up*
If it fi yuh, it fi yuh: *If it's supposed to be yours, it will be*
Jacked: *Stolen from*
Kissed my teeth: *Sound made with the mouth when upset*
Lick: *Hit, beat, thump*
Lit: *Exciting*
Low batties: *Trousers worn with the waist sitting below the bum*

M&S: *Marks & Spencer store*
Mash Get Smash Martian: *Metal Martian that advertised Smash potato*
Mavardo: *Jamaican reggae music artist*
Mick: *To mock, tease, ridicule*
Mugged off/Muggy: *Made to look stupid/two faced*
Nang: *Cool*
'oman: *Woman*
Puffing: *Smoking*
Peggy Mitchell: *Fictional former landlady of the Queen Victoria pub in BBC soap opera* EastEnders
Pickney: *Child*
Piff: *High grade marijuana*
Porkie Pies: *Lies*
Pranks: *Jokes*
Prat: *Idiot*
Raaaaah: *Exclamation of surprise*
Renk: *Rude*
Safe: *Cool*
Sliders: *Slip on sandals/flip flops*
Snap: *Shocked or surprised about a comment*
Spice: *Fake weed*
Squeeze: *Break*
Starkers: *Naked*
Tink yuh clever?: *A person who thinks they are smart*
Tooled up: *Carrying a weapon*
Triage: *The system of determining the priority of a patient's treatment in A&E*
Tripe: *Rubbish*
Under her frocktail: *mollycoddled, babied and protected*
Vex: *Upset*
Vybz Kartel: *Jamaican reggae music artist*
Wicked*: Contradictory slang meaning excellent*

Julz's Gems
At The Front of my Bookshelf

Akala: *Natives.*
ISBN: 9781473661219

Karen Allen, *Broken: Into Useful Pieces.*
ISBN: 9780956203205

Romeo Bremmer, *Hey, Black Boy!*
ISBN: 9780993316883

Original Flava, *Caribbean Cookbook.*
ISBN: 9781999806705

Dorothy Hall, *Kaye Having Downs Syndrome is not an Obstacle.*
ISBN:9781434379351

Paul Lawrence, *101 Lessons I Taught My Son.*
ISBN: 9780995703117

Angie Le Mar, *Full Circle.*
ISBN: 9781911425731

Brianna-Kayla Lynch, *Hey, Black Girl!*
ISBN: 978-0993316869

Mark Prince, *Prince of Peace.*
ISBN: 9781910335895

Jemma Regis, *God's Romantic Getaway.*
ISBN: 9781907402586

Jacqueline Robinson, *The Silence is Broken.*
ISBN: 9780956272706

Angie Thomas, *The Hate You Give.*
ISBN: 9781406384765

Gabrielle Union, *We're Gonna Need More Wine.*
ISBN: 9788925598024

Elizabeth Uviebinene & Yomi Adegoke, *Slay In Your Lane.*
ISBN: 9780008235628

Davis Williams, *No Enemy Within.*
ISBN: 9780993342301